See Madeira &
the Canaries

See Madeira & the Canaries

Annette Pink &
Paul Watkins

a complete guide
with maps

FORMAT

Front cover photo: Los Berrazales, Grand
Canary
Back cover: Curral das Freiras, Madeira
(Spectrum)
Front endpapers: Pico de Teide, Tenerife
(Peter Baker)
Back endpapers: Landscape on walk to
Boca do Risco, Madeira
Frontispiece: Dragon tree

Photographs are by Paul Watkins with the
following exceptions:
Spanish National Tourist Office: 8,42,47,
48/49, 66,78,88,92/93; Peter Baker: 14,
32/33,35; F.Rojas: 74/75; J.Allan Cash:134

First published 1976
Revised editions 1980,1990
© Paul Watkins 1976, 1980, 1990
Published by Format Books
23 Jeffreys Street, London NW1 9PS

ISBN 0 903372 13 4

Filmsetting by Oliver Burridge Filmsetting
Ltd, Crawley, Sussex

Printed by Richard Clay Ltd, Bungay, Suffolk

In the same series

**See Corfu &
the Ionians**
by Paul Watkins

See Cyprus
by Paul Watkins

See Malta & Gozo
by Inge Severin

See Sicily
by Paul Watkins

Contents

The Canary Islands

Madeira

The Canary Islands

LA PALMA

TENERIFE

S.Cru
deTene

GOMERA

HIERRO

Introduction The mystery of the origins of the Canary Islands has for centuries fascinated travellers, writers and historians. Were the islands the Garden of the Hesperides? Did they once form part of the mainland of Africa, and who were the first people to enjoy their lovely climate?

Their geological foundation is uncertain, although it is probable that they were once a single land mass, broken into islands by immense volcanic upheavals. The history of their settlement is likewise obscure, and the tantalizing question of when and by whom they were first discovered remains unanswered.

The name 'Canaries' is itself a mystery. It certainly does not derive from the yellow songbirds found there in such large numbers, but it may have come from the large fighting dogs (Latin *canis*) which were kept by the early inhabitants and brought back to Africa by the Romans.

The early writers gave each island a separate name as they became known. Pliny the Elder called one 'Capraria' (the one which swarms with lizards) referring to Lanzarote. 'Nivaria' (snow-covered) was the name given to the snow-capped peak of Tenerife. It was not until the Spaniards had completed their conquest in 1496 that the whole group became known as the Canaries.

With the eastern islands less than 60 miles from the north-west coast of Africa, and the rest of the group stretching into the Atlantic for another 250 miles, the Canaries are situated at the crossroads of sea and air routes between Europe, Africa and America. A very large number of ships call at ports in the islands from all over the world. Las Palmas in Grand Canary is one of the largest ports in the western hemisphere.

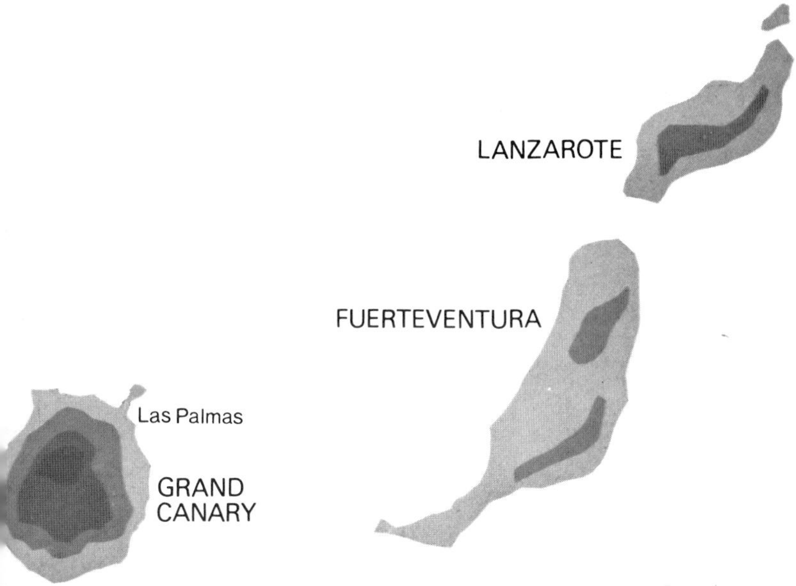

LANZAROTE

FUERTEVENTURA

Las Palmas

GRAND
CANARY

There are seven major islands. The easternmost, and nearest to Africa, are Lanzarote and Fuerteventura. Originally thought to be one island, they have only a narrow strip of ocean between them. To the south-west of the southern tip of Fuerteventura is Grand Canary, almost circular in shape, with a high point of 1949 m near the centre. These three, together with a number of small satellites, form the Las Palmas province of Spain. The other islands to the west are Tenerife with its highest point at Teide (3718 m), La Palma, Gomera and Hierro. They make up the second province of Santa Cruz de Tenerife. Gomera lies off the west coast of Tenerife, while La Palma and Hierro are north-west and south-west respectively.

All are volcanic in origin, and eruptions have occurred in La Palma as recently as 1971. The volcanic nature of the islands accounts for the extraordinary variety of their landscape. From the beauty of the great pine forests and rolling beaches to the stark desolation of the volcanic areas, the contrasts are fantastic. In Tenerife the snow-capped mountain of Teide looks down on banana plantations, and vines flourish in the lava dust of Lanzarote.

Dubbed by the Romans the 'Fortunate Isles', the Canaries have one of the most agreeable climates in the world. Until fairly recently the winter was the most popular period for visitors, but now the season is extending to cover the whole year. The summer has much to recommend it both for the warmer sea bathing and for boat travel between the islands, which is more comfortable at this time of the year.

That the islands owe their contemporary fortunes to tourism can hardly

7

be in doubt when one sees the great hotel blocks of Las Palmas, Puerto de la Cruz and other resorts. But although these are the inevitable home of the sun-seekers one should not forget that the choice extends to the tranquillity of a small pension or Government Parador in rural Gomera or La Palma.

Each of the islands has its own particular charms, and herein lies the special attraction of the Canaries. They provide all things for all men: Tenerife and Grand Canary their spectacular resorts and surrealist landscapes, La Palma, Hierro and Gomera the more intimate scale and a sense of refuge, Lanzarote and Fuerteventura the experience of another world of volcanoes, deserts and multicoloured panoramas.

Fortunate are the islands, and fortunate their travellers.

The people The Islanders (total population 1,200,000) are generally known as 'Canarios', although strictly speaking the name should only be used when speaking of the inhabitants of Grand Canary. In the same way, the name 'Guanche' should only be applied to the early natives of Tenerife (see History, p. 12).

From the evidence of the mummies and skeletons discovered in the islands, the first inhabitants have been identified as belonging to the Cro-Magnon culture predominant at the time in south-west France. This gave them a common ancestry with the Spanish, which assisted their eventual assimilation by the *conquistadores*. These early people, who reached the islands from the coast of north Africa c. 2000 BC, did not progress beyond a Neolithic culture. They lost the art of navigation and there was no further contact with the mainland or, apparently, between the islands.

Ancient travellers cast little further light. It is strange that the Romans did not make a more determined effort to take possession of the islands, which were extremely fertile. They seemed content to confine themselves to the occasional visit, which had little impact on the inhabitants. The people were left to lead their idyllic life undisturbed until the Spanish and Portuguese explorers found them and began their efforts to conquer the islands in the 14th century.

By 1496 the whole of the group had come under Spanish rule. The large number of islanders who had been killed fighting the Spanish, plus others sold into slavery, greatly reduced the native population. The Spaniards took many of the native women as wives, and their descendants form the present-day population of the islands.

Variations occur among the physical types found in the islands. The people of Gomera have a higher percentage of Guanche blood, retaining the native ancestry eliminated from the other islands by war and slave raids. Much of the population of Fuerteventura is descended from the Moorish slaves imported to the island by the Spanish in the 15th and 16th centuries.

The natives of each island have a special name. Those of Grand Canary are known as *canarios*, those of Tenerife *tinerfeños*. The others are: Lanzarote, *conejos* (rabbit people); Fuerteventura, *maioreros*; La Palma, *palmeros*; Gomera, *gomeros*; Hierro, *herreños*.

The economy of the islands is based on three main sources of revenue: agriculture, shipping and tourism.

Agriculture This is the most important activity and most of the country people work on the land, producing fruit and vegetables for export. Bananas are still one of the biggest crops, and in every port one sees the piles of boxes marked 'Canary Bananas—Extra' waiting to be loaded on to ships from all over the world. Many other kinds of fruit are grown in the islands, including citrus varieties, melons, avocados and tomatoes. Potatoes—many of them grown from seed imported from Britain—are another important crop.

In spite of the difficulties presented by the peculiar terrain of Lanzarote, the people have devised ingenious techniques of cultivation. Vines and fig trees flourish in the dry volcanic dust that covers most of the island.

Each island has its speciality. Tenerife, abundant in most things, is specially proud of its tomatoes. Grand Canary is the largest producer of bananas, while in La Palma the almond trees cover many acres of the fertile land in the valley near El Paso. In Fuerteventura potatoes and wheat are grown as well as tomatoes and in Hierro figs and cheeses are produced commercially. Gomera has its maize, Lanzarote its extraordinary vineyards.

Most of this produce is grown for export, but other crops are cultivated solely for domestic consumption. These include maize—an important cereal item in the diet of country folk—and coffee. In recent years the cultivation of tobacco has been increased, and there is a lively tobacco industry in Tenerife.

Shipping Their position in the Atlantic near the north-west coast of Africa has established the Canaries as a major port-of-call on almost all sea routes between America and the other countries of the western hemisphere. Another virtue of their ports is that they are duty free, under a special customs regime set up in 1852. The benefits deriving from this concession have made a great contribution to the economy of the islands. Las Palmas, the main port, is one of the largest oil bunkering ports in the world.

Tourism The advent of the holiday cruise put the Canaries on the map for the wealthy minority of Europeans who in the earlier part of this century were able to afford the luxury of pursuing warmer climes during the winter months. The seductive climate of the islands made their interest more enduring and many of them established winter homes in Tenerife and Grand Canary. The advent of direct air routes and package tours in recent years has brought in the less affluent tourists in large numbers, particularly from Britain, Germany and Scandinavia.

The winter season (September–March) has traditionally been the peak period for tourist travel. During this high season hotel prices are up to a third higher than in the summer months. Inevitably, the lower summer rates, coupled with the less crowded beaches and the fact that the climate is much the same all the year round, have made this period increasingly attractive to low-budget tourists. The Canaries now have a total of three million visitors each year.

Although not a major source of revenue, the *handicrafts* of the Canaries make an important supplement to the income from tourism. Drawn thread work of varying designs is a popular item with foreign visitors, as are the handmade dolls dressed in the typical Canary Island costumes. Basketwork and weaving are other crafts which are purchased in great quantity from the craft shops in the major towns and resorts.

Statue of Guanche chieftain at Candelaria, Tenerife

History

The Guanches The history of the Canaries is sparse, particularly before their capture by the Spanish in the 15th century. Although the islands were inhabited in early times, the origin of their first settlers is uncertain. The hardest evidence—the mummies, pottery and cave drawings found in the islands, points to a Cro-Magnon culture native to the south-west of France. Known in Tenerife as the Guanche people (see below), they migrated to the islands c. 2000 BC.

The vagaries of sea currents and prevailing winds, which make it easy to get to the islands from the African coast but difficult to return there, may have prevented the early settlers—after a speedy landfall—from returning to Africa or the Mediterranean. It appears that subsequent to their arrival they lost the art of navigation and did not even travel from one island to another.

The Guanches were a very religious people. They worshipped one invisible god, and the summits of mountains, where their worship was performed, were revered. In Tenerife the peak was considered the abode of the deity, and its name *Teide* or *E'Cheyde* means 'the seat of fire'.

(The name 'Guanche' means 'son of che'—an abbreviation for *E'Cheyde*. Strictly speaking this name should apply only to the ancient people of Tenerife—but for convenience is now commonly used to refer to the pre-conquest inhabitants of all the islands.)

In Grand Canary there are two sacred mountains, Bentaiga and Cuatro Puertas, on which images made by aboriginal people have been discovered. In La Palma the main place of worship was in the great central crater. In Gomera, on Alto Garajonay—the highest point in the island—there is a great circular space with seats hewn from the surrounding rocks where religious ceremonies were held.

The early people supported a large number of priests who in addition to conducting religious ceremonies made prophecies and controlled the storage of tithes of food, the surplus of which was preserved against times of famine. The priests also had the work of embalming the dead. Bodies of kings and nobles were always mummified, and the preparation of the corpse was an elaborate ritual, involving the use of vegetable extracts such as the sap of the dragon tree as preservatives. The mummies were then interred secretly in remote caves. (The museums in Las Palmas and Santa Cruz de Tenerife contain many interesting exhibits relating to these burial ceremonies.)

The first civilized people to discover the islands were the Romans. In 30 BC Juba II, Consul of Mauretania, sent an expedition to explore them, which recorded many details about the geography, flora and fauna. Among the specimens brought back to Africa were two of the 'Canary' dogs.

Juba wrote several works about the islands, among them a treatise on the cactus-like *Euphorbia canariensis*, named after his physician, Euphorbus. Although these writings have been lost, much of what he recorded is quoted in other authors' works, including Pliny and Plutarch, who refer to the 'Insulae Fortunatae'.

After Juba's death no further interest was shown in the islands, and the next reference to them is in the writings of the Arabs, who re-discovered the Canaries *c.* 1016. They did little more, however, than note their position and name them *Kaledat*, Arabic for the Roman 'Fortunate Islands'.

Jean de Bethencourt During the Middle Ages, while the Mediterranean was the focus of the struggles between Christian and Moslem, the islands were left in isolation, troubled only by the occasional slave raid. In the middle of the 14th century King Alfonso IV of Portugal sent soldiers to try and gain possession of Tenerife and Gomera, but they were repulsed. They did, however, gather information about the islands from the parts they visited.

The modern history of the Canaries really begins in 1402, when Jean de Bethencourt, a Norman, led his first expedition to the islands. But the explorers' interest in the Canaries had been as a source of slaves, rather than as colonies for settlement. This limited objective prevailed until the King of Castile financed de Bethencourt to fit out a force with the express purpose of subduing and settling the islands.

De Bethencourt first landed on Lanzarote, and finding the inhabitants much reduced by the earlier raids, he took the island with little opposition. He later crossed to Fuerteventura, but without sufficient forces to bring the whole island under his control. He built a fortress on the north coast, and leaving a garrison there, returned home to procure reinforcements and supplies. He received these from Henry III of Castile, in return for which he had to undertake to capture the islands for Castile. On his return he took over the whole of Fuerteventura, and conquered Gomera and Hierro. He was unable to secure the other three islands in the group, although La Palma offered partial submission. Tenerife and Grand Canary put up a stiff resistance and retained their independence for many years.

The conquest It was not until 1483, when the Spanish themselves were involved in the conquest, that the first of these islands was overrun. This was Grand Canary, conquered by Juan Rejón after a five-year campaign.

The conquest of La Palma and Tenerife had to await the arrival of a later *conquistador*, Don Alfonso Fernandez de Lugo. De Lugo was a Galician nobleman who had fought in many campaigns, including the defence of Granada against the Moors. He reconnoitred the coasts of both Tenerife and La Palma carefully before making a report to the court in Spain. He was appointed Captain-General of Conquests in the Canaries, and returned to attack La Palma in 1491. It took him seven months to subdue the island, and in May 1492 it was finally captured.

In the following year de Lugo attacked Tenerife. Assisted by forces from Grand Canary and Gomera, a foothold was quickly gained on the north-east coast, near present-day Santa Cruz. Here the invaders built a tower of refuge, and from it sorties were made to the interior. In 1494, however, the invaders were forced to withdraw in the face of strong resistance by the Guanche people.

They returned with more men later in the year and recaptured the settlement of Santa Cruz. At this time the natives had the misfortune to suffer from a mysterious disease known as *modorra*. This illness apparently did not affect the Spanish, but its ravages among the natives were such that they were forced to capitulate to the Spanish at Realejo Alto in 1496, thus ending the prolonged and unequal struggle.

The process of conquest was completed by the gradual assimilation of the native people by the Spanish. Many of the women married into Spanish families, took Spanish names, and were baptized into the Catholic Church. There is now little evidence, other than the Guanche sanctuaries and place names and a few relics, of the islands' former inhabitants.

British raids Since the surrender of Tenerife, the sovereignty of the Canary Islands has never been in serious dispute. Although at times both Portugal and Morocco have claimed some rights, these have not been conceded by the Spanish. Apart from occasional Moorish incursions, the only serious attacks were by the English and Dutch in the late 16th century.

The British attacks culminated in the one made by Nelson in 1797. Nelson, who at the time was assisting in the blockade of Cadiz, landed at Santa Cruz on July 21 in an attempt to capture the town. His men were repulsed and Nelson himself lost an arm, shot off by a cannon ball. The British were unable to obtain more than a brief foothold in the city, and the landing party were obliged to make terms with the Spanish which guaranteed them safe conduct back to their ships. The tattered flags which were captured from this party still hang in the Church of the Concepción in Santa Cruz.

Modern development In 1821 the Canaries were created a Province of Spain, with Santa Cruz de Tenerife as the capital and seat of government. There has always been a good deal of rivalry between the islands, which has to a certain extent prevented progress in land and industrial development. On the other hand this has maintained the individual characteristics of the islands, which has enhanced their appeal to foreign visitors.

In 1852 the ports of the Canaries were declared free, and have remained so to date. In 1883 submarine telegraph cables were laid which connected the archipelago with the rest of the world. The development of modern coaling and oil stations for shipping has made a major contribution to the economy. In 1927 two separate provinces were created, that of Las Palmas including the islands of Grand Canary, Lanzarote and Fuerteventura, and Santa Cruz de Tenerife including the islands of Tenerife, La Palma, Hierro and Gomera.

Climate An assessment of the varied climate of the Canaries is determined by a number of factors profoundly affecting weather conditions in the islands.

First is the spread of the archipelago, from 60 miles off the African coast to 300 miles into the Atlantic. Their relationship to the continent has a significant bearing on the climate of the islands, those nearest being hot and dry, those furthest away being more temperate.

Second is the existence—or lack—of mountains, and third the presence of winds, blowing in from the Atlantic (westerlies) or from the north-east (trades), which create contrasting conditions in the islands where there is a central massif. The mountains, acting as a barrier to the wind-driven clouds, mark a climatic borderline. On the north and west the islands tend to be cool and fertile, on the south and east drier and less productive. Where the contours are lower, as in Lanzarote and Fuerteventura, much drier conditions prevail—and these islands, too, are subject to the hot winds of the Sahara.

A further effect of the mountains is seen in the clouds which often surround their peaks. These are, however, usually of a transient nature and one has to be unlucky to experience a day in which the sun is permanently obscured.

A fourth factor is sea currents. The cold Canaries current, which flows down from Morocco, produces a barrier of cool air between the archipelago and the continent. The effect of the current on the islands themselves is tempered by the warm Gulf Stream, which flows into it.

All these factors have prevented the Canaries, which are situated in the latitude of the world's deserts, from becoming totally desert islands. Additionally they have created the special conditions in which the islands' diverse and prolific vegetation can flourish.

For average annual temperatures and additional weather information, see p. 27.

Cultivation Since the Spanish conquest, the islands' agriculture has been subject to a recurring pattern of success and failure. Plants have been introduced, successful commercial cultivation has followed, and then the decline has set in, caused either by falling demand or competition from abroad.

The first plant introduced, soon after the conquest, was the sugar cane. Prior to this the only exports had been pitch, obtained from the pine trees, various kinds of lichen used for dyes, and the sap of the dragon tree, regarded in the Middle Ages as having medicinal properties.

The sugar cane was introduced from Madeira, and its cultivation was made obligatory for the settlers. The methods of planting and cultivation were taught to the islanders by Portuguese specialists known as Masters of Sugar. In a few years plantations were extensive in all areas found suitable for growing the crop. Sugar mills were erected, and by 1550 it is recorded that there were twelve such mills in Tenerife alone. Many roads were built for transporting the sugar to the mills and then to the ports. Water systems were installed to provide the necessary irrigation.

The growth of the industry created a great demand for labour. Slaves were shipped from nearby Africa, and for many negroes the Canaries became the first stop on the road to America.

For more than a hundred years sugar was the most important crop in the islands, which contemporary writers called the 'Islands of Sugar'. When plantations were started in the New World, however, the competition became too much for the small insular farmers. Their difficult hilly terrain, and the problems of watering the sugar cane limited their output and made it impossible for them to compete with the comparatively cheap sugar from the West Indies. Trade gradually declined, and the people of the Canaries had to look for other means of exploiting their fertile soil. Happily the vine had already been imported from Crete, and vineyards were expanded to replace the sugar plantations.

The volcanic lava and ash which is found in the soil give a special quality and flavour to wines produced in the islands, and in a short time 'sack' and 'malvasia' became very popular in Europe and America. The roads and ports which had been built to handle the sugar crops were now employed for the wine trade, which was to become the mainstay of the islands' economy.

Unhappily the competition which had undermined the sugar trade was to have a similar effect on the islands' wine. The competition came largely from Madeira and Oporto, but in addition many wine producing countries in Europe had introduced trade protection. A run of plagues in the vineyards contributed further to the failure of the industry, and once again the people had to turn to another crop to restore their fortunes.

Production of cochineal, which had been a subsidiary crop for some years, was increased. The Nopal Cactus was brought from America specially for the nourishment of the insect, *Coccus cacti*, from which the cochineal dye is obtained. The cactus can live in sterile and dry country, so was very suitable for the arid land on the south side of the islands. Many fortunes were made and lost in pursuit of the business during the 19th century, but like its predecessors this trade also died, outmoded by the introduction of aniline dyes. (Cochineal is still produced in the islands today for the manufacture of cosmetics and the colouring of synthetic fabrics.)

Originally grown for home con-sumption, the banana's potential for the export market was realized with a growing demand from Europe. The banana, which today is by far the largest crop in the islands, is limited by local conditions to the four which are suitable for its growth: Tenerife, Grand Canary, Gomera and La Palma. The banana plants are grown near the coast (up to 300 m above sea level) and large areas of land had to be levelled for the plantations.

In growing the banana adequate preparation must be made to ensure a healthy crop. First of all, a base of small stones and gravel is laid to allow for adequate drainage. Soil is then put on top of these layers and the bananas are planted in long rows, surrounded by walls of stone or cement blocks which protect them from the heavy winds. Each plant produces one bunch or stalk of fruit which takes about six months to mature. The parent plant then produces a 'baby' beside it, and the next crop will come from this second generation. The original plant is cut down and used as cattle fodder.

Although the banana crop is all-important, memories of the failure of previous one-crop economies have today ensured a more diversified approach. Efforts have been directed towards the production of a wide variety of fruits and vegetables, including apples and citrus fruit, tomatoes and potatoes (the latter are grown from seed imported from Britain, and constitute the most important crop in the islands after bananas).

Production of cotton and coffee is being increased, but mainly for local use. Maize and tobacco are also grown, and Tenerife has a flourishing cigarette and cigar industry.

Cultivation in the eastern islands of Lanzarote and Fuerteventura, with their scant rainfall, presents special problems. The people of Fuerteventura are particularly dependent on crops such as sisal, which flourishes in desert conditions. In Lanzarote, the method of cultivation is unique. Here there is neither rain nor ground water, so the farmers have to utilize the high humidity existing in the island. They are assisted here by the volcanic ash which covers the terrain and which has the extraordinary capacity of retaining the moisture in the atmosphere. The plants' water supply is thus ensured, and in this way plentiful crops of grapes, figs, tomatoes and other fruit are grown.

The problem of water supply has been overcome in the other islands by the development of an elaborate system of aqueducts, pipes and storage tanks which are filled by water from underground springs. The search for new sources goes on continually as more and more water is needed for irrigation.

In a hilly landscape where machinery is obsolete, men and animals share the labours of cultivation. Oxen and donkeys are used for ploughing and in some areas camels can be seen working on the farms. Many fields are still dug by hand, and the long rows of peasant women in their typical straw bonnets, sowing seed for the next crop, are a familiar sight.

Plants and flowers One would have to travel far to find—in such a small total area—the diversity of plants existing in the Canaries. Variations of climate and altitude—ranging from the alpine to the sub-tropical—have provided a home for plants from many parts of the world.

The range of trees growing in the islands is illustrated by a mention of the two best-known endemic species: the Canary Pine and Canary Palm. The Canary Pine (*Pinus canariensis*) is seen at its most prolific in the forest regions of Tenerife (Bosque de la Esperanza etc.), Grand Canary (Cumbre) and La Palma (La Caldera). The Canary Palm (*Phoenix canariensis*) grows at lower levels. Between these altitudes one can see a great variety of trees, some native to the island (juniper, laurel) and some exotic (Acacia, araucaria).

Many of the endemic species of trees and plants in the islands are on the decline, and represent less than a third of the total species growing here. Both the laurel and juniper, already mentioned, have been greatly reduced by the incursions of agriculture—especially the introduction of sugar cane.

Most of the imported plants were introduced by the Spanish after the conquest. Tenerife was used as a 'hardening ground' for tropical specimens before they were taken to the harsher climate of mainland Spain. The Orotava Botanical Gardens near Puerto de la Cruz offer a rich field of study for the botanist and gardener.

The domestic species—many of which can also be seen at roadsides—adorn the gardens, balconies and patios of villas and apartments. In addition to the plants of the warmer latitudes one should not be surprised to see, in this all-embracing climate, the gentle rose and the more prosaic annuals found in any English garden.

With so little difference between the seasons, wild plants and flowers abound throughout the year in the five western islands. With their drier climate, the vegetation of Lanzarote and Fuerteventura is like that of the dry zones of the other islands, i.e. with the emphasis on the cactus-like species.

Some of the plants to look out for:

Drago or Dragon Tree (*Dracaena draco*)

The most famous native plant of the Canaries. With its thick, bulbous branches and canopy of spiky leaves the 'drago' has a strangely archaic appearance—appropriate for a plant whose age in many individual specimens has been estimated as between 2–3000 years. The tree exudes a resin which, exposed to the air, turns dark red: hence its other name 'dragon's blood tree'. This was thought by the early inhabitants to have medicinal—even magical— powers, and they used it, among other things, for preserving their mummies. The best specimens of the dragon tree will be found in Tenerife at Icod and La Laguna and in Grand Canary at Galdar.

Cardón or Candelabra Spurge (*Euphorbia canariensis*)

With its tall, cactus-like stems (branched like a candelabra from the main stem) this plant is unmistakable. It was discovered in the islands by Euphorbus, the physician to King Juba II, after whom it—and a whole family of varied plants—was named. It is found in barrancos and hillsides in the drier parts of the Canaries.

Tabaiba (*Euphorbia regis-jubae*)

This plant, most prolific in Tenerife, is named after King Juba II, who dispatched the Roman expedition to the islands. It is quite bushy and grows to waist height with tiny yellow flowers. It is found in a similar habitat to the *cardón*.

Berol (*Kleinia neriifolia*)

Like a miniature dragon tree in appearance, this plant grows, like the *cardón* and *tabaiba*, in dry areas.

Agave or Century Plant (*Agave americana*)

This species from Central America has the distinguishing features of a base cluster of large pointed leaves and a central stalk which grows up to 8 m in height with its seed pods on short branching arms. The fibre of this plant (sisal), which is taken from the leaves, has many commercial uses (rope-making, etc.) and the *agave* is cultivated for this purpose in Fuerteventura.

Of the cactus and cactus-like plants the prickly pear, aloe and numerous varieties of *sempervivum* also flourish in the Canaries.

Taginaste or 'Pride of Tenerife' (*Echium bourgaeanum*)

The most spectacular flowering plant in the Canaries, the *taginaste* is endemic to Tenerife and found only in the Las Cañadas region. Its red flowers, which bloom in early summer, form a tall tapering mass and make a brilliant display in their volcanic setting.

Retama or Teide Broom (*Sparto-cytisus nubigenus*)

Flourishing at altitudes of 3000 m or more, the *retama* is found in the higher regions of Tenerife (Las Cañadas) and La Palma, where it is endemic. The thick round bushes have pink or white blossom in the spring.

White Angel's Trumpets (*Datura arborea*)

This shrub bears its large trumpet-shaped flowers all year round, but they are most conspicuous in the early months, in the roadside plantings of Grand Canary and Tenerife. The shrub, which comes from South America, is poisonous.

Practical information

TRAVEL

Air

Flights to the Canaries are from London (Heathrow and Gatwick) with connections to other major UK airports. These flights are to Las Palmas, Grand Canary (with one stop, flying time 5hrs), Tenerife (with one or two stops, 5hrs+) and Lanzarote (via Las Palmas, 5hrs + 40min). There are also services from Manchester to Las Palmas and Tenerife. The only scheduled air service with direct flights to the Canaries from the UK is operated by the Spanish national airline **Iberia.** Details of fares and timetables from Iberia, 130 Regent St, London W1.

Air Portugal operate twice-weekly flights from Las Palmas to Funchal, Madeira. (Flying time: 1hr.)

Internal flights

Iberia operate air services between all the islands except Gomera, which has no airport.

Direct flights (*at least* one a day) are as follows:

From	To
Tenerife	all islands as above
Las Palmas,	Tenerife
Grand Canary	La Palma
	Lanzarote
	Fuerteventura
Lanzarote	Tenerife
	Las Palmas
	Fuerteventura
Fuerteventura	Tenerife
	Las Palmas
	Lanzarote
La Palma	Tenerife
	Las Palmas
	Hierro
Hierro	Tenerife
	La Palma

For details of fares and timetables apply to Iberia as above.

Airports Tenerife has two airports: *Los Rodeos* in the north (mainly domestic flights) and the newly-opened *Reina Sofia* in the south. For details of taxi services from the airports to the main holiday centres see p.20. Airport buses connect all the airports to the major towns (Iberia operates its own service in some airports), but before using them it is important to ascertain how far the bus terminus is from the hotel.

Sea

Steamship lines operating regular cruises to the Canaries from the UK are:
CTC Cruises 1/3 Regent St, London SW1
14-day cruises throughout the year

P&O Cruises 77 New Oxford St, London WC1 Apr-Dec
Fred Olsen Lines Crown House, Crown St, Ipswich, Suffolk
Fred Olsen operate 7-day fly-cruises to the Canaries which start at Madeira but which may be picked up either at Tenerife or Las Palmas. The company also offers occasional 14-day cruises from Southampton.
P&O's *Canberra* includes the Canaries on its South American and African routes.
Compania Trasmediterranea operate a passenger/car service from the Spanish mainland to the Canary Islands, sailing twice a week from Cadiz. Details from Melia Travel, 12 Dover St, London W1.

Inter-island boat services

All the islands are connected by car ferry services throughout the year. These are operated by Aucona (Compania Trasmediterranea). London Office: c/o Melia Travel, 12 Dover St, London W1.

The ports are:

Tenerife	Santa Cruz de Tenerife
	Los Cristianos
Grand Canary	Las Palmas
Lanzarote	Arrecife
Fuerteventura	Puerto del Rosario
La Palma	Santa Cruz de la Palma
Gomera	San Sebastian de la Gomera
Hierro	Valverde (Puerto Estaca)

Gomera is most conveniently reached from Los Cristianos in the south of Tenerife (1½hrs). The *Ferry Gomera*, run by Fred Olsen Lines, operates a thrice-daily service (10.00, 12.00 & 20.00), and bookings can be made at the Fred Olsen office in Santa Cruz de Tenerife (Av. de Anaga) or on the mole at Los Cristianos. Note: if the ticket is purchased in Santa Cruz de Tenerife the price includes a return bus trip to Los Cristianos.

A fast Jet-Foil service (passengers only) operated by Aucona (see below) connects Tenerife and Las Palmas to Fuerteventura's beach area at Morre Jable. Sailings are four times daily between Tenerife and Las Palmas (80 min) with connections on Mon, Thurs and Sat to Morro Jable (90 min).

Offices of Aucona:
S. Cruz de Tenerife Marina, 59
Las Palmas Muelle Ribera Oeste
Arrecife José Antonio, 90
Puerto del Rosario Leon y Castillo, 46
S. Cruz de la Palma A Perez de Brito, 2
S. Sebastian de la Gomera Gen. Franco, 35

Motoring

Motorists shipping their own vehicles to the islands should remember that they are subject to Spanish law and should make sure their insurance includes cover for legal defence (Bail Bond). Those wishing to drive in the Canaries should ensure they are in possession of a valid driving licence. Most car hire firms stipulate that drivers should be not less than 25 and have had a driving licence for at least 12 months.

Drivers in the Canaries will find the road manners of the local drivers extremely courteous, in contrast to the more hectic mainland.

Car hire

Car hire firms can be found at all the major airports and resorts. In addition to the international firms (Avis and Hertz) there are a number of local firms and one, OCCA (Organización Canaria Coches Alquiler) which has offices in the five largest islands. **Avis Rent-a-Car** offer a particularly good service in the Canaries. Agents are at:

Tenerife	*Fuerteventura*
Airports	Corralejo
Santa Cruz de Tenerife	Puerto del Rosario
Playa de las Americas	*La Palma*
Puerto de la Cruz	Santa Cruz de la
Grand Canary	Palma
Airport	*Gomera*
Las Palmas	San Sebastian
Playa del Ingles	de la Gomera
Lanzarote	*El Hierro*
Airport	Valverde
Puerto del Carmen	
Costa Teguise	

Cars may be returned to any location where there is an Avis office. A special 3-, 7- or 14-day rate operates in the Canaries. This includes unlimited mileage/kms and full third party insurance but excludes local taxes and petrol. (Allowance should also be made for two optional extras: collision damage waiver and personal accident insurance.) Details of rates in Spain and the Canaries, including special discounts, may be obtained from Avis Europe, Avis House, Station Rd, Bracknell, Berks.

Conditions for car rental with the local companies differ from those of the international firms. Unlimited mileage is not available (an additional km charge operates after 100km) but the hire charge usually includes insurances.

Roads

There are three basic types of road in the islands:

Autopista (motorway) These are either single or dual carriageway. There are *autopistas* in both the major islands. Tenerife: from Santa Cruz to Puerto de la Cruz and to Los Cristianos. Grand Canary: from Las Palmas to Maspalomas and to Guia (in construction).

Main roads These routes are numbered and connect the main towns and villages. All are surfaced but their condition varies greatly.

Side roads In the larger islands the minor roads to the smaller villages are generally surfaced. In the smaller islands they are usually earth tracks, which are reasonably easy to negotiate in dry conditions. One should, however, watch out for the roads in the remoter parts of the islands which are not clearly signposted, as these often lead into fields and vineyards and are only suitable for Landrovers.

Road signs

Continental road signs are used in the Canaries. There are however additional signs in Spanish which should be memorized:

Ceda el Paso Give Way
Despacio Slow
Desvío Diversion
Paso Prohibido No Thoroughfare
Estacionamiento Prohibido No Parking
Dirección Unica One Way Street
Obras Workmen
Peligro Danger
Cuidado Caution
Curva Peligrosa Dangerous Bend

Road maps

Maps of all seven Canary islands, which include town plans and tourist information, are:

Michelin (1:200,000)
Clyde Leisure Map (1:150,000)

Maps that divide the islands into two provinces are:

Firestone 'Islas Canarias' (1:150,000) with town plans, also available as single map
Hildebrand Grand Canary province including Grand Canary (1:100,000) and
Fuerteventura and Lanzarote (1:190,000);
Tenerife province including La Palma, Gomera and El Hierro (1:100,000) with tourist information
Daily Telegraph Grand Canary (1:150,000) and Tenerife (1:150,000) with town plans and tourist information

All these maps are obtainable from Edward Stanford Ltd., 12 Long Acre, London WC2.

Bus services

Local bus services provide a good method of seeing the islands very reasonably, though in the smaller islands it is not always possible to make a return trip from outlying places in one day. When taking a bus from the terminal it is important to see whether there is a ticket office, as tickets are sometimes bought in advance of the journey. Destinations are usually shown clearly on the front of the bus, but it is worth checking this and the time of departure with the driver. In Tenerife and Grand Canary there are special express buses which run from the capitals to the main tourist centres (e.g. Las Palmas–Maspalomas, Santa Cruz de Tenerife–Puerto de la Cruz). Here it is important to take the bus marked 'Express'—otherwise one will be visiting half the villages of the island *en route*!

All bus services, urban and rural, are centred on the major towns (see under Gazetteer entries for each town). It should be remembered that services, other than those to the resort areas, tend to be most frequent in the early mornings, late afternoon and evenings, to serve the workers from the villages. Up-to-date details of services may be obtained from tourist offices or bus stations.

Taxis

Taxis are generally equipped with meters. For the longer journeys the fare should be agreed in advance. For regular journeys, such as those from the airports to the main resorts, standard tariffs operate.

Most of the resorts and major towns have offices by the taxi ranks where one can refer to a scale of charges.

Sightseeing by taxi can be expensive, and people travelling in this way are recommended to share the journey with two or three others.

Sightseeing tours

Daily coach excursions are operated by travel agencies in the major islands. These are listed as 'Viajes' in the local directories. Among the main agencies are *CYRASA, Insular, Intersol* and *Wagon-Lits Cook*. These companies offer full-day or half-day excursions to places of interest in the islands. The prices are very reasonable and include lunch on the longer trips. Most of the larger hotels have details of these local excursions on their notice boards and will make the necessary reservations. The coaches will usually collect passengers from the hotel if convenient.

INCLUSIVE HOLIDAYS

A selection of tour operators which include the Canaries in their brochures:

Arrowsmith Holidays Royal Buildings, 2 Mosley St, Piccadilly, Manchester
Carousel Holidays 45 New St, Birmingham
Cosmos Tourama House, 17 Homesdale Rd, Bromley, Kent
Enterprise Holidays Ground Star House, London Rd, Crawley, Sussex
Falcon Holidays 33 Notting Hill Gate, London W11
Flair Holidays 4-6 Manor Mount, London SE2
Horizon Holidays Broadway, Edgbaston Fiveways, Birmingham

Hotels in Spain 310 London House, 26/40 Kensington High St London W8
Inghams Holiday House, 329 Putney Bridge Rd, London SW15
Intasun Holidays Intasun House, 2 Cromwell Ave, Bromley, Kent
Lanzarote Villas Springfield Rd, Horsham, Sussex
Martin Rooks Holidays 204 Ebury St, London SW1
Mundi Color Travel 276 Vauxhall Bridge Rd, London SW1
Portland Holidays 218 Great Portland St, London W1N 5HG
Saga Holidays The Saga Building, Middelburg Sq, Folkestone, Kent
Select Holidays Centurion House, Hertford
Thomas Cook Holidays PO Box 36, Thorpe Wood, Peterborough, Cambs
Thompson Holidays Greater London House, Hampstead Rd, London NW1
Tjaereborg 194 Campden Hill Rd, London W8

ACCOMMODATION

Hotels

Hotels in the Canaries, as in other parts of Spain, are graded on a star system. All are required to display a sign at the main entrance showing their 'star' rating. This rule includes the 'Residencias' (abbreviated HR) which are hotels without restaurants, but where one can nearly always have a continental breakfast. There are in addition the Apartment Hotels (HA) which are like Residencias but include apartments, and the smaller 'hostals' or 'pensions' which offer accommodation but no food.

The Spanish Tourist Authority runs **Paradores**, which are hotels controlled by the Government. They are either old buildings which have been converted or new buildings in the traditional style. They maintain a high standard and offer extremely good value. The Paradores in the Canaries are in Tenerife, Gomera, Hierro and Fuerteventura (for locations see *Hotels*, opposite). The former Parador in Grand Canary at Cruz de Tejeda is now a Hosteria, offering meals only.

The range of resort hotels is wide. The luxury hotels in such places as Las Palmas and Puerto de la Cruz offer every modern facility. Additional refinements found in most of the 5-star category are grill rooms, heated swimming pools and night clubs. The smaller hotels are generally clean and well run.

In the remote villages a pension or 'fonda' (small local restaurant) can usually be found, offering a cheap and simple room. The appeal of these places is of course confined to the casual traveller, as they cannot be booked in advance.

PRINCIPAL RESORTS, HOTELS AND BEACH AREAS

(Locations shown clockwise from capital, with distance from it by the shortest route)
HR: Residence Hotel HA: Apartment Hotel

TENERIFE

Santa Cruz de Tenerife (capital)
Nearest beach at *Las Teresitas* (see below)
5-star *Mencey*; 3-star *Colon Rambla* (HA), *Diplomatico* (HR), *Plaza* (HA); 2-star *Anaga, Pelinor* (HR), *Taburiente* (HR), *Tamaide* (HR); 1-star *Horizonte, San Jose* (HR); pensions

Las Caletillas (14km south)
Pebble beach on attractive coastline. Mostly apartments, similarly at town of Candelaria which also has beach.
3-star *Tenerife Tour, Los Geranios* (HA); pensions

El Medano (62km south-west)
Spacious sand beach in wide bay with safe shallow bathing and island's best windsurfing. Alternative sand beach of *Playa de la Tejita*, popular with nudists, on west side of Montaña Rosa peninsula.
3-star *Medano, Playa Sur Tenerife*; pensions

Costa del Silencio (71km south-west)
Resort area at southern tip of island including two locations. *Las Galletas* has a rock and shingle beach and fishing harbour, *Ten Bel* apartments with large swimming pools to compensate for poor beach.
2-star *Parque Ten-Bel Sol*; pensions

Los Cristianos (76km south-west)
Small harbour (boats to Gomera) whose wall protects a long, wide, sandy beach with shallow water, good for children. A second, pebble beach lies to the north.
3-star *Princesa Dacil, Tenerife Sur* (HA); 2-star *Andreas* (HR); pensions

Playa de las Americas (76km south-west)
This major resort's range of beaches includes a sandy stretch with shallow water and a less sheltered, pebbly beach with good surfing.
4-star *Bitacora* (HA), *Bouganville Playa, Club Atlantis* (HA), *Columbus* (HA), *Conquistador, Esmeralda Playa, Europe Tenerife, Gran Tenerife, Guayarmina Princess, Las Palmeras, La Siesta, Palm Beach* (HA), *Park Hotel Troya, Tenerife Princess, Tenerife Sol, Vulcano*; 3-star *Europe Park Club, La Gala, Las Dalias, Flamingo, Jardin Tropical* (HA), *Los Hibiscos* (HA), *Oasis Moreque* (HR), *Oro Negro* (HA), *Panorama* (HA), *Ponderosa* (HR), *Villamar* (HA)

Playa Paraiso (87km south-west)
New development with small beach of dark sand and rocky cove with swimming pool.
3-star *Fiesta Floral, Oasis Paraise*

Puerto de Santiago (89km west)
Series of four bays with one sandy beach (*Playa de la Arena*) shelving steeply. Old fishing village with small harbour.
4-star *Los Gigantes Sol, Santiago*

Los Gigantes (89km west)
Cliff backdrop ('The Giants') to resort terraced over harbour/marina. Adjacent beach (sand, enclosed by rocks) good for families.

Playa de San Marcos (58km west)
Black sand beach located below attractive old town of Icod de los Vinos.

Los Realejos (43km west)
Hill town above Puerto de la Cruz.
4-star *Maritim*; 3-star *Panoramica Garden*; 2-star *Reforma, Romantica*.

Puerto de la Cruz (39km west)
The lush Orotava Valley provides a backdrop to a rocky shore with black lava beaches to west as far as Punta Brava. Landscaped lido (*Lago de Martianez*) at east end of town most popular bathing place, with black sand *Playa de Martianez* to east. Island's oldest and largest resort.
5-star *Botanico Sol, San Felipe Sol, Semiramis*; 4-star *Atalaya Gran, Atlantic Playa, Dania Park, El Tope, Florida, Gran Hotel Concordia Playa, Los Dogos Sol, Bonanza Canarife, Interpalace, La Chiripa, La Paz, Las Vegas Sol, Magec, Martianez, Melia Puerto de la Cruz, Orotava Garden Sol, Parque San Antonio Sol, Tenerife Playa Sol, Tigaiga, Tryp Puerto Playa, Valle-Mar*; 3-star *Casa del Sol, Castellana Puerto, Chimisay* (HR) *Colon* (HR), *Condesa* (HR), *Don Manolito, Guacimara* (HR), *Guajara* (HA), *Ikarus, Internacional, Lavaggi, Las Aguñas Sol, Los Principes, Magec-Park, Marquesa, Marte, Martina* (HA), *Miramar, Monopol, Nopal, Onuba* (HR), *Oro Negro, San Borondon I, San Borondon II, San Telmo, Tagor* (HR) *Teide Mar* (HA), *Tropical* (HR), *Trovador, Xibana Park* (HR); 2-star *Capricho, Floralva* (HA) *Framperez, Gardenia Park* (HR), Marquesol, Monseve (HR), *Pinocho* (HR), *Puerto Azul* (HR), *San Amaro* (HR), *Tejuma* (HR); 1-star *Alfomar* (HR), *Bambi* (HR), *Casa Alta* (HR), *Catrin* (HA), *Don Candido* (HR), *Maga, Marquesita, Monica* (HR); pensions

La Laguna (10km west)
Historic university town.
1-star *Aguere*; pensions

Bajamar (20km north-west)
High cliff setting on northern Anaga peninsula with celebrated *piscinas naturales*.
4-star *Nautilus*; 3-star *Delfin-Laguna* (HR), *Neptuno, Tinguaro*

Las Teresitas (10km north-east)
Beach area nearest to Santa Cruz with sand imported from Sahara. *Playa de las Gaviotas* to the north also has fine sand.

Las Cañadas del Teide (65km south-west)
Centre for Las Canadas National Park
2-star *Parador Las Canadas del Teide*

LA PALMA

Santa Cruz de la Palma (capital)
3-star *Parador de Santa Cruz de la Palma, San Miguel*; pensions

Los Cancajos (6km south)
Sand beach with volcanic coves under development.

Mazo (El Pueblo) (14km south)
1-star *Casa Roja* (HR)

El Paso (27km west)
Good base for exploration of the Cumbre.
2-star *Nambroque* (HR); pension

Los Llanos de Aridane (32km west)
Main western centre with access (10km) to beaches at Puerto de Naos.
1-star *Eden*; pension

GOMERA

San Sebastian de la Gomera (capital)
The town has a dark volcanic beach south of the harbour and the attractive *Playa de Avalo* 4km to the north.
4-star *Parador de la Gomera*; 2-star *Garajonay*; pensions

Playa de Santiago (26km south-west)
Sheltered, cliff-backed beach, rather stony with other coves to the east.
4-star *Tecina*.
Also pension at **Vallehermoso** (42km north-west) and other beaches at Playa de Valle Gran Rey (46km west), Playa de Vallehermoso (45km north-west), Agulo (27km north-west)

HIERRO

Valverde (capital)
The nearest accessible beach is the *Playa de la Caleta* (4km) on the east coast.
3-star *Parador de la Isla de Hierro*; 2-star *Boomerang*; pensions. Also pensions at **Frontera** (33km south-west)

GRAND CANARY

Las Palmas (capital)
Major beach area *Las Canteras*, a 3km stretch on the west side of the city with fine golden sand and a protective reef 150km offshore. On the east, *Las Alcaravaneras* beach is unsuitable for swimming.
5-star *Cristina Sol, Reina Isabel, Santa Catalina*; 4-star *Concorde, Iberia Sol* (HR), *Imperial Playa, Los Bardinos Sol, Rocamar, Tigaday* (HR); 3-star *Astoria Club, Atlanta* (HR), *Banosol* (HR), *Braemar* (HR),

Cantur (HR), *Corinto* (HR), *Fataga, Faycan, Galatea* (HR), *Gran Canaria, Las Lanzas* (HR), *Mariluz* (HR), *Miraflor, Nautilus* (HR), *Olympia* (HR), *Parque* (HR), *Rosalia* (HR), *Sol* (HR), *Sorimba, Tenesoya* (HR), *Trocadero* (HR), *Utiaca* (HR), *Villa Blanca* (HR); 2-star *Alva* (HR), *Atlantida* (HR), *Cactus* (HR), *El Cisne* (HR), *Funchal* (HR), *German* (HR), *Idafe* (HR), *Majorica* (HR), *Marola* (HR), *Pujol* (HR), *Syria* (HR), *Valencia* (HR), *Verol* (HR); 1-star *Los Angeles* (HR), *Madrid* (HR); pensions

San Agustin (48km south)
Beginning of 7km stretch of coastline terminating at Maspalomas which has the finest beaches in the island. Main beach *Playa de San Agustin*, with adjacent *Las Burras* beach to west used by fishing boats.
5-star *Tamarindos Sol*; 4-star *Costa Canaria, Don Gregory, Folias*; 3-star *Ifa Beach* (HR)

Playa del Ingles (50km south)
The south's major resort has 3km of golden sand, merging to the west in the sand dunes of the Maspalomas peninsula.
4-star *Catarina Playa, Canaria Princess, Lucana, Neptuno, Rio Palmeras*; 3-star *Beverly Park, Buenaventura Playa, Continental* (HR), *Don Miguel, Eugenia Victoria, Las Margaritas, Playa del Ingles* (HA) *Waikiki*; 2-star *Escorial* (HA), *Ifa Regina Mar* (HA), *Rondo* (HA), *Sunwing Playa del Ingles* (HA)

Maspalomas (52km south)
The *Dunas de Maspalomas* are the most dramatic features of the south coast, stretching 3km from the *Playa del Ingles*. On the east they are bounded by a lagoon (*El Oasis*) and lighthouse, to the north by a golf course. The dunes, with their dips and hollows, are perfect for nudists.
5-star *Iberotel Maspalomas Oasis*; 4-star *Apolo, Corona Caserio, Ifa Dunamar, Ifa Hotel Faro de Maspalomas, Las Margaritas, Lucana, Maspalomas Palm Beach, Rio Palmera*; 3-star *Parque Tropical, Rey Carlos* (HA), *Surycan* (HA); 2-star *Inter Club Atlantic* (HR)

Puerto Rico (69km south-west)
Man-made beach of yellow sand, lido and sailing harbour set into mountainside.
4-star *Revoli* (HA); 1-star *La Riviera* (HA); pensions

Puerto de Mogan (82km south-west)
Small beach area with marine and fishing harbour

Los Berrazales (Agaete) (40km west)
Former spa at head of beautiful fertile valley.
2-star *Princesa Guayarmina*

Santa Brigida (18km south-west)
Near Caldera de Bandama and golf course.
3-star *La Posada* (HR)

LANZAROTE

Arrecife (capital)
The nearest beaches west of the town are not very accessible and it is better to go to one of the resorts.
4-star *Arrecife Gran*; 3-star *Lancelot Playa* (HR), *Miramar* (HR); 1-star *San Gines*; pensions

Playa de los Pocillos (10km south-west)
Nearest beach to airport with 3km of good sand.
4-star *La Geria, Lanzarote Palace, San Antonio*; 2-star *Playa Grande* (HA)

Playa Blanca (14km south-west)
Northern of two resorts with same name.
The 'white' beach here is nearer grey — but
with good sand.

Puerto del Carmen (16km south-west)
A wide beach backed by bungalow villages,
apartments and other tourist development in
Lanzarote's major resort.
4-star *Los Fariones*; 3-star *La Perla*

Playa Blanca (40km south-west)
Southern of two resorts with same name.
Ferry port for Fuerteventura. Small beach of
former fishing village crowded in season: a
better bet is the wide *Playa de Papagayo* to
the east (7km, rough road) with white sand
and cliff backdrop.
4-star *Lanzarote Princess, Lanzarote Park* (HA);
pensions

Playa de Famara (18km north)
3km stretch of sand beach on north coast,
location of La Santa sports centre and
holiday village.

Playa de las Conchas (Graciosa i.)
Best of Graciosa's rarely-visited beaches.

Costa Teguise (7km north-east)
Sand transported from Playa Blanca area in
south has created fine beach.
5-star *Las Salinas Sol, Teguise Playa*

FUERTEVENTURA

Puerto del Rosario (capital)
Good sand beach (*Playa Blanca*) to the
south.
3-star *Parador de Fuerteventura, Las Gavias* (HR);
2-star *Valeron*; pensions

Gran Tarajal (45km south-west)
Modest beach near port.
3-star *Los Gorriones Sol*

Tarajalejo (57km south-west)
Wide sandy beach alongside road running
through small resort.
3-star *Maxorata*

Costa Calma (72km south-west)
First resort on the 24km *Jandia Playa*, the
superb white sand beach of the southern
peninsula.
2-star *Club Solyventura*

Jandia Playa (95km south-west)
At the southern end of the Jandia's
magnificent coastline of sweeping dunes
(*Playa del Matorral*) in the area known as
Morro del Jable.
4-star *Casa Atlantica*; 3-star *Robinson Club Jandia
Playa*; 2-star *Fiesta Casa Atlantica* (HA); pensions

Corralejo (39km north)
Coastline of white sand dunes stretching
from port (ferry to Lanzarote) 10km south
along coastline (*Playas Grandes*).
5-star *Tres Islas*, 4-star *Oliva Beach*; 1-star *Corralejo*

Further details of hotels in the Canaries,
including prices, are found in the publication
Hoteles, Campings, Apartmentos (separate
booklets for each province) available from
the Spanish National Tourist Office, 57/58 St
James's St, London SW1.

Apartments and villas
'Apartmentos' are becoming increasingly
popular in the islands for visitors who prefer
independent accommodation. This is particularly true of families who enjoy the
additional space and freedom they offer. The
apartments are fully furnished and equipped
and rates depend on the number of bedrooms
required. Alternatively, villas suitable for
one or two families only are available
for those who prefer more intimate
surroundings.
Many apartments offer continental breakfast, and those who prefer not to cook the
other meals will usually find that there is a
good restaurant nearby.
The cheapest way of booking apartments and
villas is through tour operators, who now
offer them as an alternative to hotel accommodation in their package tours.

Camping
With their mild climate and attractive
countryside the Canaries are ideal for
camping. Unlike the coastline of Spain, however, the islands have very few camp sites.
The only official camp sites are in Grand
Canary at Temisas, on the mountain route
from Aguimes, and Guantanamo, Puerto de
Mogan; in Tenerife at Nauta, Las Galletas.
The lack of camp sites in the other islands
should not deter the visitor who prefers the
outdoor life. The tourist authorities in each
island will usually be able to suggest places
suitable for camping, either in woods or open
country or near a beach.
In the more remote areas local inhabitants
will often give permission for camping on
their property, but in view of recent objec-
tions to the 'hippy' type of visitor it is necessary to show that one is properly equipped
with either caravan or tent, and also to make
suitable sanitary arrangements.
Lighting fires in wooded areas is prohibited,
and the camper should be equipped with a
small stove for cooking.
For further details apply to the Spanish
National Tourist Office.

FOOD AND DRINK
Food in the Canary Islands is similar to that
of mainland Spain, but in addition there are
some interesting local dishes. Unfortunately
it is becoming increasingly difficult to find
restaurants serving such dishes in the
tourist areas as the need to cater *en masse*
for foreign palates has meant the pre-
dominance of the international restaurant.

The traditional Spanish meal is a leisurely affair. The *entremeses* (*hors d'oeuvres*) may have as many as a dozen items, including meats, shell fish, canned fish, vegetables and sausages. The soups are usually very substantial, and often include eggs or bread. *Tortillas* (omelettes) are eaten either hot or cold, and the classic *Tortilla Española* contains potatoes, red peppers and onions.

Meats are varied, and include game in some districts. Tripe and rabbit are used in many dishes. Fish is extremely good in the islands, whose waters are stocked with a great variety of species. The best introduction to the seafoods of the Canaries is by sampling the *tapas*. These are small snacks—usually cooked meats or fish—served over the bar with beer or coffee. The fish most often served in this way are *calamares fritos* (fried squid), *pulpo* (octopus), *gambas* (shrimps) or *anguilitas* (baby eels). Other popular fish are the *cherne* (cod), *merluza* (hake) and *caballa* (mackerel). Game fish include *atun* (tunny) and *espada* (swordfish).

Vegetables are often served as a separate *entrée*, and only potatoes or bread served with the meat course. The popular method of serving fish in the Canaries is with potatoes cooked in their skins (*papas arrugadas*). A red piquant sauce—*mojo picon*—is then usually added.

A traditional dish of the Canaries which is rarely served in restaurants is *gofio*. This is the basic food of the country people, and consists of grain—generally either wheat or maize—which is roasted and ground in a mill. This is then mixed with water and made into a kind of loaf.

Other typical dishes to look for are:

Paella, which in the Canaries has more fish in it than in the mainland.

Vieja A local fish eaten with oil and vinegar.

Pescado con mojo Fish eaten with a sauce made in a wooden mortar from peppers, spices and oil. Particularly good in Gomera.

Quesadilla herrena Cheesecake made with goat's milk cheese, a speciality of Hierro.

Miel de Palma Palm honey extracted from the date palm and cooked over a slow fire until thick and black. Eaten with *gofio* or used as a filling for tarts.

The most popular **drink** for the working people is rum. The main distillery is in Grand Canary, near Arucas: a 'finger' of *Ron Arehucas* costs 5ptas. From the same distillery come the liqueurs which are offered to tourists in the local *bodegas*. Their rich flavours are often too much for the uninitiated palate, but a local cheese is usually served to offset their sweetness. Flavours include banana (*platano*), orange (*naranja*), cactus (*tequila*) and mint (*menta*). Another popular drink is beer (*cerveza*), with Spanish or local labels, and wine (*vino*).

Each of the islands produces its own wine. They tend, however, to have a common characteristic: the flavour peculiar to grapes from vines grown in volcanic soil. One of the most famous wines which can be sweet or dry and served as an aperitif is *Malvasia*. This is chiefly produced in Lanzarote and the volcanic south of La Palma.

One of the best wines, *Vino del Monte* comes from the Monte district in Grand Canary. This is a fine, full-bodied red wine.

Wines served in hotels and the larger restaurants are usually from the mainland. Canary wines are inclined to be sweet, so those requiring a good dry wine should order a mainland label.

Restaurants

International cuisine is readily available in the larger towns and resorts. Unless you can find a restaurant in these places which bases its reputation on authentic Spanish cuisine, you will have to go to the smaller towns and villages for good Spanish cooking. Here the local restaurant-bars serve many exciting and well-cooked dishes at reasonable prices. Best value is often provided by the *menu del dia* (usually a set three-course meal including wine). Although prices generally include taxes and service, it is customary to leave a 5–10% tip if everything is satisfactory.

Fish is an important item in Canary Island cooking, and restaurants which serve nothing else are quite common. The best of these are—not surprisingly—in the fishing villages and small seaside resorts.

All the vegetables, fruits and spices used in Canary dishes are grown locally. The people appreciate good cooking, and are always pleased to know that a visitor has enjoyed a meal.

Details of local restaurants are available from the tourist offices in the main towns and resorts.

FOLK ART

Embroidery and drawn thread work Although many of the tourist shops employ their own embroiderers, much of this beautiful work is still done by the country women in their own homes. Each island has its own distinctive pattern. Popular articles are tablecloths, table mats, handkerchiefs and pillowcases. The work is extremely fine and intricate, and both white and coloured materials are used.

Weaving is a popular craft in the smaller villages. Traditional designs are used and articles include blankets, rugs, shoulder bags and curtain materials. It is quite a common sight in the remote villages of the western islands to see groups of women sitting outside their homes with their spindles and distaffs. The wool is very tough, and the blankets hard-wearing and almost waterproof.

Pottery It is still possible to find hand-made pottery in the islands, but most of it is now factory-produced. The genuine hand-made articles are replicas of the ancient Guanche vessels, made of red clay. *Chipude* in Gomera is a centre of this ancient craft, and the traveller who gets as far as this remote village can still see the women turning the pots by hand. Another important pottery centre is at *La Atalaya*, in Grand Canary.

LANGUAGE

The language of the Canaries is Spanish, similar to that spoken on the mainland. As in the mainland, regional differences of dialect prevail—particularly in the smaller islands.

The advent of tourism has introduced a smattering of foreign tongues (notably German and some Scandinavian languages) and in the larger towns English is understood by the staffs of most hotels, shops and travel agencies. In outlying districts, however, few people speak anything but Spanish.

A good Spanish phrase book, and a knowledge of the expressions of courtesy, basic words and numbers and the days of the week will be necessary for the visitor planning to travel outside the major resorts.

Some common words encountered by travellers in the islands:

Aldea village	*Finca* farm or villa
Ayuntamiento town hall	*Fonda* inn
Barranco ravine	*Iglesia* church
Barrio quarter	*Llano* plain
Caldera crater	*Malpais* badland
Calle street	*Monte* mountain
Camino road	*Muelle* mole
Capilla chapel	*Pico* peak
Carretera highway	*Pinar* pine forest
Casa house	*Pueblo* village
Ciudad city	*Punta* point
Cumbre mountain	*Roque* rock
range	*Vega* plain
Ermita hermitage	(cultivated)

FESTIVALS

Religious festivals are an intrinsic part of the life of the Canary Islands. A special attraction are the floral processions associated with the festivities of Corpus Christi when elaborate carpets of flowers are laid out in the streets. Every village celebrates its Saint's Day, and the traveller in the islands is sure to encounter one of these lively events during his visit.

There are so many festivals that a complete list cannot be given, but tourist offices have full details of local festivities. Some of the most important festivals are:

Jan 5	**S. Cruz de Tenerife and Las Palmas** *Procession of the Magi*
Jan 19	**S. Sebastian de la Gomera** *Festival of S. Sebastian*
Feb (2nd week)	**Aguimes, Grand Canary Puerto de la Cruz S. Cruz de Tenerife** *Winter festivals*
Mar/Apr	*Holy Week* celebrations are held throughout the islands with particularly impressive ceremonies at La Orotava and La Laguna in Tenerife and Las Palmas and Telde in Grand Canary
Apr 29	**Las Palmas** Celebration of the *Incorporation of Grand Canary in the Kingdom of Castile*
May/Jun	*Corpus Christi* The most spectacular of these festivities is at La Orotava where carpets of flowers are laid in the streets. Other fine floral displays are at Tacoronte and La Laguna in Tenerife, Las Palmas and Arucas in Grand Canary and Mazo in La Palma

May 1–15	**S. Cruz de Tenerife** *Fiestas de la Cruz* Celebration of the founding of the city
Jun 24	**Icod de los Vinos, Tenerife** *Festival of S. Juan*
Jul 15	**Puerto de la Cruz** *Festival of Gran Poder de Dios* Street processions and floral battle
Jul (3rd week)	**S. Cruz de Tenerife** *Festivals of the Sea* and *Virgen del Carmen*
Jul 25	**S. Cruz de Tenerife** *Commemoration of the Defeat of Nelson*
Jul 27	**La Laguna, Tenerife** *Festival of S. Cristóbal*
Aug 4–7	**Agaete, Puerto de las Nieves, Grand Canary** *Festival of Nuestra Señora de las Nieves* and *Bajada de la Rama*
Aug 15	**Candelaria, Tenerife** *Feast of the Assumption* (Nuestra Señora de la Candelaria)
Aug (3rd Sun)	**Bajamar, Tenerife** *Festival of Cristo del Gran Poder*
Aug 24–29	**Arrecife, Lanzarote** *Festival of S. Gines*
Sep 1–6	**S. Sebastian de la Gomera** *Christopher Columbus Week*
Sep 5	**S. Cruz de la Palma** *Festival of Nuestra Señora de las Nieves* Once every 5 years this event starts in August and continues for 1 month—the *Fiestas Lustrales*
Sep 6–8	**Teror, Grand Canary** *Festival of Nuestra Señora del Pino* Patron Saint of the Canaries
Sep 12–14	**La Laguna, Tenerife** *Festival of El Santisimo Cristo*
Sep 12–18	**Telde, Grand Canary** *Festival of Santo Cristo*
Sep 21	**Tacoronte, Tenerife** *Festival of Santisimo Cristo de Tacoronte*
Oct 10	**Valverde, Hierro** *Festival of Nuestra Señora del Rosario*
Oct 11	**Las Palmas** *Festival of Nuestra Señora de la Luz*
Nov	**Teror, Grand Canary** *Fiesta del Rancho de Animas*
Dec 8	**Jinámar, Telde, Grand Canary** *Festival of Nuestra Señora de la Concepción*
Dec 17	**Santa Lucia, Grand Canary** *Fiesta de los Labradores*

SPORT

Among the many sports enjoyed by visitors to the Canaries, **swimming** is naturally the most popular (see *Beaches and Swimming Pools*, below). **Waterskiing** and **scuba diving** are also popular, and facilities for these are available at all the major resorts.

Of the more specialist water sports, **sailing** presents the greatest challenge, particularly for those who wish to brave the windward side of the islands. Except for Hierro every island has its Yacht Club, located in the capital.

Fishing is another challenging activity and the waters of the islands (particularly Lanzarote and Fuerteventura) present marvellous opportunities for game fishing. For details about hiring of boats and tackle etc., contact the local tourist office.

The sport which one would least associate with the Canaries is **golf**. There are however two fine 18-hole courses in the islands:
El Peñon (Tenerife, near airport 15km from Santa Cruz)
Llanos de Bandama (Grand Canary, at Tafira 12km from Las Palmas)
Grand Canary has two more 18-hole courses at Maspalomas, and Lanzarote a new course 3.5km from Arrecife.

Facilities for **tennis** are extremely good in the two major islands. Most of the large apartments and hotels have courts, but failing that one can apply for temporary membership to a Tennis Club (see Las Palmas, Santa Cruz de Tenerife and Puerto de la Cruz).

Spectator sports

Some of the popular Canary Islands sports, such as cock-fighting and bull-fighting, are best avoided: but there are other sports inherited from the Guanches which are peculiar to the islands and worth seeing if one is in the right place at the right time. These include:
Lucha canaria Canary wrestling. The object of this very skilled sport is that one wrestler should be able to throw the other to the ground.
Juego de Palo Fencing match using long flexible sticks.
Garrocha Form of pole-vaulting peculiar to La Palma.

BEACHES AND SWIMMING POOLS

There is no such thing as a typical Canary beach. It can be a tiny cove formed by a seaward flow of lava or a wide golden strand stretching for miles. It can be shingle, rock or black volcanic sand. It can be yellow sand or white sand, and backed by sweeping dunes or pine trees.

The finest beaches are mainly on the south and east coasts of the islands, where the sand is generally of the golden rather than the dark volcanic variety. The best examples are the rolling dunes of Maspalomas in Grand Canary and the Jandia Playa in Fuerteventura.

For descriptions of the beach and resort areas, see ps. 21–23.

Swimming pools All 5-star and most 4-star hotels have swimming pools, as do the larger apartment buildings. The splendid new landscaped pools, such as the Lago de Martianez in Puerto de la Cruz, are a special attraction.

FOLK DANCING

Canary folk songs and dances are known the world over, and they are one of the most enjoyable forms of entertainment in the islands. In origin they are partly native, partly Spanish: lively combinations of singing and dancing known as the *tempo canario*.

The dances are performed in the colourful Canary Island costumes, and accompanied by traditional instruments (guitars, *timples*, flutes, tambourines). They can be seen at the Pueblo Canario in Las Palmas every Thursday, Sunday and holiday, as well as at special performances at the main hotels. The many festival days also have their song and dance items, many of which accompany the processions.

WEATHER

The factors influencing the climate of the Canaries (see p. 14) produce weather conditions which, though varied, suit the average holidaymaker. The most important aspect of the islands' climate is that with the exception of the highest peaks on Tenerife and Grand Canary they are never cold. The average temperatures range between 59°F (15°C) and 84°F (29°C). Hours of sunshine are generally long (the daily average in Las Palmas is 7.5 hrs).

The winter season is a little cooler than the summer, and cloud and rain may occasionally interrupt inter-island sea and air services between November and March. The summer is the best time for excursions into the mountains and more remote parts of the islands, as well as for travel between them. There is often great variation in the weather in one island on the same day. A 'microclimate', as it is called, is very typical of Grand Canary. Here, on one beach in the north, it may be cool with fine rain, while on another only a few miles down the coast the sun may be shining and the temperature in the 80s. Likewise the interior may be hot and dry while the coast is cool and windy.

The following table shows average monthly temperatures in the Canaries (°Fahrenheit):

Jan	Feb	Mar	Apr	May	Jun
64	64	65	66	68	71
Jul	Aug	Sep	Oct	Nov	Dec
74	76	75	73	69	66

CURRENCY, BANKS AND SHOPS

The monetary unit is the peseta. The coins are of 5,10,25,50,100 and 200 ptas. Notes are of 500, 1000, 2000 and 5000 ptas. There are ample facilities for changing travellers cheques or currency in the resorts and main towns. Banks are usually open Mon-Fri 09.00-14.00.

Hotels and exchange bureaux (*cambios*) will usually change travellers cheques, but at a less favourable rate of exchange.

Shopping The large towns and resorts all provide ample shopping facilities. As the Canaries are Free Ports the prices of such items as cameras, watches, electrical equipment, leather goods, wine, spirits and tobacco are low.

The special products of the islands, such as embroidery and woven goods, are excellent buys. Care should be taken, however, to ensure the goods are genuine local work, as many of the items on sale are brought into the islands from mainland Spain.

GUIDE AND REFERENCE BOOKS

The classic travel book of the Canaries is the two-volume epic of the intrepid Mrs Olivia M. Stone, *Tenerife and Its Six Satellites*. Mrs Stone travelled throughout the seven islands with her husband in the 1880s, at a time when methods of transport were totally primitive and islands like Lanzarote and Fuerteventura were 'beyond the pale of civilisation.' Published in 1887, the book may be found in the London Library.

The classic guide book is Brown's *Madeira, Canary Islands and Azores*, published by Simpkin Marshall (last edition 1932).

Four excellent walking guides to the Canaries are published by Sunflower Books in their acclaimed 'Landscapes' series. These are *Tenerife, Southern Tenerife & La Gomera, Gran Canaria* and *Lanzarote & Fuerteventura*, all by Noel Rochford.

TOURIST INFORMATION

Information on all aspects of travel to the Canary Islands is available from the Spanish National Tourist Office, 57/58 St James's St, London SW1

Tourist offices in the islands are:

Tenerife *Santa Cruz de Tenerife* Plaza de España; *Puerto de la Cruz* Plaza de la Iglesia
La Palma *Santa Cruz de la Palma* O'Daly 35
Grand Canary *Las Palmas* Parque Santa Catalina
Lanzarote *Arrecife* Parque Municipal
Fuerteventura *Puerto del Rosario* Avenida de Primero de Mayo, 33

The staff of these offices mostly speak English and they are open all day Mon-Fri and Sat a.m. For assistance in the smaller islands, try the *Cabildo Insular* (Town Hall).

Exploring the Canaries

The most daunting fact confronting travellers who wish to see the Canaries as a group is that there are seven islands, stretching over 250 miles of ocean. Although communications between the islands are excellent, an itinerary that embraced all seven in two or three weeks would be too demanding and leave little time to absorb the atmosphere of each island.

A combination of two or three islands makes a happier alternative, and here the choice is up to the individual taste of the traveller, whose preferred environment may be anything from sand dunes to pine-clad mountains. The most popular islands are Grand Canary and Tenerife, for these provide a wide range not only of tourist facilities but of the 'breathing spaces'—desert shores, misty peaks, fertile slopes—that add an extra dimension to a conventional resort holiday. But beyond these favoured shores lie the lesser-known islands which have their own special features to add to the landscape of the Canaries.

Visitors to Tenerife can conveniently fit in excursions to other islands. The most accessible by air (direct flights) are Grand Canary, La Palma and Lanzarote. Even little Hierro—usually overlooked in the tourist itineraries—has an airstrip, with direct flights from Tenerife and La

Betancuria, Fuerteventura

Palma. Boat trips are obviously slower, although there is an excellent $1\frac{1}{2}$-hour service to Gomera from Tenerife (Los Cristianos).

From Grand Canary the most accessible islands are Tenerife, Lanzarote and Fuerteventura, all of which have a direct air service. Air excursions combined with sightseeing tours are offered by travel agents in the major islands.

The strategy is choosing an island: the tactics are exploring it. Here a car is invaluable, if not essential, but car hire is expensive and one must consider the alternatives. All the islands have good bus services, based on their major towns. In the remoter islands, however, the condition of the roads is a limiting factor and one should not expect to do a whistle stop tour by public transport. Another point is that bus schedules are not geared to the tourist but to the requirements of the local population, and for this reason the services are most frequent in the early morning and evening. The range of frequency is best illustrated by the bus journeys of equivalent distance (40 km) across the islands of Tenerife and Gomera. From Santa Cruz de Tenerife to Puerto de la Cruz there is a half-hourly, 45-minute service along the *autopista*: from San Sebastian de la Gomera to Vallehermoso there is a daily run along a slow, winding road which takes $2\frac{1}{2}$ hours.

In the three major tourist islands (Tenerife, Grand Canary and Lanzarote), those who prefer more controlled sightseeing can join the coach excursions which operate from the main resorts. Like the buses, however, these have prescribed stopping points and independent spirits will prefer the flexibility of a hired car.

However he travels, the visitor to the Canaries will be impressed by the changing panoramas that unfold with every turn of the road, whether they be the lush valleys of Tenerife, the cindery craters of Lanzarote, the forests of Grand Canary or the pink deserts of Fuerteventura. Towns and villages, too, present their contrasts, from the white-painted Moorish-style hamlets of the eastern islands to the bustling city-ports of Las Palmas and Santa Cruz de Tenerife.

And the past? What can the explorer find of the story of the Guanches, those proud but primitive people whose realm this was while Spain was still a Roman province? Or of those intrepid conquerors who came in their tall ships, carrying their cannon and crucifixes on to the unsuspecting shores? So much, it seems, awaits the archaeologist and historian, and the modern traveller can do little more than follow the few signposts, the jots of information that lead to a Guanche cave or the holy image that has survived countless vicissitudes to reach its shrine in a 400-year-old church.

This is the paradox of the Canaries. Discovered by modern man more than 600 years ago and colonized by the developers and tour operators in the 20th century, they remain barely charted by history. This is perhaps one of the secrets of their appeal: that they have so much to offer, but may still have more.

Tenerife

Note on maps

Distances in km

Itinerary routes in black

These maps should be
used in conjunction with
recommended road maps
(see p. 19)

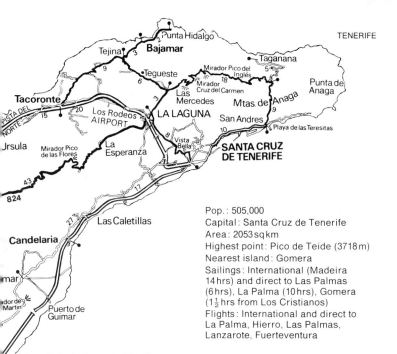

Pop.: 505,000
Capital: Santa Cruz de Tenerife
Area: 2053 sq km
Highest point: Pico de Teide (3718m)
Nearest island: Gomera
Sailings: International (Madeira 14 hrs) and direct to Las Palmas (6 hrs), La Palma (10 hrs), Gomera (1½ hrs from Los Cristianos)
Flights: International and direct to La Palma, Hierro, Las Palmas, Lanzarote, Fuerteventura

Tenerife is the largest of the Canary Islands. Its most impressive feature is the great peak of Teide, the volcanic cone which rises to a height of 3718m in the centre of the island and which can be seen from four of the other islands in the group. This mountain is the most enthralling sight in the Canaries and its setting—the bare and desolate crater bed of Las Cañadas—provides a dramatic study in contrast which typifies the landscape of the Canary Islands.

At the opposite extreme, the Orotava Valley spreads its green robe down to the coastline, a rich patchwork of fields and plantations embroidered with flowers. Unlike the stark wasteland of its summit, the coastal region of the west of the island offers its most abundant gifts: bananas and cereals, fruit trees and vines, the varied hues of hibiscus, poinsettia, and a multitude of other tropical flora.

Between the contrasts there are the shades: subtle variations of climate and vegetation which can best be seen in the steep climb up the

Orotava Valley from Puerto de la Cruz to Las Cañadas. Palm trees meet pines, the warm climate of the coastal zone meets the cooler atmosphere of the higher altitudes. And at the top— when a cloud breaks on Teide—one can experience the ultimate contrast: the weird, mist-shrouded landscape of another planet.

The activities of *this* planet are very much in evidence in the island's busy capital, Santa Cruz de Tenerife. This city of 150,000 inhabitants is also the second largest port in the Canaries, and the life of city and port are inseparable. The visitor who arrives by boat can be in the Plaza de España, at the very heart of Santa Cruz, within a few minutes' walk of the ship. The Plaza is at the southern end of a wide promenade which runs beside the harbour. At the other end is an old fort, whose battlements are commanded by the cannon which is reported to have blown off Nelson's arm in 1797. The incident, which occurred during an attempt by the redoubtable sailor to capture the city, does not loom large

31

in the annals of British naval history. For the people of Tenerife, however, the repulse of the British remains a great victory—celebrated to this day by an annual procession in the city. Elsewhere in the city the echoes of the past are in the few surviving colonial churches and in the Museo Arqueologico, which contains the most complete collection of Guanche remains and artefacts in the Canaries.

It should be mentioned here that to conquer the island the Spanish themselves had to deal with a proud race. After a tenancy of 3500 years the Guanche people were not disposed to give up their homeland without a fight and for three years (1494–96) the Spanish had to battle for every inch of ground. The struggle is recorded by such place names as La Matanza (Massacre) de Acentejo and La Victoria (Victory) de Acentejo, referring respectively to a battle lost and a battle won by the *conquistador* Alonso de Lugo.

De Lugo was the man who founded Tenerife's second most important town, La Laguna. This was once her capital and comes closer to the spirit of her colonial past than any other town in the island. Old churches and convents, and stately houses bearing the crests of their noble owners are at the turn of every street in the heart of the town. La Laguna is rightly the Canaries' principal seat of learning. The University of La Laguna, to the east of the town, is famous all over the world for its scientific research and studies. It has a particularly fine library, containing many books and manuscripts relating the early history of the Canaries.

The visitor who arrives by air at Reina Sofia Airport (*Aeropuerto del Sur*) reaches Santa Cruz in 40 minutes by car on the *Autopista del Sur*. This motorway continues as the *Autopista del Norte* to Puerto de la Cruz on the north coast (another 20 minutes). Communications in the island are good, with the *Autopista del Sur* continuing west to Los Cristianos and the opportunity of easy access to Las Cañadas by four roads from different parts of the island.

Tenerife's tradition as a resort goes back to the 19th century, when it first became a destination for the leisured classes of Europe. The tradition is maintained today in the super-resort of Puerto de la Cruz on the north coast, and in the growing number of tourist developments in the south.

The latter region has until recently been the forgotten flank of Tenerife. Starved of Atlantic rains by the barrier of the central massif, this near-desert area was a playground for lizards and little else. Now, however, the sandy beaches of the south-west, from El Medano to Playa de las Americas, are thronged with holidaymakers throughout the year.

Further up the west coast the rocky shoreline has made development more difficult, but has not deterred the creation of successful resorts at Puerto del Santiago and Los Gigantes.

Folk song and dance group, Tenerife

Itineraries

Circular tour

This one day tour of the island, starting at either Santa Cruz de Tenerife or Puerto de la Cruz, takes in the major points of interest.

Santa Cruz—Los Cristianos via Autopista del Sur—Los Gigantes— Route 823 to Las Cañadas—Route 821 to La Orotava—Puerto de la Cruz— La Laguna—Santa Cruz

This is a strenuous route and Short Tour No. 6 (omitting the south coast) may be preferred.

Short tours

From Santa Cruz

1 *Santa Cruz—La Laguna—Puerto de la Cruz—Icod—Garachico—Realejo Alto—La Orotava—Santa Cruz*

2 *Santa Cruz—La Laguna—Las Mercedes—Pico del Inglés—San Andres—Santa Cruz*

3 *Santa Cruz—La Laguna—Bajamar (via Tegueste)—Punta del Hidalgo— Tacoronte—Santa Cruz*

4 *Santa Cruz—Route 824 to Las Cañadas—Vilaflor—Granadilla— return Santa Cruz via Autopista del Sur*

5 *As No. 4, but returning via La Orotava (Route 821)*

6 *As No. 4, but returning via Tamaimo (Route 823) and Icod*

From Puerto de la Cruz

7 *Puerto de la Cruz—La Laguna— Santa Cruz (via Vista Bella)—return via Autopista del Norte*

8 *Puerto de la Cruz—Tacoronte— Bajamar—Punta del Hidalgo—Las Mercedes—Pico del Inglés—La Laguna—Puerto de la Cruz*

9 *Puerto de la Cruz—San Juan de la Rambla—Icod—Garachico—San Juan del Reparo—Realejo Alto—Puerto de la Cruz*

10 *Puerto de la Cruz—La Orotava— Route 821 to Las Cañadas—return via Tamaimo (Route 823) or La Esperanza (Route 824)*

Hotels and restaurants These are mostly concentrated in the resorts and in the capital. See Santa Cruz de Tenerife, Puerto de la Cruz and ps. 21 and 24.

Beaches The best beaches in Tenerife are at the resorts on the south coast (Playa de las Americas, Los Cristianos, El Medano, etc.) Further up this coast there are good beaches of black sand (Candelaria, Las Caletillas) and, to the north of Santa Cruz, the man-made golden sand beach of Las Teresitas. The north coast has few beaches but there are excellent natural swimming pools at Garachico and Bajamar. See also Puerto de la Cruz and p.21.

For **bus services and local excursions**, see Santa Cruz de Tenerife and Puerto de la Cruz.

Adeje Village in west of island 2km from junction with Route 822, 25km west of Granadilla.

Situated at the foot of the dramatic **Barranco del Infierno**, Adeje was the capital of one of the ancient Guanche kingdoms of Tenerife. It has a further place in the history of the island as the seat of the Counts of La Gomera. Their fortified mansion, known as the Casa Fuerte, is now a ruin (not accessible), but a number of the nobles' houses survive.

The church of *Santa Ursula* has a fine 18th c. gilded reredos (left nave). From the highest point of the village it is possible to follow a track for about 2km up the *barranco*.

Anaga Mountainous north-east peninsula of Tenerife.

Las Montañas de Anaga are explored by a circular route from Santa Cruz (Tour No. 2). The principal viewpoints are the *Mirador Pico del Inglés*, the *Mirador Cruz del Carmen* and the *Mirador Las Mercedes*, all of which offer striking panoramas of the coastline and forest regions of the peninsula. If time allows, a detour should be made to *Taganana* (see Gazetteer entry).

Bajamar Village and resort on north coast, 20km north-west of Santa Cruz. Buses from La Laguna.

German investment has done much to create this resort on the rocky north-west coast of the Anaga peninsula. The dark cliffs make an improbable setting for the montage of hotels, promenade and swimming pools— but the resort is one of the most popular in Tenerife.

The chief attraction of Bajamar is the swimming. Three of the pools are tidal, which allows visitors to enjoy swimming in natural conditions and in safety.

In the village, in August, the annual festival in honour of *Cristo del Gran Poder* is held. There are bouts of Canary wrestling, fun fairs and fireworks.

2km east of Bajamar the road ends at *Punta del Hidalgo*. Like Bajamar this was a small fishing village until the developers took over. From the point, the view of the Anaga range to the east is impressive. For accommodation, see p. 21.

Barranco del Infierno see **Adeje**

Buenavista Village in western corner of Tenerife 38.5km west of Puerto de la Cruz.

The wonderful views implied by its name may be enjoyed to the full on the drive to this village. To the west the islands of La Palma and Gomera can be seen, rising mysteriously from the Atlantic. Inland the green hills surge up to the heights of Teide. From the village one can drive up to *El Palmar* (5km) for more views.

Candelaria Town 17km south of Santa Cruz, reached by *Autopista del Sur*. Buses every half-hour from Santa Cruz (Calle Rámon y Cajal).

The significance of this town as a pilgrimage centre for the people of Tenerife is similar to that of Teror in Grand Canary. The patron saint of the island, here enshrined, is Nuestra Señora de la Candelaria.

The legend has it that in 1390 a statue of the Virgin was found by two Guanche herdsmen on a rock near the sea. The ruler of Guimar, awed by her mysterious arrival, called his fellow kings to discuss what should be done with the statue. They agreed she should be housed in a cave in the cliff, and she became an object of veneration throughout the then pagan island.

In 1464 she was seized and carried off to Fuerteventura by Sancho de Herrera, but after an outbreak of plague it was decided to return her to Tenerife. Thirty years later, immediately after the conquest of the island by the Spanish, she was installed in a church built near the original cave.

The original statue was lost as mysteriously as it was found. In 1826 a great storm caused a tidal wave which swept away the image. The present figure is the work of Fernando Estevez, and was made in 1827.

Basilica of Nuestra Señora de la Candelaria The present church is modern. Outside are large red stone figures of the Guanche people who first venerated the holy image. 3km to the north of Candelaria is the beach resort of *Las Caletillas*. For accommodation, see p. 22.

Costa del Silencio Resort area 71km south-west of Santa Cruz. For accommodation, see p. 21.

El Medano Resort on south coast, 62km south-west of Santa Cruz.

The island's best sandy beach, good for windsurfing. For accommodation, see p. 21.

El Palmar Village 5km south of Buenavista.

A drive up to this isolated village makes a good climax to a tour of the north-west. This is the heart of one of the most cultivated parts of the island and the terraced plots create a brilliant patchwork of greens and browns on the mountainside.

Garachico Town on north coast, 28.5km west of Puerto de la Cruz. Buses from Puerto de la Cruz, Santa Cruz.

In the early colonial period this was the most important town and port on the north coast. In 1705, however, a volcanic eruption destroyed Garachico, the lava stream sweeping down from the heights and engulfing both the town and the harbour.

In a brief tour of Garachico the visitor will see three of the buildings which survived the flow of lava that swamped the original town. On the east side of the main square is the convent of *San Francisco* (17th c.). Though now disused it is in process of restoration and through the gate in the corner of the square one can admire its two cloisters, with their old wooden balconies. Further west (passing the 17th c. Baroque *Palace of the Marques of Adeje* on the left) one reaches the church of *Santa Ana*. This church, founded in 1548 and rebuilt the year before the eruption (1704), contains some fine local carving and two works by the sculptor Luján Pérez.

On the waterfront (reached by continuing westwards) is the *Castle of San Miguel*, built in the 16th c. It is almost toylike in its structure, and on the tiny battlements one can imagine the early inhabitants of Garachico looking anxiously out to sea at Drake's fleet, threatening them with bombardment unless they meet his demands for a supply of their best wine. (As no shot was fired on this occasion, one can assume that Garachico's citizens acceded to the request and the English departed, suitably fortified, to continue harrying the Spanish fleet.)

A little way off shore is the *Rock of Garachico*, topped by a cross symbolizing the prayers of the town to be spared another catastrophe. Garachico is well known for its bathing facilities which include specially constructed rock pools, subject to the tides.

The best views of Garachico are from *El Tanque* (4 km to the south, on mountain road

signposted Las Cruzes) and from the viewpoint on the upper road (823) 2 km further on (*San Juan del Reparo*). Seen from above, the brown-tiled houses, clustered on their semicircular promontory of lava, make an interesting concentric pattern.

Granadilla
Village 78 km south of Santa Cruz at junction of Route 822 and southern route to Las Cañadas.

The full name of this village, Granadilla de Abona, recalls the Guanche kingdom in which it was an important settlement. Lying in the foothills within easy access of Las Cañadas (29 km) and the coast at El Medano, Granadilla is recognized as the capital of the south. It is an important agricultural centre, renowned for its oranges.

Guimar
Town 27 km south of Santa Cruz (Route 822) in centre of potato and tomato-growing area.

The seat of one of the two main Guanche kingdoms, Guimar has many links with the early history of the island. In more recent times it was popular as a winter resort, but the new *autopista* has now by-passed it, taking the tourists to the new beach resorts of the south.

South of the town (4 km) is the *Mirador of Don Martin*, which offers superb views of the Guimar Valley.

In early September the inhabitants celebrate the appearance of the Virgin on the beach of Chimisay, with a feast where the main events take place at El Socorro on the coast.

Icod Town 22.5 km west of Puerto de la Cruz (Route 820). Buses from Puerto de la Cruz. Probably best known to tourists for its famous **dragon tree**—reputed to be 3000 years old— Icod itself started life in 1501. Its proper name, Icod de los Vinos, describes its situation in a wine-growing area which is one of the most fertile parts of Tenerife. With Teide in the background and superb views down over the coast to San Marcos and San Juan de la Rambla it is one of the most attractively situated of the smaller towns. (The best views are from the *Mirador* at *La Vega*, 2.5 km south of junction 2.5 km west of Icod.)

Church of San Marcos Built over a period of two centuries (16th & 17th) this church is of mixed styles. The portal is Renaissance, the interior Baroque. The reredos is very fine and other treasures include a large filigree silver cross from Mexico.

The convents of *San Francisco* and *San Agustin* are fine old buildings, both having many carvings of the 17th c. In the architecture of Icod one finds the Canary tradition at its most appealing. The side street to the left of the dragon tree leads up to a small square that is one of the most delightful ensembles of domestic architecture in the islands.

2 km below the town is the tiny port of *San Marcos* with a restaurant and a good beach for swimming (regular bus service from Icod).

La Laguna (pop. 58,000) Second largest town in Tenerife, 7 km west of Santa Cruz (Route 820 or *Autopista del Norte*). Buses from Santa Cruz (Plaza de España), Puerto de la Cruz.

Properly called San Cristobal de la Laguna (St Christopher of the Lake), this town was founded in 1497 with the dedication of its first church, Nuestra Señora de la Concepción. The founder was the conqueror of Tenerife, Alonso de Lugo, whose troops had fought hard for the possession of the plateau on which the town (and the nearby Los Rodeos airport) now stand. The lake after which the town was named has disappeared.

La Laguna was the first capital of Tenerife and has the only university in the Canaries. It was made a Bishopric in 1818, and two previous churches were designated as the cathedral before the present building was consecrated in 1913. It is a busy yet dignified town. The long straight streets are still graced by many fine old manor houses. There are several convents and churches of note, and the Town Hall, Bishop's Palace and Nava Palace are all worth a visit (see Walking Tour below).

On the main road just outside the town stands the fine bronze statue of *Padre José Anchieta* (1533-97). This friar was a missionary born in La Laguna who worked in Brazil and converted many Indians to Christianity.

Dragon tree at Icod

La Laguna

Walking tour (see map) Starting point: **Plaza del Adelantado**.

This is the main square of La Laguna. Its name (which means 'the clever and advanced one') is an attribute bestowed on the founder of the city, Alonso de Lugo.

Nava Palace This imposing building, on the west side of the square (originally 17th c.), was rebuilt in the mid-18th c. Its original owner was the Marquis de Villaneuva del Prado, father of the man who later founded the famous Botanical Gardens at La Orotava. Also on the west side is the convent of **Santa Catalina da Sena** (in the church, a fine altar of silver repoussé), and at the south-west corner the **Town Hall** (*Ayuntamiento*). This building, in the neo-classical style, was commenced in the mid 16th c. (the façade on the Calle Obispo Rey Redondo is from this period) and completed in the 19th c. The murals on the stairway depict the presentation of the Guanche kings to the King and Queen of Spain.

The large building on the east side of the square houses the town's principal *market*. It is open on weekdays and the busiest days are Friday and Saturday, when the stallholders spill out into the square and adjoining streets.

Church and Monastery of Santo Domingo In the Calle de Santo Domingo, off the south side of the square. This former Dominican convent, set on the edge of a steep barranco, belongs to the 16th c. The church contains some curious treasures, among them the Holy Hearse used in the Holy Week processions.

In the garden of the Ecclesiastical Seminary, part of the old Dominican establishment, is a *dragon tree*—one of the oldest and largest in the island. Permission to visit the garden can be obtained at the office.

Returning to the square and going up the main east-west street (Obispo Rey Redondo) one can admire the old seigniorial houses, with their coats of arms and sculpted lava façades. One eventually reached the cathedral square, the Plaza de Fray Albino.

Cathedral La Laguna was made a Bishopric in 1818, and the present cathedral was built on the site of its predecessor, the 16th c. church of Nuestra Señora de Los Remedios (demolished 1897). The architect was José Rodrigo Vallabriga, and the new cathedral was consecrated in 1913 by the then Bishop, Nicolas Rey Redondo.

The interior is a strange mixture of Gothic and Baroque. The Gothic is most apparent in the beautiful *presbytery* with its semi-circle of pointed arches and in the decorated windows of the east end. The *tabernacle* at the high altar is the work of the celebrated Canarian sculptor Luján Pérez. The immense *Bishop's Throne* is carved out of Canary pine and the *pulpit*, made in Italy, is

Nava Palace, La Laguna   37

supported by a group of life-size figures carved from a single block of marble.

In the nave are tablets commemorating the founder of La Laguna, Alonso de Lugo (d. 1525), and the Bishop Rey Redondo, both of whom are buried in the cathedral.

The chapel of *Nuestra Señora de Los Remedios* contains an impressively elaborate *reredos* of 1715, with Flemish panels. Also in this chapel is a painting of *The Last Supper* by Miranda.

Treasury (small entrance fee) The richness of the religious heritage of La Laguna can be seen in the magnificent processional pieces in gold and silver and the embroidered robes. Also in the treasury are the life-size painted figures carried in the Christmas, Easter and Corpus Christi processions.

Continuing westwards along the Obispo Rey Redondo one reaches the Plaza Concepción.

Church of Nuestra Señora de la Concepción Founded by Alonso de Lugo in 1497, this is Tenerife's mother church. The exterior is simple, except for the elaborate *bell tower* with its six stories surmounted by an octagonal lantern. This tower, built in 1697, stands apart from the main building on the north side.

The interior of the church contains some fine carving, particularly that of the *pulpit*. The statues include a figure of *La Dolorosa*, by Luján Pérez, and a picture of *San Juan* (1592) which is said to have a miraculous image which shed real tears.

The church was declared a National Monument in 1948. At the moment it is undergoing extensive repairs and is closed to the public. Returning along the Obispo Rey Redondo, a left turn at the cathedral square leads to the Calle San Agustin. Turning right, the tour ends at the **Bishop's Palace** (No 28). This was originally the residence of the Conde de Valle de Salazar. It is a fine late 17th c. building, with a Baroque façade.

The main gate is adorned with the coat-of-arms of the Bishop. Beyond the entrance hall is a beautiful flower-filled patio, with a large magnolia tree in the centre. (Hours: Mon, Wed & Fri 10.30–13.30. Entrance free.)

Other places of interest in La Laguna

Church of San Francisco On the road to Las Mercedes, north of the town. Originally called San Miguel de las Victorias, this was the church of the Monastery of San Francisco.

It was the second church to be built in La Laguna (1513), and the main chapel was reserved by the conqueror Alonso de Lugo for his burial place. He rested here until the completion of the present cathedral, where his body was re-interred.

The Royal Sanctuary of the Holy Christ contains a much venerated image, the *Christ of La Laguna*. It is a life-size wooden figure, the work of a Spanish sculptor of the School of

Seville. It was brought to Tenerife by de Lugo in 1520. The superb altarpiece, in silver repoussé, is 18th c.

University The University of La Laguna is situated at the southern end of the town on the road to Santa Cruz. Here students from all the Canary Islands join those from Spain and many other countries in the pursuit of knowledge, particularly in the fields of natural science and history. The university has a large amphitheatre and a library which is renowned for its books on the history, flora and fauna of the Canaries.

On September 14 the town celebrates the Festival of *El Santisimo Cristo* which centres on the Christ of La Laguna, venerated in a massive procession from the church of San Francisco. At the Festival of *Corpus Christi* in May/June the streets are carpeted with flowers.

La Orotava (pop. 26,000) Also known as Villa La Orotava. Town commanding Orotava Valley in hills above Puerto de la Cruz.

In 1799 the German naturalist Humboldt, beholding the wide sweep of fertile country around La Orotava, was prompted to describe it as the most lovely prospect of all his travels. Appropriately the town of La Orotava, much of which survives from his time, is one of the most attractive in the Canaries. The town was one of the earliest to be established on the island by the Spaniards, who built it on the site of the old Guanche kingdom of Bencomo. (The original Guanche name was Araytava.) For many years only families of substance lived in the town, the poorer folk inhabiting the little port of Puerto de la Cruz 7 km below. Today it is still the home of noble and well-to-do families, whose lovely old houses, with their interior staircases and balconies of carved wood, are an indication of the town's prosperity.

If possible a visit to La Orotava should be planned to include the week of the Octave of *Corpus Christi* which falls in late May or early June. At this time the streets are covered with an extraordinary carpet of flowers which serves as a floral path for the bearers of the Host. This carpet, which runs from the cathedral through many of the streets of the town, is made by laying out the flowers—brought in at dawn from outlying fields and villages —in a continuous pattern formed by wooden stencils.

In front of the Town Hall a different method is used. Here, instead of flowers and foliage, the designs are made from the many-coloured soils found in the region of Las Cañadas. These are ground into fine powders and used to produce religious pictures of great beauty.

At the end of the festivities, the Pilgrimage of *San Isidro* is held. The image of the patron saint is carried in procession by twelve farmers, and receives symbolic offerings of fruit and earth.

Walking tour (see map) Starting point: **Calle Calvario**.

From the bridge at the west end of Calvario one can obtain the best overall view of the town. Below, clustered at the edge of a *barranco* are the old Spanish houses with their steep tiled roofs, balconies and flowering creepers. In the background are the mellowing façades of larger buildings, topped by the twin towers and dome of the Concepción church. Beyond is the blue spine of the central range, climbing to the snow-capped peak of Teide.

The little raised square at the far end of the bridge is the meeting place of La Orotava. The food kiosks and seats are always in use, and on feast days the whole square is decorated with flags and electric lights. In the corner of the square is the 18th c. convent and church of *San Francisco*. This group of buildings is now used as a tax office, and is not open to visitors.

Further on, to the left, is the *Calle de Leon*, in which there are some good examples of old Spanish houses with grilled gates opening into cool patios. The Calle Carrera, continuation of the Calle Calvario, shortly opens into the *Plaza General Franco*. This imposing square is in front of the Town Hall, and is the

La Orotava

Walking tour
1 S. Francisco
2 Town Hall
3 Casa de los Balcones
4 Hospital
5 Botanical Gardens
6 La Concepción

setting for the magnificent designs made from the coloured soils of Las Cañadas, executed for the Feast of Corpus Christi.

From the Plaza General Franco the street rises sharply and bears left into the Calle San Francisco. On the left is one of the finest old buildings in the Canaries, now much restored. This is the **Casa de los Balcones**, built in 1632, which has been cleverly adapted to house a fine collection of local arts and handicrafts. The old balconied *courtyard*, beyond the main entrance, is an attractive feature.

On the right, further on, is the old **Hospital**. Built as a convent in the 18th c. this building is now a home for old people. The main halls and chapel are open to the public (Hours: 16.00–17.00; Sun 10.30–11.30). In the main door the revolving drum which was made to receive abandoned babies can be seen. The views from the courtyard over the whole valley and down to Puerto are very fine.

Crossing to the Calle Hermano Apolinar, a right turn is made for the parish church of *San Juan*. This old church, which looks down on the whole of La Orotava, is well worth the climb up the narrow cobbled streets. It is a typical Canarian village church with a raftered wooden ceiling, tiny windows set high in the walls and a simple spacious interior. The altar is contrastingly elaborate, with a tabernacle and intricately carved reredos.

The church contains two interesting works by the sculptor Pérez: the *Virgen del Carmen* and the *Virgen de la Gloria*. An unusual statue which is also in this church is the figure of *Christ Tied to the Pillar* by Roldan (1780).

Returning downhill to Hermano Apolinar, continue east to the Calle Tomas Pérez. A visit may now be made to the *Botanical Gardens*, which contain many rare plants and trees from different parts of the world. From here the tour continues north, across the Calle Carrera, to the Plaza de la Concepción.

Church of La Concepción This is the town's principal church. The convoluted façade, flanked by two bell towers, is most attractive and has an unusual feature: a balconied doorway set above the main entrance.

The *interior* is neo-classical in style with a cupola over the crossing and barrel vaults over the nave and aisles. The main *altar* is an ornate marble and alabaster work by the 16th c. Italian artist Giuseppe Gagini. The statues include a *St Peter* by Rodriguez de la Oliva and *La Dolorosa* by Luján Pérez.

Among the church's treasures is a set of altar pieces in silver repoussé, in rococo style (18th c.).

To the north of La Orotava (see map) is the *Mirador Humboldt*, a viewpoint of the Orotava Valley named after the German naturalist.

Las Cañadas

Extinct volcanic crater forming plateau at highest point in island accessible by car, with the peak of Teide (Pico de Teide) as its centrepiece rising to 3718 m.

In such a small island as Tenerife the spectacle of this vast flat desert is astonishing. The crater rim surrounding it forms a circular mountain barrier, preserving the view for the visitor until he has broken through and entered the wilderness. The emptiness and space which make the initial impact on mind and eye are followed by other impressions, no less forceful. The silence is at first unnerving but then stimulating, acting as a vacuum in which the chirp of a chaffinch or the tinkle of a sheep's bell strikes the ear with a crystal clarity. (The presence of life in this lunar landscape is a reassurance, and it is interesting to recall that the name Las Cañadas refers to the sheep trails that have long existed as the route for the shepherds across the mountains.)

The natural colours of the area make a similar impression. Like the sounds, the dramatic hues of the volcanic rocks scattered in the area known as Los Roques stand out from the sombre background of the crater bed. The brown flanks of Teide, too, provide a rich contrast to the white crust of snow that lies for much of the year on its peak.

Another phenomenon of Las Cañadas—unexpected in such desolation—is the appearance of flowers. These include the aromatic broom-like *retama*, the red poker-shaped *taginaste*—both found on the floor of the crater—and the delicate *violeta del Teide*, found on Teide itself.

Route across Las Cañadas from El Portillo to Boca de Tauce (21 km)

At *El Portillo* (2020m), at the threshold of Las Cañadas, is the *Visitor Centre of ICONA*, responsible for the Las Cañadas National Park. There are refreshments here and at the Park entrance, 1.5km further on.

7km from here, an opening to the right marked Montaña Blanca indicates the route to the peak (see **Ascent of Teide**). 2km further on, the cableway is off to the right.

Continuing 3.5km on the main road, a parking area on the right opposite the entrance to the Parador leads to the extraordinary area of *Los Roques*. Here the scattered rocks thrown out by the volcano offer a striking range of shapes and colours, the black lava contrasting with the red magma and white pumice. Perhaps the strangest colour is the brilliant green of the rocks, tinted by copper oxide, through which the road is carved further on. From the *Mirador de los Roques* one can gaze on the looming mass of Teide to the north, or the flat, ghostly expanse of the *Llano de Ucanca* (Plain of Ucanca) to the west.

The road continues for another 7km to the

pass of *La Boca de Tauce*. On the way, note the oddly-shaped rock to the south of the road known as the *Zapato de la Reina* (Queen's Boot).

Ascent of Teide

On foot (from Montanã Blanca, see below). This is a long climb (c. 1300m) up a trail of 5km (driveable part of the way only). Climbers are recommended to arrange a night's rest at the Refugio de Altavista (closed 15 Dec-31 Mar). Applications for accommodation and guide should be made to ICONA (Instituto Nacional Para la Conservacion de la Naturaleza) in Santa Cruz. ICONA also operate a Visitor Centre at El Portillo, with information about footpaths and guided tours.

The trail commences at the foot of the *Montaña Blanca*, so named for its covering of white pumice. On the way up there are many interesting volcanic features, including the strange *Huevos del Teide*.

From *Altavista* (3260m) a dawn start should be made for the summit for the climactic view of the Canary Islands. The crater here is 50m wide and 25m deep, and from the fissures in the floor issue the ever-present fumes of sulphur.

From the summit one's gaze embraces the shoulders of the volcano with the old peak (*Pico Viejo*) to the west, the bowl and rim of Las Cañadas, the forest-covered slopes falling away to the coastline, and on a clear day the islands of Grand Canary, La Palma, Gomera and Hierro.

The first recorded eruption of Teide was in 1393: the last in 1909.

Cableway (Teleferico al Pico de Teide) The quick way to the summit. The trip from the lower station (2356m) to the upper station (3555m) takes 8 min. From here there is a short climb to the edge of the cone. (Hours: Outward 09.00–16.00; Return 09.00–17.00. Tickets 500ptas return.)

Routes to Las Cañadas

Las Cañadas may be approached by four different routes:

East

Route 824 from La Laguna to El Portillo (43km)

Excellent road along spine of northern range. Gradual ascent. Main viewpoints: 13km, *Mirador Pico de las Flores* (views of pine forest of Bosque de la Esperanza). 37km + 3km side road, *Observatorio de Izaña* (views of Guimar Valley to the east, Orotava Valley to the west).

Route 821 from La Orotava to El Portillo (27km)

Shortest route from coast. This route, strongly recommended, offers the traveller a fascinating experience: a rapid climb (2000m) through the different zones of climate and vegetation that lie between coast and mountains.

From the coast and up to 300 m the banana flourishes, although the bunches are smaller at the higher levels away from the warmer coastal region. Where the bananas give up the vines take over, and flourish up to 1000 m. Between these altitudes, too, the vegetables are in abundance, most notably potatoes and tomatoes. Water to irrigate the fields comes from canals fed by underground streams running out of horizontal galleries cut in the mountains. (The pipes from these galleries may be seen protruding from the rocks.)

Deciduous trees—notably the chestnut—take over from the palms, though some of these survive at 1000 m. At this altitude the first Canary pines can be seen (watch out for them at *Las Fuentes* near the Aguamansa wood). These trees show an amazing capacity for survival, apparently growing straight out of the rock. Their hard wood is virtually fire-resistant and their roots so vigorous that they break up the rock in which they are embedded. The pine needles are used for packing bananas for export. Another tree which is put to good use is the graceful araucaria from South America, whose branches are used for supporting vines.

At 2000 m the pines thin out and give way to Spanish broom. This level is usually snow-covered between December and March. At the small pass of *El Portillo de Las Cañadas* (2020 m) the trees end and the crater area is entered.

West

Route 823 from Tamaimo to La Boca de Tauce (29.5 km)

Route 821 from Granadilla to La Boca de Tauce (29 km)
This route climbs steeply from 654 m (Granadilla) to 2050 m (La Boca de Tauce). The road between Granadilla and Vilaflor has many hairpin bends.

Las Mercedes Forest region in north-eastern Tenerife (see **Anaga**).

Los Cristianos Resort 74.5 km south-west of Santa Cruz (*Autopista del Sur*).
This rapidly growing resort, 15 km from the new airport of Reina Sofia, is also a port. From here there is a regular ferry service to the island of Gomera, a $1\frac{1}{2}$ hr trip. (See Boat Services, p. 18).
For accommodation, see p. 22.

Los Gigantes Resort 103 km west of Santa Cruz on west coast (Puerto Santiago).
For accommodation, see p. 22.

Los Realejos Town comprising adjacent villages of Realejo Alto and Realejo Baja between coastal road (820) and upper road from La Orotava to Icod.
These villages have a typical Canarian as-

pect, with winding streets and red-tiled houses. In Realejo Alto stands the church of **Santiago**, topped by a four-storied bell-tower and spire. This church—the oldest in Tenerife —was built in 1498 on the site of the surrender of the last defenders of the island to the conqueror Alonso de Lugo. (To add to their injury, the Guanche chieftains were then baptized in the church.) The church has been rebuilt many times.

Orotava Valley see La Orotava

Playa de las Americas Resort 76 km south-west of Santa Cruz (*Autopista del Sur*). For accommodation, see p. 22.

Puerto de la Cruz Town and resort on north coast, 39 km from Santa Cruz.
In less than two decades Puerto de la Cruz— once a small port for the produce of the Orotava Valley—has come to symbolize the international resort. Fulfilling the image of this 20th-century phenomenon are the concrete blocks of the hotels and apartment buildings and their satellite growth of gift shops, discotheques and bars. The latter line an English-type 'prom', and it is easy for the foreign visitor wandering along it to forget that he is in a far-flung province of Spain, off the north-west coast of Africa.

The old part of the town has all but disappeared. The traditional Canarian houses that survive, with their balconies and pitched roofs, huddle uncomfortably beneath the encroaching walls of the new hotels. Even at the town's original centre, the Plaza de la Iglesia, the old church of Nuestra Señora de la Peña is faced symbolically by the hacienda-style building of the Tourist Information Office.

The delights of the resort represented by this office do not immediately communicate with the first-time visitor. The black lava beaches and pounding Atlantic seas offer little compensation for the overpowering modern architecture, and one wonders what magic ingredient—other than the justly extolled climate—makes this such a popular resort for the out-of-season traveller. The exhilarating presence of Teide, breaking the clouds in the distance, is one obvious bonus, as is the proximity of the lush Orotava Valley. But one can be sure that the physical charms of Puerto's setting are quite incidental to its popularity. The secrets of the resort's success will only be found by a patient exploration of its possibilities, for which the developers must be given every credit.

The streets are wide and flower-filled, and the front laid out with gardens. Following the Lido de San Telmo development, the most spectacular creation is the *Lago de Martianez*, a salt-water lake contained by a sea wall.

For a small admission fee, the sun-seeker can enjoy the diversions of this elaborately landscaped complex with its circular lagoon and islands of rugged lava planted with cactus and palms. This artificial 'natural' playground more than compensates for the deficiencies of nature, represented below the sea wall to the east by the black lava beach of the *Playa de Martianez*.

Opportunities for recreation and entertainment in Puerto are endless. In addition to watersports, golf, horse-riding and tennis, there are the special amusement parks with the family in mind, such as Loro Parque (see p.48). Evening entertainment ranges from informal discos to the more lavish night clubs and the casino.

Places of interest (see map)

Tourist Information Office In the Plaza de la Iglesia opposite the church. (Hours 08.30–19.00; Sat 09.30–12.00. Closed Sun).

Puerto Pesquero (Fishing Port) The open air market here is lively and the offerings predictable: African wood carvings, ponchos and belts, straw baskets and sea shells.

Nuestra Señora de la Peña The main church of Puerto, whose bell tower was once the town's dominant feature, stands in the Plaza de la Iglesia. Built in the early 17th c., it is very typical of the churches of the period found throughout the Spanish Empire. In the spacious interior, note the exuberant Baroque altarpiece in gilded wood and the raised choir to the rear of the church.

Casa Iriarte This 18th c. house, on the corner of the Calle de Iriarte and the Calle de José Antonio, is the town's best surviving example of traditional domestic architecture.

Chapel of San Telmo Built in 1626 by the local fishermen on the very edge of the rocky shore, this tiny chapel was dedicated to their patron saint, San Pedro Gonzalez Telmo. Set in a large paved area where palms shade the benches and local artists hold exhibitions of their work, the chapel is an attractive place of worship. The interior has a fine painted ceiling and reredos, and an unusual black and white tiled floor. There is a modern figure of Christ on the altar, contrasting with the old figures of the Virgin and Saints elsewhere. The chapel is now used by Catholic tourists, and masses are said in German, Spanish and Scandinavian. Services are held every Sunday and the chapel is open to the public.

Castillo de San Felipe This little 17th c. fortress, part of the sea defences of the old port, stands to the west of the town. Threatened— but not yet engulfed—by the resort, it remains as an isolated memorial to the days when the raiders came in ships rather than bulldozers. Generally closed to the public, the castle is occasionally used for exhibitions.

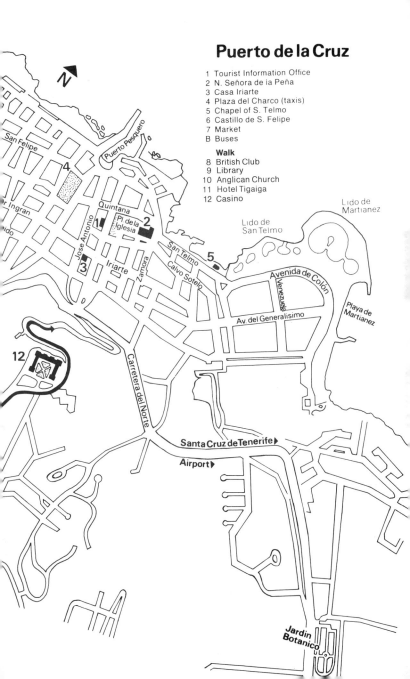

Puerto de la Cruz

1 Tourist Information Office
2 N. Señora de la Peña
3 Casa Iriarte
4 Plaza del Charco (taxis)
5 Chapel of S. Telmo
6 Castillo de S. Felipe
7 Market
B Buses

Walk

8 British Club
9 Library
10 Anglican Church
11 Hotel Tigaiga
12 Casino

Orotava Botanical Gardens (Jardin Botanico) These gardens lie 2km to the south of Puerto de la Cruz on the road to Santa Cruz de Tenerife (Autopista del Norte). Bus from central station (Calle del Pozo) marked 'Jardin Botanico' departs every hour. Admission to gardens 100ptas (Hours 09.00-19.00 daily).

Founded in 1788 for the purpose of acclimatizing the exotic plants brought back by the Spanish conquerors of the New World, the gardens contain an encyclopedic variety of species. Many plants that would have perished in the harsher climate of Spain flourish as well here, in Tenerife's temperate climate, as in their natural habitat. The species, collected from tropical and subtropical regions throughout the world, range from the giant *ficus* of tropical South America to the delicate Bird-of-Paradise flower (*strelitzia*) from South Africa, which has now adopted the Canaries as a second home. The more delicate plants, such as the orchids, are cultivated in a tropical greenhouse.

The excellent guide to the gardens (50ptas) is obligatory for all but the expert botanist. Every distinguishable plant bears a number, which corresponds to a description in the guide. Those who have had difficulty in identifying some of the Canarian species in their travels in the islands will be well informed after their visit.

Walks

Puerto de la Cruz, situated at the foot of the beautiful Orotava Valley, makes an excellent base for some pleasant walks. To make the walks easier a bus should be taken out of the town—an uphill journey—the walker returning downhill.

Recommended walk
From the San Antonio Park down to town via the British Club, Library, Church and Hotel Taoro

For this walk first take a bus from the central station (Calle del Pozo) going to La Orotava (via Las Arenas) or Icod and ask for the Parque San Antonio. This is at the junction of the Carretera General and the Carretera del Taoro (see map).

The entrance to the *British Country Club* is on the right, and visitors are welcome to visit the clubhouse and pleasant grounds which surround it. The club, correctly called the British Games Club, was founded in 1916 as the Orotava British Outdoor Games Club. Originally designed as a facility for British residents of the Orotava Valley, the membership is now divided equally between British and Spanish. In the club grounds, in addition to the spacious clubhouse with lounge, bar and card room, there are tennis courts, a bowling green and croquet lawn. (Applications for temporary membership should be made through the Secretary.)

Across the main road from the club entrance down a narrow lane is the building which houses the *Library*. It contains over 16,000 volumes, and is open on Mondays and Fridays 16.30-18.00. (Temporary membership can be arranged through the Librarian.)

Taking the Carretera del Taoro from the back of the Library proceed towards Puerto. A little way down this quiet road is the *Anglican Church*. Set back from the road in its own simple garden this might well be a small parish church in a corner of rural England. The Church of All Saints, as it is called, was built in 1880 for the resident British community. There is a resident chaplain, and services are held every Sunday throughout the year.

The road continues down to Puerto past the *Hotel Tigaiga*, where the many rare plants in the garden are labelled for the information of visitors. Further down the Carretera del Taoro is the old *Hotel Taoro*, built in the late 19th c. when Puerto first became popular as a winter resort. Recently modernised, this hotel has now become a casino.

The road winds down to the intersection of the Carretera Botanico just behind the Hotel Belair.

Giant ficus, Orotava Botanical Gardens
Right: San Telmo Lido, Puerto de la Cruz

Hotels

Puerto's hotel accommodation justifies its status as one of the great international resorts. The choice of hotels is extremely varied, from the large 5-star hotels to the small 1-star 'hostals' (pensions). Locations are equally varied: either the luxuriant subtropical setting of the hillside overlooking the town (*Hotel Botanico, Hotel Parque San Antonio*) or the bustle of the seafront (*Hotel San Felipe, Hotel Semiramis*). For those preferring to stay in the old town, the *Hotel Monopol* and *Hotel Marquesa* offer a more intimate Spanish atmosphere. (For more details of accommodation see p. 21.)

Restaurants

As well as the excellent hotel restaurants there are others which provide cuisine from every part of the world.

Visitors with wide-ranging tastes in food will enjoy themselves to the full in Puerto. They can choose from smart indoor restaurants with international menus and wine lists, open air restaurants by the sea serving fish dishes, or a back street 'local'.

Although most restaurants serve a good choice of Spanish dishes, it is not easy to find typical Canarian cuisine. The best restaurants for this are to be found in the older part of the town (Calle Iriarte, Calle de San Felipe). Canarian specialities, together with folk dancing, are on offer at *El Guanche*, behind the Atalaya Gran Hotel (reached by the Carretera del Taoro).

Beaches and swimming pools

Anyone going to Puerto de la Cruz with stretches of golden sand in mind will be disappointed. The beaches, such as they are, are of black lava—but this is finely ground and an acceptable substitute for all but the purist. The shoreline of the town itself is rocky, and the best beaches are the *Playa de Martianez*, east of the town, and the beach to the west of the Castillo de San Felipe. These beaches are used largely by the Spanish residents of Puerto, and are only safe for good swimmers unless the sea is calm—something which rarely occurs.

The best swimming for tourists is at the magnificent complex of pools at the east and of the resort. Here are perfect facilities for sunbathing on spacious terraces and a choice of sea water pools (five in the *Lido de San Telmo*, plus the impressive *Lago de Martianez*, well worth the small entrance fee.

Sports

Skin diving Equipment and lessons at the International Diving School, Lido San Telmo.
Fishing Details from Tourist Office.
Golf At the *Campo de Golf*, El Peñon (18 holes) near the airport.
Tennis Several of the hotels have their own courts, open to non-residents. There is also a club (*Las Adelfas*) open to visitors, and the British Games Club has two courts where visitors can play if introduced by a member. (This can usually be arranged through the hotel's information staff.)

Horse riding can be enjoyed at several near-by country locations. One of the best is *La Dehesa Baja* at La Orotava. The *Picadero* in the Plaza Toros in Puerto is another good riding establishment.

Loro Parque This amusement park is situated at the Punta Brava, to the west of the town. Free bus every 20 min from Café Columbus (east end of Avenida de Colón).

The garden of Loro Parque offers an attractive diversion for visitors to the resort. Filled with exotic plants and birds, its special feature is the parrot show in which the feathered performers give an exhibition of extraordinary intelligence. The park also has a cafe and orchid house, and—a recent popular new feature—a dolphinarium. (Hours 08.00–18.00.)

Shopping

Puerto de la Cruz has a wide range of gift shops and supermarkets. For the souvenir hunter there are speciality shops with beautiful pottery, embroidery and leather work. Most of these shops are concentrated in the area around the lively Plaza General Franco —a square, incidentally, where one can buy the local nougat, the celebrated *turron*.

Bus services

Buses from Puerto de la Cruz mainly serve Santa Cruz and the villages on the north coast. (For Bajamar, change at La Laguna and for the south coast change at Santa Cruz.) There is, however, a long-distance twice-weekly service to Los Cristianos via Las Cañadas.

The departure point for all buses is the Calle del Pozo (see map), where details of services can be obtained.

Special notes

There are two different buses for *Santa Cruz*. The *Express* is a direct service using the *Autopista* which takes about 45 min. The *Ordinario* is a slow bus which goes up to La Orotava and follows the old road (Route 820) to Santa Cruz. Although a journey of 1½ hrs, this is a pleasant alternative for those wishing to see something of the villages and countryside of the region.

La Orotava is served by two different routes: one via *Las Arenas* and one via the *Jardin Botanico*.

Taxis

There is a large taxi rank in the Plaza del Charco with an authorised list of charges (available at the kiosk) for local trips (Icod, La Orotava, etc.). It is a good idea to check these prices before engaging a taxi.

Local tours and inter-island excursions

Most hotels offer excursions organized by local agents, who provide conducted tours around the island. For the longer distance journeys lunch is usually included in the fare. One of the best local tours, offering the most comprehensive view of the island, is Puerto de la Cruz—La Orotava—Las Cañadas—Granadilla—El Medano—Los Cristianos—Los Gigantes—Garachico—Icod—Puerto de la Cruz.

It is also possible to arrange through these agents air excursions to Las Palmas, Lanzarote and the Sahara (El Aaiun).

Puerto de Santiago
Resort on west coast, 89km west of Santa Cruz. This old fishing village, south of the cliffs of Los Gigantes, is now a growing resort. For accommodation see p. 21.

San Andres
Village on coastline 10km north of Santa Cruz. Destination of buses from Santa Cruz for the *Playa de las Teresitas*, the best—and only—bathing beach to the north of the city.

San Juan de la Rambla
Village 14km west of Puerto de la Cruz.

With the old part of the neighbouring Icod, this is the most representative traditional Canary village. The church square is particularly attractive.

Santa Cruz de Tenerife (pop. 150,000)

Seaport capital of Tenerife and of the province which bears its name.

Although Tenerife was discovered at the end of the 14th c., the resistance of the Guanche people prevented serious Spanish colonization for another century. Santa Cruz began with a settlement of Alonso Fernandez de Lugo, who landed here in 1494. This settlement was concentrated on the banks of the river (now the dry *Barranco de Santos*) near the church of La Concepción.

The virtues of Santa Cruz as a harbour put it squarely on the map for the *conquistadores en route* for the New World, and in their wake the pirates. In 1797 the arrival of Nelson's flagship signalled a momentous event in Santa Cruz' history: the repulse of the British by the cannon of the Spanish—one of which accounted for Nelson's right arm. In more recent times (1936) Santa Cruz was the departure point for General Franco on the mission which was to carry him, after three years of civil war, to supreme power in Spain.

Before the division of the islands into two provinces Santa Cruz was (from 1821) the capital city of the Canaries.

The city The modern Santa Cruz is still dominated by its port. The main square, the Plaza de España, opens on to the sea and the main route through the town to the north-east runs along the waterfront. The mountains of Anaga to the north provide a natural shield for the port from the winds of the Atlantic.

The city has a more dignified atmosphere than its boisterous rival Las Palmas. Its older buildings are not, however, as clearly segregated as in the other capital and one has to search harder for the original character of the city.

Apart from the activities centring on its port and its status as the seat of government for its province, Santa Cruz is one of the capitals of the Canarian *fiesta* (see ps. 25–26).

Walking tour (see map)

Plaza de España—Plaza de la Candelaria—Church of La Concepción—Church of San Francisco—Plaza del Principe—Parque Municipal—Avenida 25 de Julio—Plaza de Weyler—Calle Castillo

This tour should be commenced reasonably early in the morning to allow visitors to see the churches and museums first (these are closed in the early afternoon).

Plaza de España This modern square occupies the site of the old Castillo de San Cristobal built in the reign of Philip II, which defended the port from foreign attacks in the 16th–18th c. In the square stands the *Civil War Monument*. The square, which overlooks the sea, has buildings on two sides only. To the south is the monumental *Cabildo Insular*, the seat of the Island Council. This building incorporates the Tourist Office, Archaeological Museum and an art gallery. *Tourist Information Office* (Hours 09.00–13.00, 16.00–18.00; Sat 09.00–13.00. Closed Sun & hol.)

Archaeological Museum (Museo Arqueologico) This museum contains the finest collection of Guanche relics in the Canaries. (Hours 09.00–13.00, 16.00–18.00. Closed Sun & hol. Small entrance fee: illustrated guide available.)

The west side of the square opens into the **Plaza de la Candelaria**. The *monument* here is to the Virgin of Candelaria, whose figure, with the Holy Child, stands atop an obelisk. At the foot are three Guanche kings, expressing the devotion of the Canary Islanders to their patron saint. The statue is by the Italian sculptor Canova (1778). The elaborate building overlooking the monument is the *Casino*, a popular club and meeting place. The restaurant here is open to non-members.

The Calle Candelaria leads off the south side of the square to the church of **La Concepción**, marked by its tall lantern-topped tower which was once a landmark for sailors approaching Santa Cruz. This church, built originally in the 16th c., was rebuilt after a fire in the 18th c. It is sometimes referred to as the cathedral, but this is incorrect (the Cathedral of Tenerife, and the Bishop's seat, is at La Laguna).

The dusty *barranco* and derelict buildings around it provide a rather down-at-heel setting for the mother church of Santa Cruz. The dull exterior, and curious balconied entrance, are an inadequate preparation for a church which contains many treasures. Most revered is the image of the *Virgen de la Consolación*, set in the magnificent 18th c. reredos, which was brought to Santa Cruz by the conqueror Alonso de Lugo. Also here, in the chapel at the end of the left aisle, is the *cross* that he carried on his arrival in the island in 1494, and before which, on the shores of 'Anaza' he celebrated the first Mass.

Most celebrated, however, are the two *flags* captured from the landing party of Horatio Nelson in 1797, during his unsuccessful attempt to seize the port. Their dusty remains lie in glass cases on either side of the *Capilla de Santiago* (3rd chapel, north aisle).

A particularly fine chapel is the *Capilla de Carta* (reached through door to right of chancel) which has some superb carving—unusual in that it is not gilded.

Santa Cruz de Tenerife

Walking tour
1 Cabildo Insular
  Archaeological Museum
  Tourist Information Office
2 La Concepción
3 S. Francisco
4 Municipal Museum
5 Parque Municipal
6 Plaza 25 de Julio
7 Capitania General
8 Market
9 Aucona (boat services)
B1 Main bus terminal
B2 Bus for La Laguna
B3 Bus for Las Teresitas

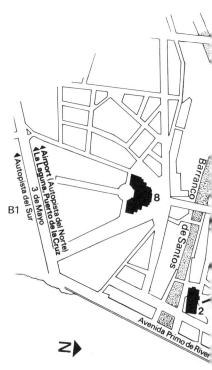

The *Barranco de Santos* to the south of the church was the site of the earliest Spanish settlement in Tenerife. In the *barranco*, which is now dry, are the old bridges which used to connect the old and the new parts of the city. They are now used as footpaths. The goats grazing along the banks of the *barranco* and the chickens scratching amidst the washing laid out to dry on the rocks give this backwater of Santa Cruz a pleasantly rural character.

Returning to the Plaza de la Candelaria, follow the street at its west end (San Francisco) to the church of **San Francisco**. This church belongs to the 18th c. and is a fine example of the simple colonial style of the period found throughout the Canaries. The only concession to Baroque extravagance is the *portal* with its twisted columns (note the use of lava). The *interior* of the church is more elaborate, with altars of gilded wood. The ceiling of trussed beams is another feature of the traditional Canary church.

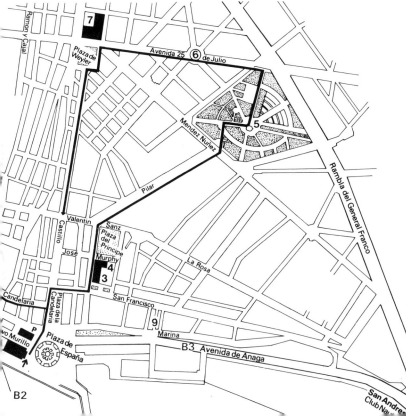

Next to the church the former convent (entered from the Plaza del Principe to the west) houses the *Library* and the *Municipal Museum and Art Gallery*, which possesses a collection of the works of Ribera and other Spanish artists. (Hours: 14.00–19.00; Sat 14.00–18.00.)

The **Plaza del Principe**, with its shady trees and bandstand, is the setting for many of the capital's folk dances and other festival events. On Sundays and holidays one can usually see a gathering of young Tinerfeños in their traditional costumes.

From the Calle Valentin Sanz the Calle del Pilar leads to the **Parque Municipal**. The park is laid out on a radial plan with a monumental fountain, dedicated to the city's architect Sanabria, at the centre. Sub-tropical trees and plants abound in the park, and at the entrance is a floral clock. In the southwest corner of the park, off one of the footpaths, is a 'lovers' nook' which can be easily overlooked by the casual stroller but which is worth a momentary pause to admire the ceramic seats whose backs have scenes, painted on a single tile, representing episodes from Tenerife history.

From the north-west corner of the park the Avenida 25 de Julio leads to one of the city's most photographed squares, the small **Plaza 25 de Julio**, which has an ornamental ceramic fountain and 20 ceramic seats similar to those in the park. The designs on these seats—advertisements for match manufacturers, motor and tyre companies and the like—date them firmly in the 20's. On the east side of this square, and adding very much to its charm with its well-kept garden is the *Anglican Church*.

The Avenida 25 de Julio leads on to the **Plaza de Weyler**, dominated by the impressive building of the *Capitania General*, seat of the Captain-General of the Canaries. This office was held by Franco prior to the Civil War, and it was here that he and his fellow officers planned their national rising.

To return to the Plaza de España, take the Calle del Castillo to the east. This is one of the main shopping thoroughfares in Santa Cruz.

Other places of interest in Santa Cruz

Port A walk along the front from the *Muelle Sur* to the *Muelle Norte* (Club Nautico) is a bracing experience. For 2km the quays are a scene of continuous activity. The ships which come and go include the inter-island steamers, the big liners bringing passengers from Europe and America to enjoy the Canary sun, and the endless freighters, displaying the flags of many nations.

Club Nautico On the seafront immediately to the north of the port. A sports and sailing club, with two swimming pools, this is the recreation centre of Santa Cruz (not open to

visitors). Just beyond the Club Nautico is part of an old fort, the *Castillo de Paso Alto*, which has been laid out as a garden. Displayed here are the *cannon* which fired on Admiral Nelson, including the one named 'El Tigre' which is claimed to have accounted for his right arm.

Market On the south side of the Barranco de Santos, near the Puente Serrador. (Hours 09.00–14.00. Closed Sun.)

This splendid market building is an emporium for the produce of Tenerife. The fruits of the island's rich soil are arrayed in the open square in the centre of the building: a colourful mixture of flowers, vegetables and fruits. On a lower floor are meats and fishes and outside the market are clothing stalls and souvenir kiosks.

Vista Bella The best view of Santa Cruz is from this point, reached by the old road out of the capital. Buses from Santa Cruz to La Laguna pass this point.

Hotels and restaurants
The hotels in Santa Cruz are mainly commercial, the tourist hotels being concentrated in Puerto de la Cruz. The most distinguished hotel in the city, and one of the finest in the island is the 5-star *Mencey*, at the north-east corner of the Parque Municipal. For other accommodation see p.21. Two good restaurants are the *Estancia* (Calle Mendez Nuñez) and the *Atlantico*, overlooking the Plaza de Espanã (also a popular bar and meeting-place). A restaurant with a good choice of Canarian dishes is *La Riviera* on the Rambla Gen Franco.

Beaches and swimming pools
Facilities for bathing in Santa Cruz are limited. The best beach is *Playa de las Teresitas* at San Andres 9km north of the city (see also p. 21). There is a good bus service to the beach, every 10 min from the Avenida de Anaga, marked 'San Andres'. The nearest beach to the south of the city (*Las Caletillas*, 14km) is reached by the local bus to Candelaria.

4km north of Santa Cruz, on the road to San Andres is *Balneario*, a popular swimming pool with a restaurant. On the way to the airport (junction of the Avenida Tres de Mayo and Avenida de los Reyes Catolicos) is the *Municipal Pool*.

Shopping
The shops in Santa Cruz offer a wide range of goods, from imported luxuries to the more reasonably priced goods of local or Spanish manufacture. Of these leather, shoes and jewellery are among the best bargains. Of special interest are the many tiny stores run by Asians who have a varied stock of every kind of merchandise.

The main shopping streets are the Calle de la Rosa, del Castillo and Valentin Sanz.

Bus services
Buses operate from three points (see map):
Avenida Tres de Mayo (main terminal)
Avenida de Anaga (for Las Teresitas)
Avenida Primo de Rivera (La Laguna)

Local tours and inter-island excursions
Coach tours to places of interest in Tenerife are available through agents in Santa Cruz. Air excursions to other islands are also available through these agents. For details of steamship and Jet-Foil services to the other islands, see p. 18.

Festivals
On January 5 Santa Cruz celebrates its most important local event, the *Festival of the Three Kings*. The cavalcade of the Kings disembarks at the quayside and proceeds through the streets to pay homage to a live tableau of the stable in Bethlehem. Later there is a parade of decorated coaches and singing and dancing groups.

Tenerife's capital is well-endowed with festivals. From February 9-16 it celebrates its Winter Festivals, with street processions and carnival events, and in the first two weeks of May it has its Spring Festivals (*Fiestas de la Cruz*) with funfairs, regattas and sports.

On July 25 there is a festival of particular interest to British visitors when the city celebrates the defeat of Horatio Nelson in his assault on Santa Cruz.

Santiago del Teide
Village situated in beautiful valley 44 km west of Puerto de la Cruz (Route 823) on west side of the island. 11 km to the south is its port, Puerto de Santiago, near the new resort of Los Gigantes. Boats may be hired for fishing.

Tacoronte
Village 20 km west of Santa Cruz on Route 820, 2 km from junction with *Autopista del Norte*.
This old village is of great religious significance to the islanders. It is here, in the chapel of what was once an Augustinian convent, that the precious image of Cristo de los Dolores is kept. Passing through the new section of the village one continues down towards the sea and the old quarter. On the east side of the main square stand the former church and convent of **San Agustin** (1662). The convent is disused, and the church is now known as the *Cristo de Tacoronte*. Above the fine silver altar is the image, a 17th c. wooden figure of *Christ* embracing the Cross. Many miracles have been attributed to this statue and on September 15 a feast is held in its honour. The ceiling over the presbytery is finely carved and painted, in the Mudejar style.

Further on, towards the sea, is the church of **Santa Catalina**. Built in the 17th c., it has a fine altarpiece of the same period, and a carving of the Virgen del Carmen by Luján Pérez.

Church of Santa Catalina, Tacoronte

Taganana
Village in Anaga peninsula 5 km north of circular route (see **Anaga**). This village stands in one of the first areas in which sugar was grown in the island. The road to La Laguna (called the *Vueltas de Taganana* and now part of the circular route) was in fact built early in the 16th c. for the conveyance of the sugar crop to the town, which was then the capital. Along this road the sea can be seen on both sides of the peninsula, and the whole area is one of great beauty.
The church of *Nuestra Señora de las Nieves* in the village has an interesting work in the form of a Gothic triptych of the *Adoration of the Kings*. It is of the 16th c. Spanish-Flemish school.

Teide
(3718 m) Highest mountain in the Canaries (see **Las Cañadas**).

Ten-Bel
Resort 4.5 km from junction 65 km south-west of Santa Cruz (*Autopista del Sur*). For accommodation see p. 22.

Vilaflor
(1161 m) Highest village in Tenerife, on southern flank of mountains 14 km west of Granadilla. Buses from Granadilla. The farming here is done on terraces, and there are good crops of potatoes, tomatoes and maize. Its altitude and location amidst beautiful pine forest make Vilaflor a popular place for hikers. There is no hotel, but accommodation can sometimes be arranged in a private house through the shopkeepers.

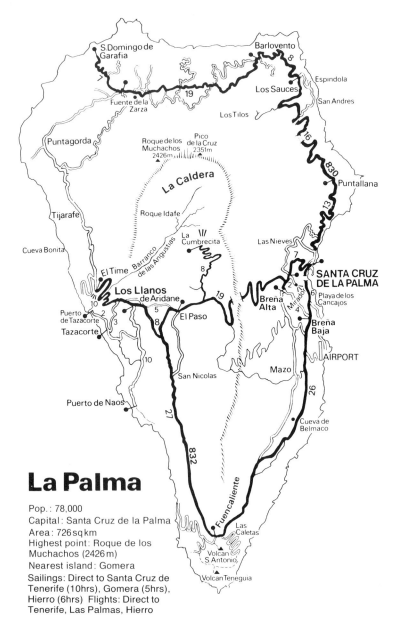

La Palma

Pop.: 78,000
Capital: Santa Cruz de la Palma
Area: 726 sq km
Highest point: Roque de los
Muchachos (2426 m)
Nearest island: Gomera
Sailings: Direct to Santa Cruz de
Tenerife (10hrs), Gomera (5hrs),
Hierro (6hrs) Flights: Direct to
Tenerife, Las Palmas, Hierro

Shaped like a flint axe-head, the island of La Palma lies to the north-west of Tenerife. Fifth in size, it has the third largest population in the Canaries. It is also considered by many visitors to be the most beautiful of the islands, largely on account of its extreme fertility, peaceful atmosphere and unique landscape.

The word 'unique' is appropriate to an island which in relation to its area achieves a greater height from sea level than any other inhabited island. This might imply a spectacular rise to a peak dominating the whole island, but in fact much of the altitude is gained near the coastline and the rise is then gradual—not to a mountain peak but to the rim of a volcanic crater whose highest point touches 2426 m. La Caldera (The Cauldron) is estimated to be the world's largest volcanic crater. Its interior is extremely beautiful. Its slopes, densely wooded with Canary pine, enclose the great bowl which was once the place where the ancient inhabitants worshipped their gods.

This was the realm of Tanausu, the Guanche king who made the tragic last stand against the Spanish invaders led by Alonso de Lugo. The year was 1493, and de Lugo had come to the island to confirm the submission of its inhabitants, who had bowed peacefully to the earlier expeditions of de Bethencourt.

Of the twelve native kingdoms in the island all but one had submitted to the Spanish. This was Tanausu's Ecero, which lay within the walls of La Caldera. The natural fortress proved too great an obstacle for the Spaniards, who had to resort to subterfuge to win the day. Offering negotiations to the native defenders, they enticed them to their camp and then dispatched them, either by sword or—perhaps a worse fate—by prison ship to Spain.

With its single opening to the south-west (Barranco de las Angustias) the crater is still one of the most inaccessible areas in the Canary Islands. To reach the viewpoint at La Cumbrecita the traveller from Santa Cruz de la Palma will have followed the thread-like road looping in and out of the *barrancos* above the town, passed through the needle's eye of the tunnel in the Cumbre Nueva, and then branched north on the road which twists in a separate strand up to the vantage point. His reward will be a view of the inner slope of the crater, cloaked with pine and sub-tropical vegetation, dipping down to its green-carpeted floor.

Such views must be achieved and are the better enjoyed for it. This is the essence of La Palma, whose small area, containing most of the best features of the other islands, deserves a leisurely exploration.

The roads, though well-made, are time-consuming, weaving their way around the corrugated coastline. The best round trip, which offers a good opportunity to see the island's volcanic formations, is from Santa Cruz de la Palma down to Fuencaliente at the southern tip and then up to Los Llanos on the west, returning to Santa Cruz by the central route.

The fertility of La Palma's soil is largely due to its volcanic content, the powdered lava in which the vines, almond trees, tomatoes and tobacco plants flourish with equal success. Flowers are plentiful too, particularly in April and May. A copious water supply and an equable climate create the right conditions for a rich variety of produce which is exported to the other islands and abroad.

Cigars are a speciality of the island, the tobacco grown from seed imported from Havana. These cigars are cheap but very good, and are sold separately or in bags of any quantity at the kiosks and bars.

La Palma's capital, Santa Cruz de la Palma, was an important seaport during the colonial period, when the Spanish had to defend their empire against the assaults of the British, French and Dutch. Its defences, including the Castillo Real, still survive in part, and there are many other fine buildings of the period.

Despite the beauty and variety of the island there has been virtually no tourist development in La Palma to date. Work has commenced, however, on a new Parador and tourist complex at Breña Baja, and there are 'urbanization' plans for the Caldereta. La Palma's airport (flights to and from Tenerife 7 times daily) is 7 km to the south of the capital.

Hotels and **restaurants** Most of the hotels are in the capital, Santa Cruz de la Palma, which has three of 3-star category including the Parador on the seafront. Elsewhere in the island, accommodation is mainly limited to pensions and *residencias*.

Visitors to La Palma should remember that tourism in the island is embryonic and that there is a shortage of accommodation even out of season. Bookings should, therefore, be made in advance (see Accommodation, p. 23).

Restaurants are almost exclusively the local type with a bar as their main attraction. Most are in and around the capital, but there are some in the smaller villages.

Beaches There are very few beaches in La Palma. The best are on the west coast near Puerto de Naos, but there is one, now being developed, to the south of Santa Cruz de la Palma (*Los Cancajos*).

Bus services There are regular bus services from Santa Cruz de la Palma to other parts of the island, with particularly good connections to Los Llanos on the west. All buses leave from the promenade (Avenida de Blás Pérez González, otherwise known as the Maratima).

Itineraries

1 *Santa Cruz de la Palma—Breña Baja—Fuencaliente—Los Llanos (with excursions to El Time, Tazacorte, Puerto de Naos)—El Paso —La Cumbrecita—Breña Alta—Santa Cruz*

This is a full day's excursion. For those who can spare another day, a night's stay in Los Llanos is recommended. This will provide a better opportunity to enjoy the short excursions from Los Llanos, and more time at La Cumbrecita.

En route the driver will see much evidence of La Palma's volcanic activity, both ancient and modern. Immediately to the south of the capital is La Caldereta, a small extinct crater through which a tunnel has been driven to take the road southward. Near Fuencaliente at the tip of the island is the Volcan de San Antonio, another volcano which erupted in 1677. On the west side of the island near Puerto de Naos (excursion from Los Llanos) the shape of the coastline was dramatically changed when a flow of lava from the island's last major eruption (1949) created a new wedge of land jutting into the sea. The return journey by the central route passes to the south of La Caldera and through the spine of the Cumbre Nueva, both volcanic creations. A diversion should be made to La Cumbrecita (8 km) for a view of the interior of the crater.

2 *Santa Cruz de la Palma—Breña Alta—La Cumbrecita—Return same route*

Half-day excursion to view crater of La Caldera.

3 *Santa Cruz de la Palma—Los Sauces—Barlovento—Garafia—Return same route*

Route to northern part of island. The roads, which have to bridge a succession of deep ravines, are more tortuous than in the south. But the country is greener, with abundant woods inland and continuous banana plantations along the coast.

Aridane, Valle de Fertile valley on west side of island with Los Llanos at its centre. Named after one of the island's early kingdoms.

Barlovento Northernmost village in La Palma, 37 km north of Santa Cruz.
The terminus for most of the buses from the capital. Only two a day continue round the forest road to Garafía.

Breña Alta Name given to upper part of two villages (Las Breñas) near airport, reached by upper road from Santa Cruz (9 km).
The village church (16th c.), was the scene of the baptism of many of the natives after the conquest. On the outskirts of the village is the *Mirador de la Concepción*, from which there are fine views of the capital and the coast.

Breña Baja 4 km below Breña Alta, and reached by lower road from Santa Cruz (6 km).
From the village, a road leads in 1 km to the *Playa de los Cancajos*, a sand beach which has the additional attraction of a series of coves formed by the volcanic lava.

Cueva Bonita Attractive cave in sea cliff on west side of island north of El Time, accessible only by boat (from Tazacorte).

Cueva de Belmaco Ancient site 8.5 km south of Breña Baja.
Guanche kings once inhabited this roadside cave with its whorl-shaped stone engravings, whose significance is yet to be interpreted. There are similar engravings at Fuente de la Zarza in the north.

El Paso Village 26 km west of Santa Cruz, centre of the silk and cigar manufacturing industries.
The village is surrounded by almond groves, which makes February and March the best months to visit the area. From the terraced courtyard of the church, at one of the high points of the village, the views are magnificent.
El Paso has two hotels and a good bus link with Santa Cruz.

El Time (594 km) Mountain overlooking coast north-west of Los Llanos.
The main road between Los Llanos and Tijarafe climbs to the summit of this mountain. This is the island's most spectacular drive (10 km from Los Llanos), along facing flanks of the deep and rugged *Barranco de las Angustias*, crossing at a narrow point 2 km inland.
From El Time the view of the *Valley of Aridane* to the south is superb. So too is the sight of

the immense *barranco* immediately below. Site of a new lookout and restaurant, this is the place to watch La Palma's sunsets.

Fuente de la Zarza Ancient site 13 km east of Puntagorda. Here are more prehistoric stone engravings, similar to those at the Cueva de Belmaco.

Fuencaliente Village 32 km from Santa Cruz at southern tip of island, reached by regular buses from the capital.
This is the centre of the island's small wine industry. A local co-operative produces a *Malvasia* wine which though palatable is tinged with the peculiar flavour associated with vines grown in volcanic soil.
The village is reached through an area of abundant pine forest where one can see good examples of the Canary pine. Beyond the village lies the most volcanic part of the island (recently active) at the southern tip. The main features here are the crater of the volcano San Antonio, scene of a large eruption in 1677, and the crater of Teneguia, site of the island's most recent eruption (1971).
A *Ruta Turistica* has been created to these volcanic sites, utilizing in part the existing roads to the vineyards, which flourish on the cindery slopes. From the main road, descend 1 km to the start of the trail to the *Volcano of San Antonio* (signposted). From here one should continue *on foot* for the view of the crater. (There are car tracks around the crater but these are strictly for Landrovers.) Returning to the road, continue 2 km south for the trail to the volcano Teneguia (this is driveable). After 2 km one can explore the **Rock of Teneguia**. This was sacred to the early inhabitants of the island and ancient 'petroglifos' or inscriptions may be found here. In this alien pasture a rare and only recently discovered plant may also be seen:

Volcano of Teneguia

the *centaurea junoniana*. Further on, after 1 km, lies the trail to the dramatically-hued **Volcano of Teneguia**, site of the Canaries' most recent eruption. From here one can return to the main road via *Las Caletas* (8 km), an uphill climb through vineyards.

Garafia (Santo Domingo de Garafia) Village in north-west of island 7 km from main road (830).

The large church and town hall mark the status of this village, the administrative centre of the region. There is also a *fonda* or local restaurant, and the buses from both Los Llanos and Santa Cruz stop here. There are beautiful walks in the woods and along the cliffs.

La Caldera The immense volcanic crater in the centre of La Palma is claimed as the largest and deepest in the world (diameter at widest point 9 km, circumference 28 km, depth 707 m). Unlike most extinct craters it is very fertile and thickly wooded from floor to rim. The best viewpoint is at La Cumbrecita,

from which the whole area can be surveyed. The road to *La Cumbrecita* is entered from the main road east of El Paso. It is a pleasant journey of 8 km through thick pine forest, climbing gradually to the *Mirador de la Caldera*. Another viewpoint is at the *Lomo de las Chozas*, 1 km further on.

The north rim of the crater rises to considerable heights (the *Roque de los Muchachos* touches 2426 m, the *Pico de la Cruz* 2351 m). One great rock in the heart of La Caldera, the *Idafe*, was one of the sacred places of the ancient inhabitants.

The crater, which is a National Park, has good tracks for hiking, but it would be advisable to get clear directions before exploring far into the interior, as the weather is very changeable there. (There are two refuges available for walkers.) Information about the area can be obtained from the Town Hall or the Tourist Office in Santa Cruz de la Palma.

La Caldereta Small crater, open on seaward side immediately to the south of Santa Cruz de la Palma.

Los Llanos Town on west side of island 31.5 km west of Santa Cruz by central route. The full name of this town, Los Llanos de Aridane (Plains of Aridane) recalls one of the original native kingdoms of the island. With a population of more than 11,000 Los Llanos is now the centre of much of La Palma's agriculture and industry, and home for many of her foreign residents.

There are three pensions and good bus services to Santa Cruz de la Palma. Good swimming is available at *Puerto de Naos* (10 km).

Los Sauces Village 28.5 km north of Santa Cruz.

The prosperity of this village owes much to the fertility of the region. Springs in the nearby forest (*Los Tilos*) have been channelled to irrigate the hillside terraces. An important crop here is sugar cane, distilled for making brandy. There are three pensions here and a good bus service to Santa Cruz de la Palma. Below Los Sauces are the twin fishing villages of *Espindola* and *San Andres* with good fish restaurants and swimming in natural pools.

Los Tilos Forest area in north-east of island near Los Sauces, noted for its laurel trees and giant ferns.

San Nicolas Village in west of island 9 km south of Los Llanos partly destroyed by volcanic eruption of 1949.

The road cuts through the lava flow to the south of the village. This lava formed a new cape at Puerto de Naos.

Santa Cruz de la Palma (pop. 20,000) Capital and port of La Palma.

Given the title 'The Noble and Loyal City of Santa Cruz de la Palma' by Philip II of Spain, this graceful old town is an appropriate capital for the island considered by many to be the most beautiful of all the Canaries.

Protected by the steeply rising hills to the west and enclosed to the south by the flank of La Caldereta, the port offers excellent anchorage for the ships which call here, mostly from the other islands or Spain. Like its namesake in Tenerife, the harbour of Santa Cruz is an integral part of the town, and arriving by ship the visitor is immediately in the middle of 'La Ciudad', as it is known by its inhabitants.

The town is built along the shelf of land between hills and sea. Although there is no beach on the seafront there is a wide promenade, following the line of the old sea wall as far as the Barranco de las Nieves in the north. There are many fine old buildings in Santa Cruz, described in the walking tour.

Communications by sea and air are good. Inter-island steamers arrive each day from Tenerife, and there are several flights daily to Tenerife from the nearby airport.

The main *fiesta* is that celebrated in honour of the island's patron saint, Our Lady of the Snows. This takes place on September 5, but every five years there is a special celebration known as the *Fiestas Lustrales*, which continues through the month of August. The festival, which began in 1680, includes a magnificent procession (*Bajada de la Virgen*) from the chapel where the image is kept. This is the Santuario de Nuestra Señora de las Nieves, 3.5 km inland from the town. From here the image is brought down to the capital to the mother church of El Salvador.

Tourist Information Office This is located on the Calle Real (O'Daly) and can be visited on the walking tour (below). (Hours: 09.00–13.00, 15.00–18.00; Sat 09.00–13.00. Closed Sun & hol.).

Walking tour (see map)

Harbour—Calle Real—Plaza Santo Domingo—Plaza España—Avenida de las Nieves—Seafront

From the harbour, cross the wide plaza at the end of the mole and turn right to enter the Calle Real (O'Daly). This is the main shopping street of Santa Cruz, which contains most of the town's older houses.

One block up on the left is Blas Simon, a steep street with steps leading up to the Plaza Santo Domingo. On a terrace overlooking the west side of this square is the one-time convent of **Santo Domingo**, now used as a school. The original tower and part of the 16th c. building are still intact, and permission to see them can be obtained from the school office.

*Church of El Salvador
Santa Cruz de la Palma*

Plaza de España, Santa Cruz de la Palma   Right: The 'Santa Maria'

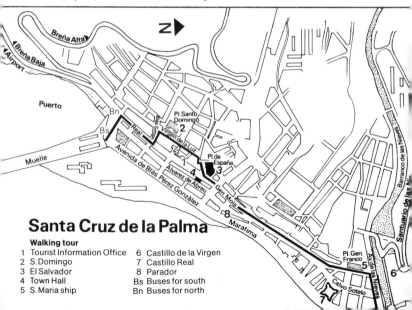

Santa Cruz de la Palma

Walking tour

1 Tourist Information Office
2 S. Domingo
3 El Salvador
4 Town Hall
5 S. Maria ship
6 Castillo de la Virgen
7 Castillo Real
8 Parador
Bs Buses for south
Bn Buses for north

Continuing northwards, turn right at the end of the street (Calle Virgen de la Luz) and descend to the cathedral square (Plaza de España). On the way, on a raised terrace in the Calle van de Walle, is the *Public Library* and *Museum*. The latter is of limited interest, being confined to natural history.

Steps lead down to the **Plaza de España**. This is the historical centre of Santa Cruz. On it are the beautiful church of El Salvador, the Town Hall, and some of the original houses belonging to the noble families who were among the early colonists.

Church of El Salvador The *portal* of this church (built in 1500) is a splendid example of Renaissance stone carving. The *interior* of the church is particularly fine, with the

ceiling of the nave and aisles carved in the Portuguese-Moorish style—a reminder of the many Portuguese craftsmen who worked in the town in the 16th c.

The Renaissance-style altarpiece—a break from the conventional gilded reredos—shows the antiquity of this church in relation to the other major churches in the Canaries. The painting of the *Transfiguration* here is by Esquivel, of the Seville School. Also Renaissance are the four *stoops* of Carrara marble.

By contrast, the vault of the *sacristy* (entrance to right of chancel) is Gothic: the only example of this style in the island.

Town Hall Overlooking the Calle Real, this buildings belongs to the reign of Philip II (1563). Its Renaissance *portico* is a good example of the period. Note also the beautifully carved *ceilings*, under the portico and in the main rooms.

Continuing along the Calle Mola one reaches the Plaza General Franco. At the end of the square stands the stone replica of the *Santa Maria*, the ship in which Columbus sailed on his first voyage to America. During the month-long *Fiestas Lustrales* (see above) the model—built to the same size as the original—is fully rigged and decorated. The interior of the 'ship' is shortly to become a naval museum.

The square opens into the Avenida de las Nieves. At this point lies the great *barranco* which divides the town from the countryside. 3 km distant at the head of this valley is the shrine of *Nuestra Señora de las Nieves*, patroness of the city. To visit it, one can either walk or take a bus (marked Breña Alta) from the Maratima (near Parador).

Turning right down the Avenida de las Nieves one reaches the seafront. To the left is the old fort of the *Castillo de la Virgen*. To the right, on the esplanade, is another fort, the *Castillo Real*, now a National Monument. Both these strongpoints were built in the 17th c. to repel the privateers—French, Dutch and British—who were constantly attacking the island.

Continuing southwards along the front one passes many old balconied houses and the attractive *Parador*, the hotel run by the Spanish Government.

Tazacorte Small port on west side of island at outlet of Barranco de las Angustias, 3 km from Los Llanos.

This was the landing-place, in 1493, of the conqueror Alonso de Lugo. It was one of the first Spanish settlements in La Palma, and there are some attractive old houses here. There are also three restaurants and some good beaches. Boats may be hired for a trip to the *Cueva Bonita* (see Gazetteer entry). Tazacorte is the centre of the island's banana production.

Balconied houses on the Maratima, Santa Cruz de la Palma

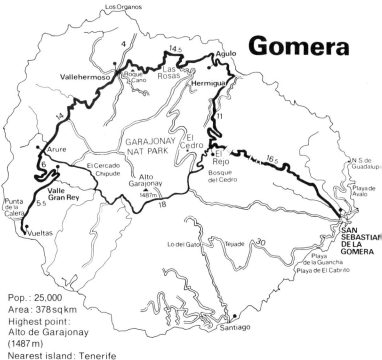

Gomera

Los Organos

Vallehermoso

4

14.5

Agulo

Roque Cano

Las Rosas

Hermigua

Arure

GARAJONAY NAT PARK

El Cedro

14

11

El Cercado
Chipude

Valle Gran Rey

Alto Garajonay
▲
1487m

El Rejo

Bosque del Cedro

16.5

N.S. de Guadalupe

Playa de Avalo

Punta de la Calera

5.5

18

Vueltas

Lo del Gato

Tejiade

30

SAN SEBASTIAN DE LA GOMERA

Playa de la Guancha

Playa de El Cabrito

Santiago

Pop.: 25,000
Area: 378 sq km
Highest point:
Alto de Garajonay
(1487 m)
Nearest island: Tenerife
Sailings: Direct to Santa Cruz de
Tenerife (7hrs), Los Cristianos
(1½hrs), La Palma (5hrs), Hierro (5hrs)

Rising in a gentle curve on Tenerife's horizon, Gomera remains a mystery to most of the visitors to the larger island. It has, however, a reward for those who can spare it more than a distant glance. The island can only be reached by sea. There is no airport yet, and the collective conscience must forbid it as much as the precipitous terrain. Gomera is an island which needs to be approached, and enjoyed, slowly.

The view of Gomera from the sea is misleading. The coast on the east side where the port is located appears barren and desolate, but if the boat were to continue to the north coast the visitor would again behold the extraordinary fertility of the Canaries, at its richest in the great valley of Hermigua, with its lush, steeply-banked terraces. There are similar fertile valleys in many other parts of the north and east, dotted with innumerable tiny villages. These valleys are blessed with an abundant supply of water from the underground streams which are a special feature of the island.

The little town of San Sebastian, the capital and port, has some interesting old buildings, including the church in which Columbus is said to have attended his last Mass before setting sail for America. This was one episode in a history which—considering Gomera's small size—was remarkably full of incident.

Columbus had dropped anchor in an island that had been colonized for Spain fifty years before by Hernan Peraza (the Elder). To achieve this new territory Peraza had first to dislodge the Portuguese, who had established themselves in the south of the island, and then gain the submission of the natives. The first task was achieved by agreement—the second took years of repression and persuasion. Peraza was succeeded in these efforts by his son-in-law Diego and grandson Hernan the Younger.

The Perazas, who had inherited the conquests of Bethencourt (Lanzarote, Fuerteventura and Hierro), were given the title Conde de la Gomera (Count of La Gomera). This was a special concession by the Spanish king to curb their ambitions towards the three remaining islands in the group, where their rivals were making their own territorial claims.

In 1481 this rivalry led to the death of Juan Rejón, the conqueror of Grand Canary, who was murdered by the Perazas when he landed briefly in Gomera on his way to La Palma. To atone for this crime, Hernan the Younger was ordered to Tenerife to assist Alonso de Lugo in his repression of the Guanche people of Grand Canary. The ultimate capitulation of the people of Gomera to their Spanish masters was shown by the fact that Hernan was able to take a contingent of *gomeros* with him on the expedition.

In 1488 Hernan the Younger met his inevitable fate. This was at the hands of a native chieftain, who, incensed at the Count's abduction of his daughter, cut him down while he was visiting her in a cave in the west of the island.

A revolt followed in which Hernan's widow, Beatriz de Bobadilla, was besieged in the fortress of San Sebastian, the Torre del Conde. She was finally rescued by a relief force from Grand Canary under Pedro de Vera, and the reprisals that followed against the natives of Gomera achieved the first real conquest of the island.

Beatriz de Bobadilla is an historical figure in her own right. Not only was she the wife of Hernan de Peraza but later the wife of the conqueror of Tenerife, Alonso de Lugo. She is also supposed to have had a liaison with Columbus, whom she entertained during his visits to the island in 1492 and 1493. This was on the occasion of his first two voyages to America, and it was Beatriz who arranged for the provisioning of his ships.

Gomera was also Columbus' last port of call on his third voyage (1498). Its name is therefore enduringly linked with the history of Spanish exploration and discovery.

For the modern explorer, Gomera presents something of a challenge—but by no means an insuperable one. The roads leading from San Sebastian to the north of the island (Carretera del Norte) and to the centre and south (Carretera del Centro, del Sur) wind painstakingly along the flanks and over the tops of the steep barrancos, but eventually find their way to their common destination — the group of villages in the beautiful western valley, the Valle Gran Rey. Here you can pause at a *fonda* for a meal or a drink under the vines, or sample the small beaches tucked into the coastline. It is all a far cry from the large Canary resorts like Las Palmas, and one can understand why many tourists, having sampled the 'high life', choose Gomera as a further line of retreat.

Peculiar to the island is the *silbo*, the whistling language evolved over the centuries as a means of communication across the great ravines which divide the little villages. As a form of 'telegraph' it is unique. Each word is relayed separately, and people using it recognize individuals as though hearing their voices. Men working in the valleys will whistle instructions or questions to each other, for distances up to a mile. Parents use it to call their children, and one often hears a man whistling into the distance to a child who may be tending goats on the far side of a wide *barranco*.

Apart from their unique customs, the people of Gomera have a special identity through their continuing descent from the original inhabitants, who did not suffer the same depletion of population through butchery or bondage that was the lot of the other islands. As a result their physical characteristics are closer to the Guanche type than elsewhere in the Canaries.

Los Organos This impressive group of basalt pillars on the north coast is accessible only by boat (apply to Club Nautico in San Sebastian).

Accommodation See **San Sebastian**.

Beaches The island has few accessible beaches. These are at San Sebastian (see town), Agulo, Puerto de Vallehermoso, Valle Gran Rey and Santiago.

Buses A bus runs once a day from San Sebastian to the north coast villages and returns the next day.

Tour from San Sebastian

San Sebastian—El Rejo—Hermigua—Agulo —Vallehermoso—Valle Gran Rey—Vueltas —Arure—El Cercado, Chipude—Alto Garajonay—El Rejo—San Sebastian

Gomera's principal road (Carretera del Norte) connects San Sebastian with Vallehermoso in the island's north-east (42km) from which minor roads continue to the village of Valle Gran Rey (a further 20km) and the coast at Vueltas (5.5km). There is a daily bus service from San Sebastian to Valle Gran Rey, but the bus does not return until the following morning and an overnight stop must be made at Valle Gran Rey.

Car drivers may feel similarly disposed after a tiring journey. An indication of the complexity of the route, engineered around the deeply indented *barrancos*, is that although its distance is only 62km, few drivers can do it in less than three hours. The advantage of the private motorist is that he can opt to return to San Sebastian by the central route (34.5km), starting at Arure 6km north of Valle Gran Rey and rejoining the main road 16km from San Sebastian.

On the tour a diversion may be made to El Cedro, at the heart of the Garajonay National Park. This village, in a beautiful forest area, is reached by either the northern or central routes, but the roads are rough and vertiginous. (Advice may be obtained *en route* from the National Park Visitors Centre, 3km from Las Rosas.)

Allow 7hrs, with stops, for the total trip.

From San Sebastian the road winds up the side of the great *barranco* behind the port. It is a well engineered road and despite the successive bends one can enjoy superb views of the neatly terraced hillsides. 2km before El Rejo, a tunnel 1km long cuts

through a mountain spur. On leaving the tunnel one has a marvellous view to the north of the island's most fertile valley, into which the road rapidly descends. The valley, green with banana plantations, is the most populated part of Gomera after San Sebastian. Its principal village is *Hermigua*, which has a pension.

27.5km from San Sebastian the road rises to *Agulo*. This old village is on the edge of the cliff and has magnificent views over the whole region and eastwards to the island of Tenerife. There are several good restaurants here, and a centre where native crafts are taught. Pottery, weaving and basket work can be purchased in the shop at the school. From here the road climbs inland until it reaches the mountain town of *Vallehermoso*. This is an important agricultural centre and has two pensions and two restaurants. It is here that the delicious *miel de palma* is produced. This is the palm honey, peculiar to Gomera, which is made by draining a liquid (*garapo*) from the palm and cooling it slowly until it becomes thick and black. The volcanic soil in which the palm trees grow imparts a spicy tang to the honey, which is usually eaten with bread or *gofio*, the local maize meal.

To the east of the village stands the striking monolith of the *Roque Cano* (650m). The main road leads north from here (4km) to the harbour, but a minor road continues the tour southwards down the deep barranco to *Arure*. Here, beneath the peak of *Cementerio* (914m) it joins another *barranco* which is one of the most beautiful in the island. In the *Barranco de Valle Gran Rey* flourishes every offspring of the rich Canary soil, from the elegant date palm to the humble potato, grown on the cultivated terraces on either side of the valley.

Good beaches lie to the south, at the outlet to the sea. These are located near the villages at the end of two roads (*Punta de la Calera* to the west, *Vueltas* to the east.) Accommodation can be found at both these places. (Ask at the beach cafes where excellent fish menus are served.)

From Valle Gran Rey the return journey to San Sebastian can be made by taking the road across the centre of the island, turning right at Arure, and going through the villages of *El Cercado* (5km) and *Chipude* (5.5km). These remote settlements are of particular interest, as it is here that the Chipude pottery is made. The women use no wheel, but fashion the red pots by hand. The shapes are the same as those of the Guanche pottery in the Archaeological Museum in Santa Cruz de Tenerife. In El Cercado and the surrounding hamlets the women spin and weave the wool from their hardy sheep. The articles they make are extremely durable: blankets, bags and rugs.

Torre del Conde, Gomera

The road now winds across the island past the great peak of *Garajonay* (1487 m) and then through the cedar forests of *El Cedro* (Bosque del Cedro). It is well signposted, and although very little traffic will be encountered (only the odd forest warden or woodman with a battered truck), it is not difficult to find the way to the main road at El Rejo, and thence back to the capital.

Other short trips may be made elsewhere in the island, but drivers should obtain advice about the condition of the roads before embarking on their journey.

A short excursion may be made to the south of the island (Playa de Santiago, 30km), where the best swimming can be enjoyed.

Beyond San Sebastian the route touches the coast twice (*Playa de la Guancha, Playa de El Cabrito*) and then goes inland to *Tejiade* (17 km). At *Lo del Gato* a left turn is made for the road to *Santiago*. This road is little used, for traditionally the fishing village has always been approached from San Sebastian by sea. The unexpected prosperity of the village is due to the presence here of a canning factory supplied by a large agricultural estate to the north. The beach, though stony, is warmer than that of San Sebastian, as it is protected by the mountains to the north.

San Sebastian de la Gomera (pop. 8000) The capital of Gomera is a neat little town situated at the mouth of a wide *barranco*. Here the land is flat, and the streets laid out in a grid pattern. The beach curves round to a busy little harbour, established by the *conquistadores* when they landed here in the mid 15th c.

This miniature capital has many links with history. In the centre of the town is what is probably the oldest building still in use in the Canary Islands. This is the **Torre del Conde**, the Count's Tower, a square fortress of three storeys. Today it stands among banana plantations, but when it was constructed by Hernan Peraza in 1450, as a stronghold against the attacks of the native inhabitants,

the sea lapped round its walls. The Spanish invaders, finding the fierce *gomeros* very difficult to subdue, used the tower as their place of refuge when the natives rushed down from their mountain strongholds in their attempts to drive out the invaders. It was in this tower that Beatriz de Bobadilla took refuge with her children after the death of her husband at the hands of the native princes (1488). The tower now contains a small museum (Hours: 10.00–13.00, 16.00–18.00; Mon 16.00–18.00.)

Elsewhere in the town (Calle General Franco) is the church of the **Ascension**. This is very much as it was in Columbus' time, and it is a fair supposition that the great man heard his last Mass in this church before embarking on his momentous voyage. The church has an interesting *mural*, painted in 1780 (left transept), the scene depicting a Dutch fleet attacking Gomera.

A number of houses in San Sebastian date back to the early colonial period and some bear the coats-of-arms of the *conquistadores* and their descendants. One of them in the Calle General Franco (No 60) is reckoned to be the house where Columbus stayed during his brief sojourn in the port. Columbus' special identification with Gomera is recognized in a week of festivities in September in commemoration of his first voyage.

Today the harbour is a busy outlet for the island's produce, and a destination for the many fishing boats and tourist launches from Tenerife. By contrast the life of San Sebastian itself is quiet and relaxed, and a favourite pastime for visitors is to sit in the plaza at the end of the promenade and watch the world of Gomera go about its leisurely business.

7 km north of the town is the shrine of *Nuestra Señora de Guadalupe*, patroness of the island. On her feast day in October the venerated image is brought by boat to the capital for a special festival in her honour.

Hotels

The Spanish Government operate a splendid new Parador on the cliff above the harbour. It is an elegant hotel in the old Spanish style, with gardens and a swimming pool, and authentic Spanish cuisine. Every room has a balcony overlooking the sea.

There is also a hotel in the centre of the town and some pensions which offer good accommodation at very reasonable rates. These are located in the street (Ruiz de Padron) to the east of the Torre del Conde.

Beaches

Good swimming is available at the beach to the south of the harbour (*Playa de San Sebastian*). Two other good beaches lie to the south of the capital: *Playa de la Guancha* (4km) and *Playa de El Cabrito* (8km). 4km to the north of San Sebastian is the attractive little cove of *Avalo*, reached by a pleasant coastal road.

Valle Gran Rey

Hierro

Pop: 7000
Area: 278 sq km
Highest point: Alto de Malpaso
(1500m)
Nearest island: Gomera
Sailings: Direct to La Palma (6hrs) and
Gomera (5hrs) continuing to Tenerife
Flights: Direct to Tenerife, La Palma

The smallest and most westerly of the
Canaries, Hierro is surprisingly
different to its nearest neighbour,
Gomera.
Shaped like a boot, the semi-circle
formed by the toe and instep are
thought to be the rim of an extinct
volcanic crater, the north side of
which has disappeared into the sea.
The sides of the 'boot' fall sheer into
the sea, and the only relatively flat
part is at the ankle in the north. Here
stands the main town of the island,
Valverde—the only capital in the
Canaries not located on the coast.

The region around Valverde, with its
dependent hamlets, is known as El
Barrio ('Suburb'). The other regions
are El Golfo ('Gulf' or 'Crater') and El
Pinar ('Pine'). The latter refers to the
heel or southern part of Hierro which
has, in its higher altitudes, the
greatest concentration of forest
vegetation in the island.
This vegetation, notably the pine,
beech and giant heather peculiar to
the western islands, is dependent for
moisture on the mists which
accumulate at higher levels. These
mists are in fact the islanders' main

source of water, apart from the almost non-existent rainfall. Any additional water has to be imported —and here is another contrast to Gomera, with its plentiful underground supply. Despite this lack of water the soil of Hierro is productive and the island is well known for its figs, tobacco and wine.

The *herreños* too—the people of Hierro—are a different breed to the *gomeros*. As in Gomera the original inhabitants were Guanche, but few of them survived the arrival of the Spanish. When Juan de Bethencourt arrived in the island in 1402 the inhabitants fled to the hinterland. When they were persuaded to present themselves to their invaders through an intermediary, Bethencourt committed the unchivalrous act of seizing them and selling them into slavery. By this means the island was virtually cleared of its indigenous population, and the modern *herreño* is of largely Spanish descent, unlike the people of Gomera who still have a lot of native blood.

Hierro has a Parador and accommodation in Valverde, Restinga and Frontera. The main port is at Puerto Estaca and there is an airstrip with flights from Tenerife and La Palma. Approached by air or sea the island has a rather barren and forbidding appearance, but once the interior and west coast are reached this impression is dispelled. There are magnificent pine forests both to north and south of the central route (best viewed from the highest point, Alto del Malpaso) and the views from the crater rim of El Golfo are fantastic, especially at sunset.

The island has only a few towns, all small and rather poor. The capital, Valverde, Tamaduste on the north-east coast, Frontera in the centre and Sabinosa in the west make up the main centres of the small population. Although most of the south and west of the island is now uninhabited, there are many indications that the primitive people lived here, including cave inscriptions. (These are unfortunately in inaccessible parts of the island.)

Travelling in Hierro With the exception of Restinga all the main villages on the island are connected by bus. The bus which takes visitors from the landing stage at Puerto Estaca to Valverde also serves the villages of El Barrio, and another service goes all the way round the island from Valverde to Sabinosa in the north-west. These services, however, are not frequent and progress around the island is a slow and leisurely business due to the poor condition of the roads.

The visitor wishing to do his own driving may hire a car in Valverde, or

El Golfo, Hierro

—if he has his own car in Tenerife—bring it over by inter-island steamer (see Boat Services, p. 18).

Taxi drivers can be found who will show visitors the country, but the limitations of the roads prevent them from taking people to the more remote areas.

The best way to see the island is, of course, on foot, and few places can offer a more enchanting setting for a hiking holiday. One is never far from a village, and having the sea on all sides it is almost impossible to get lost, even in the deep pine forests of the interior.

Tours from Valverde

1 *Valverde—San Andres—Frontera—Sabinosa—return same route*

Leaving Valverde the road passes through *San Andres*, a village in the centre of a good agricultural area, and continues west along the central ridge of the island to a fork on the right which leads down to the village of Frontera. From here the winding route offers superb views of *El Golfo*. Continuing through the hamlets of *Tigaday* and *Los Llanillos* it then goes on to the westernmost village in the Canary Islands, *Sabinosa*. From here it is a short distance to the *Balneario*.

This curious little spa on the windswept north-west coast has thermal waters with medicinal properties, and is open in the summer months to visitors. There is no pension at Sabinosa, but a room can sometimes be found for overnight accommodation by enquiring at the local post office. It is a good centre for exploring the tracks of the western region of the island.

2 *Valverde—San Andres—Taibique—Restinga—return same route*

After San Andres a turning to the left (1 km) leads to the twin villages of *Las Casas* and *Taibique*. Beyond Taibique the road deteriorates but can be followed to *Restinga*.

This little fishing village, at the southernmost tip of the southernmost island, must be the most isolated in the Canaries. Access is still mainly by sea from Puerto Estaca. Despite this there are a couple of bars here and the beaches offer reasonable swimming.

3 *Valverde — Mocanal — Jarales — return same route*

This short route is possible by bus, taxi or car. Leaving Valverde take the road northwest to *Mocanal* and on to *Guarazoca*. At the end of this road at *Jarales* is a look-out with tremendous views over the wide bay of *El Golfo*. This is the home of innumerable birds and the haunt of the giant lizard *Lacerte Simonyi*. This species, found only in Hierro, can grow to a length of two feet.

Below the village is the hermitage of the *Virgen de la Peña*.

Valverde (pop. 5000) or La Villa as it is known to its inhabitants, stands at a height of 571 m, 7.5 km inland from the port of Puerto Estaca. It is not a very prepossessing place. There is a little plaza, on which stands the church, Town Hall and two restaurants. It is from here that the buses leave for the outlying villages. Valverde has a hotel and two pensions. 20 km to the south is the *Parador Nacional de Hierro*. Bookings for this and other accommodation in the island can be made in Tenerife (Tourist Office, steamship line).

The nearest swimming places are the *Balneario* at Tamaduste (by footpath 2 km, by road 7.5 km) or the *Playa de la Caleta* (4.5 km by road).

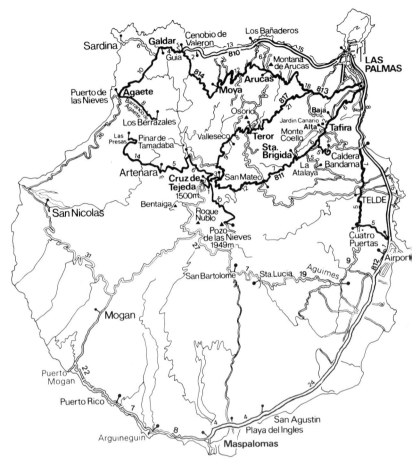

Grand Canary

Pop.: 535,000
Capital: Las Palmas
Area: 1532 sq km
Highest point: Pozo de las Nieves
(1949 m)
Nearest island: Tenerife

Sailings: International and direct to
Santa Cruz de Tenerife (3hrs),
Lanzarote (10hrs), Fuerteventura
(10hrs) For Jet-Foil service, see p.18
Flights: International (Madeira 1hr)
and direct to Tenerife, Lanzarote and
Fuerteventura

Grand Canary owes its name not to its size (it is smaller than Tenerife) but to the bravery of its early inhabitants, who for five years defied the Spanish invaders. In recognition of their stalwart resistance the Spanish gave the island the title 'Grand' or 'Great' after the conquest in 1483.

Its greatness continues today in the status of its port, Las Palmas. Commanding the principal sea-routes from Europe to America and Africa, Las Palmas has been a familiar port of call not only for the merchant adventurers of Spain but for generations of British on their way to the distant corners of the Empire. Today its harbour is still full of steamers, fuelled by the giant oil tanks which dominate the Puerto de la Luz.

The first Europeans to take an interest in Grand Canary were sailors from the merchant cities of Italy, and Majorcan traders who raided the island for slaves.

The native Guanches, led by their two kings Doramas of Telde and Tenesor of Galdar, put up a strong resistance to these incursions. Later on, they repelled attempts by de Bethencourt and his followers to invade the island.

In 1478 the Spanish under Juan Rejón made a concerted attempt to capture the island, landing their troops at the place now known as Las Palmas. In spite of their advanced weapons, which included the first cannon, the Spanish took five years to conquer the island. Their ultimate triumph was the death of Doramas and the capture of Tenesor, who was taken to Spain and converted to Christianity. Two leaders who followed Rejón were Pedro de Vera and Alonso de Lugo, who joined forces to defeat the last Guanche stronghold at Galdar.

After the conquest Las Palmas became a threshold port for Spain's newly-founded empire. The dominant figure of the period was, of course, Columbus, who fitted up his ships here for the epic voyages across the Atlantic.

The strategic importance of Grand Canary was recognized by the other maritime powers—notably the British and Dutch—who raided Las Palmas in the 16th and 17th centuries. The Barbary pirates, too, were attracted by Las Palmas, and raids continued until the mid-18th century.

For many years, when the Canary Islands were administered as one province, Grand Canary was in a state of bitter rivalry with Tenerife as to which was the most important island of the group. The issue was finally resolved by the Spanish Government in 1927 when the islands were divided into two provinces. Las Palmas is now the capital of the eastern group made up of Grand Canary, Lanzarote and Fuerteventura, while Tenerife and the western islands form the other province.

The island of Grand Canary is almost circular in shape. Its dominant feature, the central massif—known as the 'Cumbre'—provides striking scenery. The fertile slopes and valleys below the central range sweep down to a coastline which varies from the dark rocks of the north-west coast to the sand dunes of Maspalomas. Such variety has earned Grand Canary the title 'Continent in Miniature'.

The country on the east side of the island is somewhat barren, and the first impression received on the drive from the airport to Las Palmas or Maspalomas is uninspiring. But this road is probably the single exception to the network of routes that reveal the unusual beauty of the island.

The rewards for the explorer are numerous. All round the north and west coast there are attractive fishing villages, their houses clustered above small coves where the boats bob against a sheltering quay or breakwater. The aspect of this coastline is North Atlantic, with rocks and waves in eternal conflict: by contrast one can find the balm of the South Pacific on the other side of the island at Maspalomas where the palm trees and sand dunes stretch for miles.

Inland, the forest regions above Teror and Los Berrazales are ideal for

houses of the Spanish nobles, with their coats-of-arms carved over the entrances. Churches also survive from the period, both in these towns and in the remoter villages.

One should come to these country places, too, for the celebration of the dramatic folk and religious festivals which are so much a part of Canary Island life.

Hotels and **restaurants** Grand Canary's hotels are mainly centred on the resorts (Las Palmas, Maspalomas, San Agustin, Playa del Inglés, etc., see p. 22). These resorts all have good international restaurants: those with a local flavour are found in the more isolated villages on the coast and in the mountains (see p. 24).

Beaches There are excellent sandy beaches in Las Palmas and on the east and south coasts of the island. Maspalomas, the major resort in the south, is located near a huge peninsula of sand, characterized by its rolling dunes, which offers perfect bathing—both in sun and sea.

For **bus services** and **local excursions**, see Las Palmas.

walking and camping. From here the pine trees flourish right up to the summit of the island at Cruz de Tejeda. Near Tejeda itself the National Parador is an excellent centre from which to explore the country. It is superbly sited and has panoramic views over the great Cumbre. The architecture and decorations of the Parador are the work of the Canary artist Néstor de la Torre.

Wherever one travels in Grand Canary, all roads seem to lead back to Las Palmas, the modern metropolis which draws the rest of the island to it like a magnet. This magnetic effect extends, through its great port, to the shipping of the world, and to international tourism through the splendid beach resort of Las Canteras.

Another face of Las Palmas—and of the island—is in the old town, site of the first Spanish stronghold. In this quarter one meets the history of the *conquistadores* at every corner. The old balconied houses, quiet plazas and ancient churches look much the same as they did in the early days of Spanish rule.

The traveller escaping the magnet of Las Palmas will find further echoes of the past in the country towns of Teror and Telde, once the seats of the *conquistadores*. Here are the fine

Itineraries

Circular tour (Route 812, 810)
Las Palmas—Maspalomas—Mogan —San Nicolas—Agaete—Los Bañaderos—Las Palmas
(This is an arduous drive, only for the dedicated explorer. An overnight stay in San Nicolas is advised.)
Short tours
From Las Palmas
1 *Las Palmas—Telde—Cuatro Puertas—Gando—Maspalomas— direct return by coastal road*
2 *Las Palmas—Arucas—Moya— Galdar—Agaete—Los Berrazales— Cenobio de Valeron—Los Bañaderos —Las Palmas*
3 *Las Palmas—Tafira Alta—Caldera Bandama—Santa Brigida—Cruz de Tejeda—Valleseco—Teror— Tamaraceite—Las Palmas*
From Cruz de Tejeda
4 *Cruz de Tejeda—Artenara— Tamadaba—return*
5 *Pozo de las Nieves*

Agaete Village on north-west coast, 53 km west of Las Palmas, 2 km from fishing port of Puerto de las Nieves.

At the foot of the fertile valley of the Barranco de Agaete, this attractive old town has a place in history as the site of the garrison of Pedro de Vera who had come over from Gomera in 1482 to assist the military commander Alonso de Lugo in his protracted campaign against the Guanche people. It was from here that de Vera launched the successful attack on the Guanche stronghold at Galdar, which was to prove the Spaniards' decisive victory.

For de Lugo the spoils of war were a large estate in the valley, where he planted sugar cane and built one of the island's first sugar refineries. Today Agaete is still an important agricultural centre, the outlet for the valley's rich produce which now includes bananas and coffee. From the sea, too, come riches, and the local fishermen look to the Virgin of the Snows (Nuestra Señora de las Nieves) for protection. Her image, preserved in a precious Flemish triptych, is in the *church* of that name.

Between August 4-7 is celebrated the Feast of the *Bajada de la Rama* (Descent of the Branch), which has its origin in an ancient fertility rite. Huge branches of the Tamadaba pine are carried down to the sea. Here they are submerged in the water as an invocation to the Almighty for adequate rain in the forthcoming year. The feast also includes a procession with bands, giant figures and decorations and an offering to the Virgin (see also **Puerto de las Nieves**).

Artenara (1219 m) Mountain village 45 km west of Las Palmas (via Route 811) and 12 km west of Cruz de Tejeda (Parador Nacional). The highest village in Grand Canary, Artenara also has the curious distinction of being a village of caves. More strangely, their inhabitants live in them not through poverty but by choice, in the tradition of the early Guanche people of the region who were the original occupants.

Today the cave dwellings—excavated from the soft rock of the hill side—have all the comforts of a conventional home. They are served by electricity and running water and have the added virtue of being cool in summer and warm in winter.

The Guanche tradition of this village is inescapable when one looks across the *barranco* to the rock of Bentaiga which was their principal place of worship. (View from *Mirador la Silla*, reached by turning up slip road immediately west of village and walking through tunnel entrance of *Meson la Silla* restaurant.)

After the conquest the power of the ancient beliefs had to be overcome by the spirit of the Christian church. Like so many Canary Island villages Artenara has its holy image, the Virgin of the Cave (Virgen de la Cuevita). This is enshrined in a little *cave church* of the same name, on a terrace overlooking the valley. (Go up steep lane behind village—the Camino de la Cuevita—and follow path.) Inside the church, the simplicity of the altar and pulpit—carved, like the rest of the church, from the rock—present a pleasant contrast to the ostentation of church decoration elsewhere.

The surrounding views of the Cumbre and lower slopes are superb and it is worth pursuing them another 14 km to the end of the road (*Las Presas*).

Arucas (pop. 25,000) Town 18 km west of Las Palmas (Route 810), situated in valley at centre of the island's main banana growing area.

One of the most surprising sights in Grand Canary is the giant Gothic *cathedral* that rises from the midst of the orchards and banana plantations of Arucas. The cathedral (more properly—if more modestly—the Parish Church of St John the Baptist) was built under the patronage of the Marquesa de Arucas (1875-1973). The foundation stone was laid in 1909, which makes the church an anachronism even as a Gothic revival.

The cathedral square, graced by its tulip trees, is a scene of great festivity on three important occasions during the year: the

Cathedral, Arucas

festivals of Corpus Christi, St John the Baptist and St Lucy. Elsewhere in the town is a fine *Municipal Park* which has one of the most varied collections of exotic flowers and plants in the island.

From Arucas one can quickly reach the summit of the nearby *Montaña de Arucas*, an extinct volcanic cone which rises to a height of 412 m. From here one can enjoy a view of almost the entire northern coastline, from La Isleta to the Pico de Galdar.

Caldera Bandama
Volcanic crater 5 km from junction on Route 811 9.5 km south-west of Las Palmas.

A popular diversion for sightseers on their way to Tejeda, this crater is 200 m deep and more than 1 km wide. Its floor is cultivated and there is even a farmhouse, now abandoned. At the *Pico de Bandama* (569 m) are tourist shops and a restaurant.

Cenobio de Valeron
Ancient site, 37 km west of Las Palmas on road to Galdar (Route 810).

Honeycombing the cliff known as the Cuesta de Silva, the Cenobio de Valeron is a group of caves used as a sanctuary in ancient times by the Guanche people. A popular tradition is that the local virgins or *harimaguadas* were kept in isolation here prior to marriage, and given special food to make them fat and comely.

The caves were also used for grain storage, and as a stronghold during the Spanish invasion.

View from Cruz de Tejeda, showing Roque Nublo (left) and Bentaiga (right). In the distance, Teide

Cruz de Tejeda (1500m) The highest pass in the Cumbre mountains, 35km south-west of Las Palmas on Route 811.

Looking out at the massive turbulence of crag and crevice, of forest and bare rock that marks the climax of the Cumbre, one might imagine oneself at the heart of a continent rather than an island. What the Spanish poet Unamuno described as a 'petrified tempest' is of a scale more befitting the massifs of France or Spain; a spectacle for which one is completely unprepared, even after the steep climb from the coast.

Here is the pinnacle view of Grand Canary. To the west is the fortress rock of *Bentaiga* (1404m), to the south the strange monolith of the Roque Nublo (1803m). Both of these rocks were sacred to the Guanches. To the

east is the *Pico* or *Pozo de las Nieves* (1949m). (The 'pozo' was a well in which snow was preserved for use in summer.) The latter peak, we are told, is the highest in the island. But what is that other mountain, breaking through the clouds on the western horizon? Unbelievably it is the great peak of Teide on Tenerife, sixty miles away.

The meeting place of travellers to the summit of Grand Canary is the *Parador Nacional*, run by the Spanish National Tourist Office. This inn was designed by the island's great native artist, Néstor de la Torre, in the traditional Canary style. A day or two here can be the most rewarding of a visit to Grand Canary, following excursions which take one even deeper into the heart of its most dramatic landscape.

Excursions from Cruz de Tejeda
Pozo de las Nieves (10 km) Highest point in Grand Canary
Pinar de Tamadaba via Artenara (27 km)
San Mateo and Teror returning via Valleseco
(Round trip 52 km)

Cuatro Puertas Ancient site, 20 km south of Las Palmas (Route 812).

The 'Four Doors' are all that remains of a Guanche sanctuary. They are the four openings of a sacred cave in a hill of the same name, reached by turning off the main road and following a rough track to a footpath which leads to the summit.

The function of the cave is uncertain, but it is thought that it was used either as an embalming place or as a retreat for vestal virgins.

Cumbre The central mountain range of Grand Canary, best seen from the Cruz de Tejeda.

Galdar Town 43.5 km west of Las Palmas (Route 810).

This was the capital of the ancient Guanche kingdom, centre of resistance to the Spanish invaders. The site of the royal palace of the Guanarteme or Guanche king was near the present *church*, and the font here is supposed to be the one used to baptise the Guanche people converted to the Christian faith.

Some relics of the Guanche period are in the *Town Hall* (south side of church square). In the courtyard of this building is one of the island's few ancient dragon trees—reckoned to be more than 2000 years old.

Going out of the town towards Agaete, a road to the right leads up to the *Cueva Pintada*. In this cave, discovered in 1881, are Guanche rock paintings in red, ochre and black. The designs are geometric and have not as yet been deciphered.

There is further evidence of Guanche habitation in the remains of *stone dwellings* and circular *grave enclosures* on the coast 2 km to the north of the town. (Follow road behind church down to sea, then track to east of restaurant.) Archaeologists suggest that one of the enclosures—with two central graves and a number of smaller ones radiating out from them—contained the tombs of a Guanarteme and his wife and other members of their family.

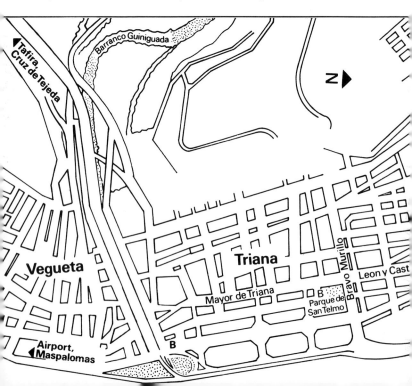

La Atalaya Village 5 km from junction (signpost *Telde*) on Route 811, 12 km south-west of Las Palmas.

This is a glimpse of pre-conquest—and pre-historic—Grand Canary. Behind white-washed façades are caves once inhabited by the Guanche people. The local craft, pottery, is practised exactly as in neolithic times, the large red storage jars modelled by hand and without the use of a wheel.

La Isleta Promontory at north-east corner of Grand Canary (see **Las Palmas**).

Las Palmas de Gran Canaria (pop. 285,000) Capital of Grand Canary and of the province of Las Palmas. Largest port in Spain.

Las Palmas was founded in 1478 as the settlement of the first Spanish invaders, and was their base during their conquest of the island, which took five years. (The name 'Las Palmas' comes from the Spanish for 'palms' —used in the construction of their defensive stockades.) The Spanish made good use of the natural harbour, protected by the knob-like peninsula known as the Isleta, and from the time that Columbus sailed from here on his voyage to America (1491) it has been the major port of call for ships bound for the New World.

The city Las Palmas stretches about 9 km along the east coast, and it is difficult for the visitor observing the mushroom development of recent years to imagine the original settlement at the mouth of the River Guiniguada, now a dry *barranco*, in the southern part of the modern city. This is the quarter known as Vegueta, dominated by the cathedral, where one may find buildings going back to the time of the *conquistadores*. The narrow balconied streets of Vegueta are in striking contrast to the hotel blocks lining Canteras beach 4 km to the north, which seem to belong to another world. This is the world of international tourism, in which Las Palmas is the supreme metropolis, crammed with its hotels and apartments, girdled by its fine sandy beaches, and filled with its tenant population of holidaymakers from all over the world.

Places of Interest (north to south)

Isleta This promontory to the north-east of Las Palmas is really a small island joined to the main island by a sandbank (Isthmus of

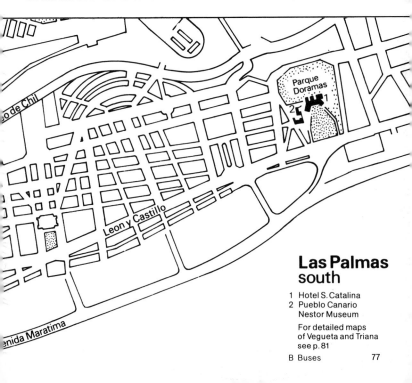

Las Palmas south

1 Hotel S. Catalina
2 Pueblo Canario
  Nestor Museum

For detailed maps
of Vegueta and Triana
see p. 81

B Buses

Paseo de Chil

▲ Arucas,
Cruz de Tejeda

▲ Arucas,
Cruz de Tejeda

Avenida Maratima

Leon y Castillo

Playa de las Alcaravaneras

Av. de Mesa y

Guanarteme). This strip of land has now been consolidated into an extension of the port area, and a continuation of the hotel development of the Canteras beach. Apart from the built-up area on the north side of the port, the Isleta is desolate. It is, in fact, a military zone and closed to the public.

Puerto de la Luz The port of Las Palmas, and the largest port in Spain. Its quays, stretching for more than two miles, serve over 10,000 vessels a year, carrying 250,000 passengers to various parts of Europe, Africa and the New World. In addition it offers vital oil bunkering facilities and is a major fishing port. Evidence of the first is in the huge silver oil tanks on the north-east side of the port, and the even huger tankers, standing out to sea, that must be the largest ships in the world. Evidence of the second is in the innumerable fishing vessels clustered against the quays, and the fishing nets spread like great unravelled skeins on the Muelle de Santa Catalina.

Visitors to Las Palmas should be aware that this is a major Spanish port, where street life is geared to a mobile population 'on the make'. The rules are simple: never leave baggage in a car; never carry valuables, passports etc. while sightseeing; always observe the security advice of the hotel or apartment.

Las Palmas
north

1 Castillo de la Luz
2 Casa Turismo
  (Tourist Information Office)
3 Aucona (boat services)
B Buses

Las Canteras This 3km stretch of sandy beach on the west side of the isthmus has given its name to Grand Canary's most popular resort. For most of its length the beach is backed by an esplanade and hotels and is protected by a long reef (*La Barra*) which makes swimming safe and pleasant.

Las Alcaravaneras This beach ($\frac{1}{2}$ km) is immediately to the south of the port.

Parque Doramas Following the Calle de Leon y Castillo southwards, a square is reached with gardens to the west. This is the Parque Doramas, a large public park with gardens, swimming pool and tennis courts. Here stands the luxury *Hotel Santa Catalina* whose architecture is a splendid replica of the 16th c. Canarian style.

A walk on this quay in the early hours of the morning, to see the fishermen at work and the great ships waking up, is one of the pleasures of a visit to Las Palmas.

Castillo de la Luz This fortress stands on the north side of the port by the Muelle Pesquero (Fishing Mole). Originally constructed in 1492, it was rebuilt in 1599. Its guns repelled the raids of English and Dutch fleets at the end of the 16th c.

Parque de Santa Catalina Visitors to Las Palmas staying in the resort area will come here for buses to Vegueta and the southern part of the city. Here too is the Provincial Tourist Office (*Casa del Turismo*), housed in an attractive building designed by Néstor de la Torre. (Hours: 09.00–13.30, 15.00–18.00; Sat 09.00–13.30. Closed Sun & hol.)

Pueblo Canario A further evocation of the past—on a grand scale—may be found in this model Canary village, also in the Parque Doramas. It was created in memory of Néstor de la Torre (1887-1938), who did much to promote a concern for the traditional architecture and culture of the islands. The 'village', based on the artist's designs, includes a chapel, an inn, and other 'period' buildings, grouped around a central plaza. A fine exhibition of Canary Islands crafts may be seen here, and the numerous snops offer the best opportunity for gift shopping in the island. Those who enjoy the music and dancing of the Canary Islands should come here on Thursdays (17.30-19.00) and Sundays or holidays (12.00-13.30) when local groups perform.

Néstor Museum (Hours: Mon-Fri 10.00–13.00, 16.00–19.00; Sat 10.00–12.00; Sun 10.30–13.30; Closed Mon). In the Pueblo Canario, a fine collection of the work of the man who inspired it.

Walking tour of Triana (see map)
This tour is of secondary interest to the tour of Vegueta, for those who have time for additional sightseeing.

Parque de San Telmo This square, located at the point where the Calle Leon y Castillo joins the Calle de Triana, provides a pleasant respite from the bustle of the city. In one corner is the tiny church of *San Telmo*, dedicated to sailors and fishermen. The church contains fine carving, notably in the ceiling. A statue of San Telmo on the altar on the right of the nave holds a model of a ship.

From the square, follow the *Calle de Triana* southwards. This is one of the main shopping streets of Las Palmas. The Calle Torres, on the right, leads up to the Calle Cano. At No. 33 (turn left) is the **Pérez Galdós Museum**. This is the birthplace of the writer Pérez Galdós (1843–1920). Galdós is celebrated for his books on the Spanish War of Independence, and his work has been compared with that of his friend and contemporary, Tolstoy. The museum contains the writer's personal belongings, furniture, photographs and drawings and a collection of letters to other literary figures. There is also a fine library of Spanish literature. (Hours: 09.00–13.00. Closed Sun & hol. Library Mon-Fri 16.00–20.00).

From Calle Cano the Calle de Malteses leads up to the Calle General Bravo. To the south is the *Plaza de Colón* (otherwise known as Columbus Gardens), in which stands the church of *San Francisco*. This church was built in 1689 on the site of a Franciscan monastery, established here in 1506. The altar is by Luján Pérez, and there are some fine silver ornaments in the treasury.

Opposite the Plaza de Colón is another small square, the *Plaza Cairasco*. The statue here is of Bartolome Cairasco de Figueroa, a poet born in Grand Canary in 1538. To the north of the square is the graceful building housing the *Gabinete Literario*. This is the home of the literary club of Las Palmas, and visitors can see the main rooms by asking at the secretary's office.

From the Plaza Cairasco the Calle Muro leads south over the wide Barranco Guiniguada to the old city, Vegueta. It was near here that the Spanish conquerors built their first stockade of palms, which gave the city its name. Once a huge rocky river bed, the *barranco* is now almost hidden by the new *autopista* which is being built to carry traffic from the city to the centre of the island.

Walking tour of Vegueta (see map)

Cathedral—Plaza de Santa Ana—Plaza Espiritu Santo—Church of Santo Domingo —Museo Canario—Casa de Colón—Church of San Antonio Abad—Mercado—Teatro Pérez Galdós

Cathedral (Santa Ana) The present building stands on the site of the old church of Santa Ana, founded by the *conquistadores*. This old church was partially demolished in 1780 by Bishop Joaquin de Herrera and work on the new building commenced. The first Mass in the new cathedral was said in 1805, but it was not until 1891 that the façade was completed. Today the north side of the cathedral is still unfinished.

In the long period of its construction the building's architecture passed from the Gothic to the neo-classical. The former is the predominant style of the interior, the latter the style of the façade. This imposing front was designed by Luján Pérez, the island's greatest native sculptor. It has two towers and a rose window (an odd note, echoing the cathedral's Gothic interior).

Interior The vaults of the nave and side aisles —which are equal in height—and the slender columns give the interior of the cathedral a feeling of spaciousness and light. Elegance is added by the palmate groining in the vault —the only example of this in the Canaries. There is much fine gilt work to be seen, particularly in the side chapels and in the magnificent Gothic reredos behind the high altar. There are also three fine sculptures by Pérez. In the chapel of the right transept is the *Dolorosa*. To the right of the chancel is *Christ*, to the left *Our Lady of the Assumption*. In the side chapels fine paintings of the *Stations of the Cross* are by R. de Lasada.

Treasury (small entrance fee) This contains some of the finest church treasures in the islands. In three large rooms are cases containing magnificent silver and gold items and a collection of vestments, richly jewelled and worked in gold thread. A gold *chalice* ornamented with emeralds was presented to the church by King Philip IV of Spain, and there is a *pyx* of gold and enamel made by Benvenuto Cellini (viewed by special permission only). Some of the plate is believed to have come from St Paul's Cathedral in London, sold by Cromwell during the Commonwealth to the Spanish Government.

Among the paintings is a portrait of *Bishop Verdugo* attributed to Goya, and a *St Ana* by Roelas, a pupil of the Spanish painter Zurburan. Another prized exhibit is a *Banner of the Conquest*, embroidered by Queen Isabella of Castile in the late 15th c.

A good day to visit the cathedral is Sunday, as one is sure of it being open and well illuminated. On weekdays the hours of opening vary, but it is usually open between 10 am and midday and again in the late afternoon. In the Columbus Chapel behind the cathedral Mass is said on Sundays at 11 am in English for the benefit of English-speaking Catholics. Leaving the cathedral, cross the road into the wide *Plaza de Santa Ana*. The bronze dogs sitting placidly at the foot of the square are supposed to be the fierce *canes* who gave the islands their name. In the 15th c. these dogs were used by the natives to defend themselves against the Spanish. That such savage beasts were the inspiration for the docile creatures that represent them here is hard to believe, but they make an attractive ornament to the square, and it is seldom that they are not in use for riding and sitting on by some young *canario*.

At the end of the square opposite the cathedral is the imposing *Town Hall* (*Ayuntamiento*), and on the north side the *Bishop's Palace*. Leaving the plaza by the street to the left of the Town Hall, one comes immediately into the *Plaza Espiritu Santo*. Here a little triangular garden with a fountain faces a small chapel, used only during the Feast of Corpus Christi. At this time the streets and plazas are laid with floral carpets for the processions which mark the festival.

Turning east, one enters the Calle de Dr Chil. (Dr Chil, an eminent physician, wrote important historical and geological studies of the islands.) Immediately to the right is the Calle L. Millares, which leads to the Plaza de Santo Domingo.

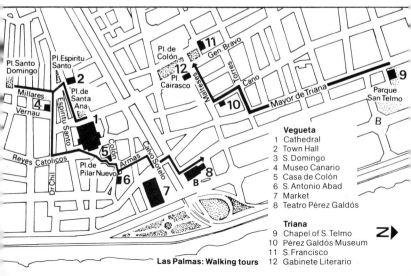

Las Palmas: Walking tours

Vegueta
1 Cathedral
2 Town Hall
3 S. Domingo
4 Museo Canario
5 Casa de Colón
6 S. Antonio Abad
7 Market
8 Teatro Pérez Galdós

Triana
9 Chapel of S. Telmo
10 Pérez Galdós Museum
11 S. Francisco
12 Gabinete Literario

This quiet square is in the very heart of the old city. The church of *Santo Domingo*, on the south side, was built on the site of a Dominican monastery in the 16th c. Although very little of the original church remains (the present building dates from the 18th c.), it is the burial place of many of the *conquistadores*.

Returning to the Calle de Dr Chil, continue eastwards. At the corner of the next street is the **Museo Canario** (Canary Museum). This museum (Hours: 10.00–13.00, 16.00–20.00; Sat/Sun 10.00–13.00) contains relics of the Guanche people who were the first inhabitants of the Canaries. Also here is a collection of *pintaderas*, the terracotta seals whose designs were stamped on their clothing and bodies. Other exhibits relate to the geography and biology of the islands, and on the ground floor is an extensive library. The museum was founded by the Dr Chil after whom the street is named.

Further down the street, at No 17, note the fine Renaissance-style entrance of the *Seminary Church*. Turning left at the Calle de los Reyes Catolicos, continue north to the Plaza del Pilar Nuevo at the east end of the cathedral. Here, over the doorway of a house on the right, is a fine coat of arms—one of the few that still embellish the old seigniorial houses of Vegueta.

Casa de Colón (House of Columbus) This fine building, with its elaborately sculptured entrance, stands in a small square just off the Plaza del Pilar Nuevo. The residence of Columbus at the outset of three of his voyages to the New World, it later became the official seat of the military governors of the island.

The building now houses the *Provincial Historical Archive*, and the *Museum of Fine Arts*. To the rear is the entrance to the *Columbus Museum*.

This museum (on the Calle Colón, reached by the passage to the right of the building) contains maps and documents relating to the explorer's voyages and a collection of furniture, armour and paintings. (Hours: 09.00–14.00; Sat 09.00–13.00; Sun 10.00–13.00. Library Mon-Fri 16.00–20.00).

One of the most touching items in the collection is the little figure of Santa Ana to which Columbus addressed his prayers before going on his voyages. There are also fine models of his ships, many of the flags and banners taken on the voyages, and the muskets, pistols and swords carried by his crew.

Much of the house is a restoration of the 17th c. It is nice to imagine, though, that the delightful patio, with its 15th c. well and tropical plants—and the occasional screech of a parrot (albeit a landlubber)—is as the great man would remember it.

At the bottom of the adjacent Calle de Colón is the little church of *San Antonio Abad*. Believed to have been built on the ruins of the first church on the island (where Columbus prayed before setting out to discover America) this church belongs to the late 18th c.

From the church, walk down the steep Calle Armas to the Calle Calvo Sotelo. This leads to the city's principal market, the *Mercado de Las Palmas*. Like all markets this is at its busiest early in the morning, but is open all day during the week until about 4 pm. It is a big general market, housed on two floors of a well-ventilated building in the Plaza del Mercado. A feature of the Las Palmas market are the bird sellers, who offer all kinds of exotic birds from Africa and South America. Parrots and macaws, minah birds and canaries are on display in many of the little shops and stalls.

After visiting the market cross the *barranco* towards the centre of the city and then turn right. On the left is the *Teatro Pérez Galdós*. This fine opera house and theatre was designed by Néstor de la Torre and opened in 1927. The huge foyer is decorated with paintings of Canary fruits, and the carved balustrade has the same motif.

Beside the theatre is the bus terminus, from which one can take a bus back to the port and resort area.

Casa de Colón, Las Palmas

Hotels and restaurants

In its choice of hotels and restaurants, Las Palmas is still the capital city of the Canaries. The hotels cover every category and are mostly in the Las Canteras area.

Restaurants are equally varied. They are, however, mainly international or national (French, Italian, Scandinavian, Chinese) and only a few offer a specifically Spanish cuisine. Those in search of Canary Island specialities will have more luck outside the capital. A complete list of restaurants in Las Palmas and elsewhere in the island is available from the tourist office.

Beaches and swimming pools

Las Palmas has two beaches, Las Canteras and Las Alcaravaneras (see under *Places of Interest*). There is a good public swimming pool in the Parque Doramas.

Sports and entertainment

Water sports For details, apply Tourist Office.
Golf The Golf Club of Las Palmas is at Bandama, 12km from Las Palmas.
Tennis The Club de Tenis (hard courts) is at the Parque Doramas.
Canary dancing At the Pueblo Canario, Parque Doramas, Thurs and Sun.

Shopping

Las Palmas is a free port where one can obtain many foreign goods duty free. Shops are open all day, and the main shopping centre is the Calle de Triana. Canary Island crafts are sold at the Pueblo Canario.

Bus services

City

Details of times and routes of city bus services may be obtained from the Tourist Information Office. Most lines commence either at the port ('Puerto') or in the old town ('Mercadillos' or 'Teatro'). For the old town (Vegueta) the most direct route is No 1, which tourists at Las Canteras can catch at the Parque de Santa Catalina. From here the route follows the sea front and the streets Leon y Castillo and Triana to the theatre (Teatro Pérez Galdós) from whence the barranco may be crossed into Vegueta.

Other points

Bus services to other towns and villages in the island start at the Parque de San Telmo.

Excursions

A number of companies offer excellent excursions by coach from Las Palmas to different parts of the island. Most popular are the tours to Agaete, Cruz de Tejeda and Maspalomas.

These companies also offer air excursions to Tenerife, Lanzarote and the Sahara (El Aaiun).

For details of agents offering tours see p. 20.

Los Berrazales 8 km south-east of Agaete, at the head of the Barranco de Agaete.

This is the site of the *Balneario de Berrazales*, once a popular spa. Here the therapeutic properties of the waters were used for the treatment of rheumatism and other ailments. Although the thermal establishment is no longer operating, the journey is justified by the view alone. The valley is one of the most fertile and beautiful areas in the island. The road up from the sea, flanked by hibiscus and poinsettias, runs through plantations where coffee, almonds and avocados vie for space with the more familiar bananas and tomatoes. At the end of the road, the views from the balcony of the hotel are superb, encompassing the great pine forest of Tamadaba and the cultivated slopes below, sweeping down to Agaete.

Maspalomas Village 52 km from Las Palmas, 28 km from Gando Airport, whose name has now been taken over by one of the major south coast resorts (Maspalomas Costa Canaria). This resort is focused on the Playa de Maspalomas, a large stretch of beach and sand dunes built up by the tides to the west of the promontory on which the village stands.

In the midst of the feverish 'urbanization' of this area it is worth noting that the name 'Maspalomas' means 'more pigeons'—a name which seems almost quaint now and should perhaps be changed to 'Masturistas'. The pigeons are among a large number of bird migrants attracted to the natural refuge offered by the oasis at the tip of the sandy peninsula. The existence of palm trees and a lagoon in the midst of sand dunes, within a stone's throw of the ocean, is an unusual feature whose natural qualities are unhappily now being reduced by tourist development. The lagoon is now a boating lake and luxury hotels, holiday chalets and golf-courses have appeared among the palm trees. The sand dunes—one of the great areas of natural beauty in the Canaries—stretch along 7 km of coastline. Rippled and curved by wind, scattered with shady clumps of tamarisk, this little Sahara is the sun-bather's nirvana. Development, happily, is being confined to the north.

To the east of Maspalomas are the popular resorts of Playa del Ingles and San Agustin. (See *Playa del Ingles* for details of local sports and entertainments.)

Mogan Village at head of *barranco* 8 km north of south-west coast (Puerto de Mogan). The road up the *barranco* to the village is one of the most beautiful in the island.

Monte Coello Popular residential area 10 km south-west of Las Palmas (Route 811). It is from the vineyards of this region that the *Vino del Monte* is produced. It is a fine red wine, which like the wines of Lanzarote owes much of its quality to the conditions in which the vines are grown. Here, as in Lanzarote, they take their moisture from the volcanic ash which absorbs dew during the night.

Barranco de Agaete near Los Berrazales

'Finger of God', Puerto de las Nieves

Moya Hill town between Arucas and Galdar, 30 km west of Las Palmas.

Dramatically situated on the edge of a steep *barranco*, the village is dominated by the twin towers of its *church*. Although the present building was consecrated as recently as 1957 the history of the church goes back to 1515 when the first congregation assembled in a small chapel to make their devotions to their patron saint (Nuestra Señora de la Candelaria). Since then a number of churches built on the exposed site fell prey to violent storms and it was not until 1944 that the foundation stone of the present church was laid.

Among the church treasures is a 16th c. *carving* of the patron saint and a statue of *San Judas Tadeo* by Luján Pérez.

The Moyans revere two very different 'sons'. One is Doramas, the last king of the Guanches, whose stronghold was in these mountains; the other the modern poet, Tomas Morales (1884–1921), whose tomb is in Las Palmas.

Playa del Inglés Resort on south-east coast 50 km from Las Palmas. For details of accommodation see p. 22.

The beach of Playa del Ingles has given its name to the island's fastest-growing resort. With its sister resorts of Maspalomas and San Agustin, Playa del Ingles is now rivalling Las Palmas as an international tourist centre. It is a town built for, and occupied by tourists, with shopping centres, hotels, apartments and restaurants.

Sand dunes at Maspalomas

Getting around the place is no problem, with a transport system that includes a mini-train, taxis, beach-buggies, bicycles and mopeds. There are also local buses to San Agustin, Maspalomas and Puerto Rico and a long-distance bus to Las Palmas.

Night clubs and discos abound and there is a casino in nearby San Agustin (Hotel Tamarindos).

Watersports are best at Pasito Blanco marina beyond Maspalomas, and further west at Arguineguin (12 km) and Puerto Rico (19 km). In addition to waterskiing and sailing, these places are suitable for the new sport of wind-surfing.

Golf and riding are available at Maspalomas. (The golf course is divided into two areas of 18 holes each and open throughout the year.) The following special attractions may be reached by a free bus from Playa del Ingles:
Cañon del Aguila 2 km east of San Agustin. Wild West movie set with special shows.
Los Palmitos Park 2.5 km west of Playa del Ingles. Exotic birds and landscaped park.
Greyhound racing At Playa del Ingles.
Go-kart racing 4 km west of Playa del Ingles.
Excursions to different parts of the island are available from Playa del Ingles, San Agustin and Maspalomas.

Pozo de las Nieves (1949m) Highest peak in Grand Canary, reached by road from Cruz de Tejeda (10km).

Puerto de Mogan Resort on south-west coast 82km from Las Palmas (see p.22).

Puerto de las Nieves Fishing port 54 km west of Las Palmas (Route 810) 1 km from Agaete. The name of this village, meaning 'Port of the Snows' has its origin in the distant views of snow-capped Teide on Tenerife. The village is well known for its dramatic coastline and its excellent fish restaurants (specialities squid, octopus, red mullet) which together merit a day's excursion. It is also the scene of the great feast of dedication to the patron saint whom it shares with Agaete, the Virgin of the Snows (Nuestra Señora de las Nieves). This is the *Bajada de la Rama* (see Agaete).

The village church is extremely simple and typical of Spanish mission churches of the early 17th c. Simple too are the tiny white-washed cottages clustered around it, and the little windmill by the harbour.

One of the best views of the island's north-west coast can be obtained from the harbour's fishing mole. On the south side of the bay is the extraordinary rock formation known as the *Finger of God* (Dedo de Dios) which points to the sky from the base of the cliff.

Puerto Rico Resort on south-west coast 69km from Las Palmas. Apartments and villas, and marina with sports facilities.

Roque Nublo (1803m) Pillar-shaped peak in the Cumbre, best viewed from the Cruz de Tejeda. This peak (its name means 'Cloudy Rock') was sacred to the Guanches.

San Agustin Resort on south-east coast 48km from Las Palmas.
San Agustin lies immediately to the east of the larger resort of Playa del Ingles. Its sandy beach stretches for 1 km.
For accommodation see p. 22. See also **Playa del Ingles**.

Grand Canary, northern coastline
Inset: Casa de Cho Zacharias

San Mateo Mountain village on Route 811 to Cruz de Tejeda, 21 km south-west of Las Palmas.

In the village is the *Casa de Cho Zacharias*, an old farmhouse which has been converted into a tourist curiosity. Wine and cheese are offered. (Entrance fee, hours 10.00–13.00.)

San Nicolas Village 90 km . from Las Palmas (Route 810) on west coast, 36 km south of Agaete.

Situated at the foot of the deep Barranco de la Aldea, San Nicolas is also known simply as La Aldea ('The Village') as it was once the only village for miles. Its isolation makes it attractive to explorers with a car who are prepared to undertake the cliff-hanging drive from Agaete in the north or Mogan in the south. There are pensions in the village for those who wish to stay overnight.

Santa Lucia Village on south flank of Pozo de las Nieves, 19 km from Aguimes.

Beautifully situated amidst palm trees, the village has an interesting Guanche museum.

Sardina Fishing port at north-west corner of Grand Canary 49 km west of Las Palmas, reached by junction west of Galdar.

This attractive village, at the end of the old road to the west coast, has a good beach and some tourist facilities.

Tafira Residential district south-west of Las Palmas on Route 811 consisting of Tafira Baja (6 km) and Tafira Alta (8 km).

Lush and fertile, this is one of the primary agricultural regions in the island. It is also popular as a retirement place for foreigners, as is shown by the many splendid villas and gardens. Between the two villages is a fine botanical garden, the **Jardin Canario**, where most of the indigenous plant species of the Canaries are cultivated. The planting has been done with great ingenuity on the steep slope of a *barranco*. (Hours: 08.00–17.30; Sat 08.00–12.00, 15.00–19.00. Closed Sun & hol.)

Tamadaba Forest area (also known as the Pinar de Tamadaba) in the western Cumbre. The route to this area, via Artenara, is precipitous but quite safe for the careful driver. The magnificent views and peaceful beauty of the pine tree forest are best enjoyed at the end of the road at Las Presas (60 km from Las Palmas).

Tejeda see **Cruz de Tejeda**

Telde (pop. 40,000) Second largest town in Grand Canary 14 km south of Las Palmas (Route 812).

This was the capital of the ancient Guanche province of Telde, from which King Doramas launched his attack on the Spanish in Las Palmas. In the 15th c., after the Spanish conquest, it became one of their most important settlements.

Modern Telde with its factories, shops and apartment blocks is a long way removed from the early settlements. One does not, however, have to search too far for its past. On the main road, half-way through the town, is a shady plaza surrounded by balconied houses.

Here is the town's principal church of **San Juan Bautista**, which belongs to the original settlement (the towers are a modern addition). It is built from the multi-coloured lava of the region which makes a pleasing, informal exterior. Inside is a magnificent 15th c. Flemish *reredos* presented to the church by a wealthy *conquistador*. Its six panels of gilded wood depict the *Nativity* and feature such curious details as shepherds with bagpipes and St Simeon wearing spectacles.

The *Christ* over the high altar is a strange and much revered piece, imported from Spain's new-found Mexican colony in the 16th c. The figure, the work of Mexican Indians, is made from a paste of crushed maize stalks and though life size weighs only 15 lbs.

Near the church is the 17th c. *Leon y Castillo House and Museum*. This is one of the old seigniorial houses of Telde, built for the family of one of the *conquistadores*. It contains an interesting collection of furniture and household objects from the colonial period.

San Francisco This attractive old quarter of Telde lies less than 1 km from the centre of the town, towards the sea. In a quiet square at the end of a cobbled street is the monastery church of the same name, a charming example of early colonial architecture.

Teror Town 21 km south-west of Las Palmas (Route 817).

This lovely old town, deep in the hill country on the way up to the Cumbre, is one of the most interesting places in Grand Canary and makes an ideal centre for visiting the mountain region and north coast of the island.

Its special significance for the people of Grand Canary is that it is the home of the island's patron saint, the Virgin of the Pine (Nuestra Señora del Pino). Every year, in December, the devotion of the islanders to their saint is shown by the great procession of her image to the cathedral in Las Palmas, attended by as much as a third of the island's population.

The venerated statue of the Virgin may be seen in the church of **Nuestra Señora del Pino**, in the main square. The figure of the Virgin is said to have appeared miraculously in the branches of a pine tree which grew near the site of the church. The spot where

Above: Teror   Right: Ox plough, Grand Canary

the tree stood is marked by a monument, and a descendant of the original pine now grows there. In the same way, the present church was built (1765) on the site of an earlier building, founded to commemorate the miracle.

The statue of the Virgin in the church is approached by a staircase behind the altar. She is dressed in splendid robes, covered with jewels, and stands in a massive silver *shrine* (late 18th c.), the work of the silversmith Antonio Juan Correa of La Laguna, Tenerife. In the rooms beside the shrine are dozens of gifts to the Virgin, ranging from priceless jewels to a football from a sports club. Particularly touching are the toys from children, and crutches and wax models of limbs given in thanks for recovery from sickness and accidents. There are also many beautiful vestments, candlesticks and other altar furnishings.

On September 8 the whole town is *en fête* for the festival of its saint. Pilgrims arrive in the town from all parts of the island, bearing offerings of their best produce. The festival opens with a re-enactment of the Virgin's miraculous appearance, and in the three days of celebrations there are painting exhibitions, dancing and theatrical displays, and music.

Apart from the church, the other important buildings in Teror are the *Bishop's Palace*, formerly a convent, which is immediately behind the church, and two other *convents*, Cistercian and Dominican. The *Town Hall*, to the south of the square beside the Bishop's Palace, is a good example of late 18th c. architecture.

There are several very old balconied houses, built round shady patios with wrought iron grilles on the windows. On the south side of the street opposite the church is an interesting museum in one of the oldest of the early Spanish houses, the *Casa de los Patronos de la Virgen* (17th c.). Here can be seen typical furnishings of the well-to-do household, a coach house with vehicles and harness, the servants' quarters across a tiny paved courtyard, and some old farm implements. (Hours: 10.00–13.30, 16.00–18.00.)

In addition to its religious and historic significance, Teror is an important agricultural centre and produces a popular mineral water.

From *Mt Osorio* (968 m) to the north of Teror, one can obtain fine views of the valley of the Barranco de Tenoya, which the town commands.

Valleseco

Mountain village 13 km north of Cruz de Tejeda on road to Teror.

From the *Mirador de Zamora* (restaurant) beyond the village to the north is a splendid view of Teror in the valley below and beyond it Las Palmas.

Lanzarote

The most easterly of the Canary
Islands is also the most extraordinary.
The traveller who has already visited
Tenerife or Grand Canary will find it
difficult to believe that this stark,
uncompromising island is in the same
group. Not for the Fire Island those
verdant ravines, pine forests and
plantations: only a volcanic emptiness
which creates the feeling not merely of
another place but of another planet.
There is no water source on
Lanzarote, and little rainfall. From
north to south it is a landscape of
sand and black lava, raked by the
wind and punctured by the empty
sockets of extinct craters. There are
few trees and little natural vegetation,
no wildlife apart from rabbits, lizards
and birds. One might question how in
these circumstances it comes to be
inhabited and why it was not
abandoned long ago: in the answer to
this lies the true fascination of
Lanzarote.

Pop: 60,000
Capital: Arrecife
Area: 795 sq km
Highest point: Peñas del Chache
(671m)
Nearest island: Fuerteventura
Sailings: Direct to Las Palmas (13hrs),
Fuerteventura (6hrs from Arrecife to
Puerto del Rosario, 40min from
southern Playa Blanca to Corralejo)
Flights: Direct to Tenerife, Las
Palmas, Fuerteventura

The nearest of the islands to Europe, Lanzarote was the first to be settled in the period of conquest. This was in the 1330's, a clear century before the *conquistadores* had secured more than a token grip on the islands. The flag planted here was not Spanish but Genoese, and the man who bore it, Lancelotto Malocello, gave the Latin version of his name 'Lanzarotus' to the island.

Later on (1403) the island was secured by the Norman adventurers Jean de Bethencourt and Gadifer de la Salle, who had also pacified Fuerteventura. This was achieved by either killing or forcibly baptising the native population—the same method later used by the Spanish in the other islands. It was the Spanish, in fact, who had financed the Normans' expedition, and they later took control of the island.

The Spanish were not to have it all their own way. In the late 16th c. the island—a bare 65 miles from the coast of Africa—was invaded by forces of Moroccans and Algerians, more as a reprisal for Spanish attacks on Barbary than to pillage the poverty-stricken island. The British were here, too, at about the same time, but found little to plunder.

In 1730 the island was devastated by a series of volcanic eruptions which continued for six years. Before these eruptions Lanzarote was reasonably fertile, and the wasteland of black lava that we see today is largely a legacy of that disaster and a smaller lava flow in 1824. Since then there have been no further eruptions in Lanzarote, but the evidence of the island's volcanic activity—both past and present—is everywhere.

Most dramatic are the Montañas del Fuego (Fire Mountains) in the south-west of the island. The underground temperature here, only 60 cm below the surface, reaches 400 C—hot enough to set fire to dry brushwood or to hard-boil an egg. The surroundings are appropriately infernal: a vast rolling sea of red and black lava.

The strange blackness of Lanzarote's landscape can be explained in part by the special farming methods peculiar to the island. These methods have enabled her people to redeem Lanzarote from the fate decreed for her by nature, of becoming an uninhabited desert island. The fields of black ash that patch the interior have been spread by diligent farmers over the soil in which the crops are sown, a necessary defence against the hostile conditions of weather and climate. In the low-lying, windswept island, the layer of ash prevents the topsoil from blowing away. In an atmosphere of high humidity, it also has the capacity of retaining moisture, essential for the nourishment of the plants.

The hand of man has worked bizarre rhythms on this landscape. Most extraordinary is the scalloped effect produced by the innumerable semi-circular walls, built of lava, which protect the vines from the high winds. To give added protection, these vines are planted in deep holes, so that only the upper branches are visible on the surface. Rooted in volcanic soil, the vines obtain their moisture from the ash laid at their base, which acts as a reservoir for the nightly dew. The wine which is the end product of this unusual method of cultivation (*Malvasia*) is considered the finest in the Canaries.

Fig trees and citrus are grown in the same way, shielded from the winds. Other produce includes potatoes, maize, onions, tomatoes, melons and tobacco. In the north-east of the island (Guatiza) the cochineal insect is bred on the prickly pear. This insect, when crushed, produces a red dye, still in demand for the colouring of Persian carpets.

The sea, too, produces its harvest. The fishing industry serves both the home and overseas market, with a canning factory at Arrecife. Near Arrecife, and in the north and west of the island (La Punta and Janubio) are extensive salt works. Here wind pumps raise the sea water into shallow pans, which after evaporation leaves deposits of salt, raked by the salt workers into large white pyramids. (This salt is in great demand by the fishing fleet, which uses it to preserve the catch during the long voyages from Africa.)

A further exploitation of salt water, becoming increasingly essential for an island with a growing tourist industry, is desalination. Until recently water had to be imported into the island from Grand Canary and Tenerife, but now many of the hotels have their own desalination plants, which convert the salt water into drinking water.

The future of tourism is being watched keenly in Lanzarote, the third island (after Grand Canary and Tenerife) to be developed to any serious extent for this new industry. With such a bizarre landscape its appeal to tourists had at first appeared dubious, but this very difference has materialized as the island's biggest asset. The Fire Mountains are an obvious draw, as are the volcanic phenomena such as the Cueva de los Verdes in the north.

The other, more subtle attraction is the absence of the high-rise hotels which mar the landscape of the two major islands. The houses of Lanzarote are 'low-profile', and the hotels, villas and other new buildings largely conform to the same principle. The man who has given direction to this enlightened approach (in which buildings integrate with the landscape rather than dominate it) is a native architect and interior designer, Cesar Manrique. In addition to various villa developments he was responsible for the imaginative night club at Jameos del Agua and the restaurants at Islote de Hilario and Bateria.

The creation of a viable economy in a desert island is a tribute to the tenacity and ingenuity of her people, the *conejos* ('rabbit people'). A journey into the interior is enlivened by the sight of the peasant women working in the fields, wearing their distinctive 'balaclava' headgear and wide-brimmed bonnets (an interesting detail here is that it is only the unmarried women who wear bonnets: the married ones wear hats). The *conejos* are among the friendliest people in the Canaries and it is worth going out to meet them. Lanzarote, after all, is the last place on earth where the visitor should stand still.

The joy of this island lies in its discovery.

To the north of Lanzarote are her satellite islands of Graciosa and Alegranza. To the south, across the Strait of Bocayna, lies her sister island Fuerteventura.

Travelling in Lanzarote The flatness of the island and the good quality of her roads make driving a pleasure. There are a number of car-hire firms in Arrecife and arrangements for rental can be made through the hotel. Taxis can be shared to reduce the cost, and coach excursions are available. There are also three bus lines (see **Arrecife**).

Hotels and apartments The rapid tourist development of recent years has now brought 'urbanizacion' to Lanzarote. These complexes of hotels, villas and self-catering apartments are centred on beach areas. (See Accommodation, p. 22.)

Restaurants in tourist complexes usually offer Spanish specialities. Good country inns with local cuisine are at Yaiza, Mozaga, Arrieta and other villages (for Arrecife, see p. 94).

Beaches Fine sandy beaches lie to the west of Arrecife at various points along the coast as far as *Playa Blanca* (40 km). *El Golfo* is a good place for swimming and the *Playa Famara* is the best beach in the north. A superb beach on the north side of the island of Graciosa is the *Playa de las Conchas*.

Sports The best sport on Lanzarote is undoubtedly fishing. The sea here is well stocked with game fish such as tuna and barracuda, but the calmer, eastern coast is recommended for those unfamiliar with the island. For details of facilities, inquire at the Tourist Office. For those who prefer a quiet game of golf there is a new course 3.5 km from Arrecife on the Teguise road.

Itineraries
North
Arrecife—Teguise—Los Valles—Haria—Bateria—Jameos del Agua and Cueva de los Verdes—Guatiza—Arrecife
Centre and south
Arrecife—Tinajo—Montañas del Fuego—Yaiza—Janubio—El Golfo—Playa Blanca—return via airport

Alegranza, Isla de Islet to north of Lanzarote. Features volcanic crater rising to height of 289 m.

Arrecife (pop. 20,500) Capital and seaport on south coast.

The name of this town comes from the Spanish word for 'reef'. This reef, which takes the form of a series of islands linked by causeways, is the most remarkable feature of a town which otherwise has little to distinguish it. The reef offers protection to the largest fishing fleet in the Canaries, whose catch is largely culled from the coast of Africa to the east.

Most of the fishing vessels are moored in the inlet known as the *Charco de San Gines*, a popular fishing place for the menfolk of Arrecife. At low tide the vessels are left lying high and dry on the mud—a strangely desolate sight. The new port of Arrecife, completed in 1960, is 4 km to the east of the town.

Like Puerto del Rosario in Fuerteventura, Arrecife only became the island's capital in the 18th c., when the threat of pirate raids no longer endangered the coastal settlements. Before that the capital had been Teguise, 12 km inland.

Little of the 18th c. town survives, apart from its fortifications. The most prominent landmark is the 16th c. *Castillo de San Gabriel*, a square squat castle situated on a part of the reef known as the *Islote de los Ingleses* and reached by an old bridge, the *Puente de las Bolas*. This castle is now used as a museum of archaeology and anthropology (Hours 10.00–13.00).

The second fortification (built 1779) is the *Castillo de San José*, about 2 km to the east. This houses a museum of contemporary art (Hours 11.00–21.00) and a bar-restaurant. The most important church in Arrecife takes the name of the island's patron saint, *San Gines*. The festival of the saint takes place from August 24–29 and features Canary Island music and dances.

The *Tourist Information Office* is situated on the promenade (see map). 08.00–15.00, 17.30–19.30; Sat 09.00–13.00. Closed Sun & hol.

Hotels and restaurants

Arrecife has one 4-star, two 3-star hotels and a number of pensions (see p.22). The hotels have restaurants with international cuisine: elsewhere the restaurants have a purely local appeal. The *Abdon*, is a side street opposite the *Arrecife Gran* hotel, has an excellent fish and seafood menu.

Bus services

There are three bus lines operating from Arrecife. These are village buses, bringing workers into the capital, and their frequency varies greatly. There are for example several buses daily to San Bartolomé, but only one a day to the remote Playa Blanca. The three lines are *Linea Norte* (Teguise and Maguez), *Linea Centro* (San Bartolomé, Montaña Blanca, Tinajo, Soó) *Linea Sur* (Yaiza, Puerto Carmen, Playa Blanca). The departure point for buses in Arrecife is the Calle Garcia Escames (see map).

Bateria A disused battery and now a viewpoint (*Mirador del Rio*, 479 m) at the northern tip of the island.

The journey from Arrecife (38 km) is well rewarded by the sublime view, from the cliffs of Guinate, of the Strait of El Rio and the peaceful islands of La Graciosa, Montaña Clara and Alegranza.

Built into the headland is a cleverly concealed cafeteria, the *Mirador del Rio*.

Costa Teguise Developing resort area 7 km north of Arrecife (see p.22).

Cueva de los Verdes Volcanic cavern located 2 km east of road junction on Arrecife–Bateria road, 29 km north of Arrecife. This spectacular underground gallery, formed by gases escaping from a lava flow, is one of the sights of Lanzarote. The lava is multi-coloured and assumes eerie and fascinating shapes.

The cave is 6 km in length and stretches from the sea to the volcano Corona, the site of the eruption which created it. The entrance is 700 m from the sea, and the cave is illuminated for 1 km. The guided tour, conducted every hour from 11.00–18.00, takes approx. 50 min.

Church of San Gines, Arrecife
Above right: Castillo de San Gabriel

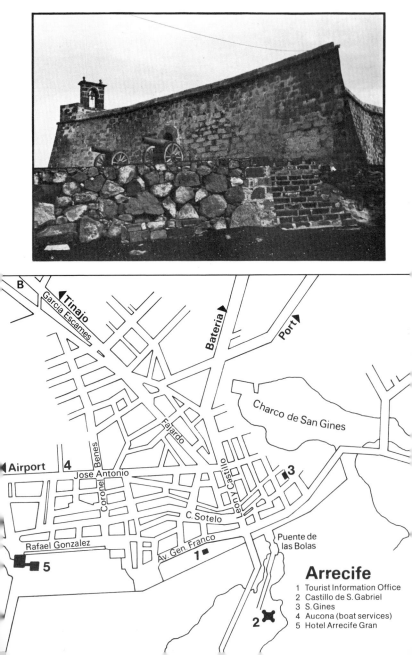

Arrecife

1 Tourist Information Office
2 Castillo de S. Gabriel
3 S. Gines
4 Aucona (boat services)
5 Hotel Arrecife Gran

El Golfo Beauty spot 38 km west of Arrecife.
This placid lagoon—unrivalled as a picnic place—is the flooded crater of an extinct volcanic cone, one wall of which has fallen away into the sea. A sandbank keeps the ocean at bay, and the luminous green water, though very salty, makes pleasant bathing.

Graciosa, Isla de Islet (area 27 sq km) off northern tip of Lanzarote, separated from it by Strait of El Rio. Reached by boat from Orzola.
Crossing the narrow stretch of water to this tranquil little island, the visitor will feel its separate identity. The small population of fishermen, who live in the settlements of *Caleta del Sebo* and *Pedro Barba*, are proudly self-sufficient. The families work together as teams, the women helping to unload their husbands' fishing boats and the children helping to clean and dry the fish.
The island has a fine beach on the north (*Playa de las Conchas*) and a dramatic landscape of sand-dunes and volcanoes (highest point *Pedro Barba*, 266 m).
To cross to Graciosa one should arrive as early as possible at the pier at the little fishing village of *Orzola* in the north of Lanzarote, where boats are usually available for the trip.

Guanapay, Castillo de see **Teguise**

Haria Village in north of island 7 km from junction with Arrecife–Bateria road, 25.5 km north of Arrecife.
In the midst of the bleak mountain country which typifies the north of the island, this village of white houses shaded by palm trees has the appearance of an oasis. The valley in which it stands is, in fact, one of the most fertile in the island.
A new church here contains a figure of the *Virgin of the Assumption* by the Canaries' leading sculptor, Luján Pérez. A popular local craft is the manufacture of mosaics, used for flooring.
Above Haria on the main road are a *tourist shop* (2 km) and a *restaurant* (2.5 km) which offer good views of the village and eastern coastline.

Islote de Hilario The phenomena of the Montanas̃ del Fuego are best observed at this spot, reached by a side road off the main road through the National Park. The special charge includes the coach tour of the volcanic area (see below).
On one of the lower summits is a circular *restaurant*. With great ingenuity, the management have utilized the subterranean temperature (400°C). A grill has been laid over a deep pit, and the heat that rises is sufficient to fry eggs, barbecue meat, etc.

Timanfaya, Montañas del Fuego

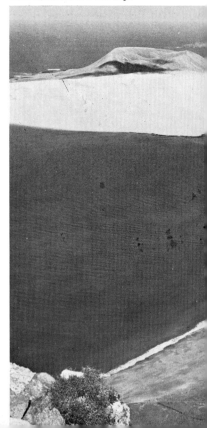

Graciosa from Bateria

Islote de Hilario

Outside the restaurant, further demonstrations of the intense heat beneath the ground are given. These include pouring water down a pipe sunk into the earth, which spurts out as a geyser of steam, and kindling brushwood in a hole in the ground. Even volcanoes, it seems, can be fun.

The Islote de Hilario is the starting point for the *Ruta de los Volcanes*, a special bus tour of the area devastated by the great eruptions of 1730–36. This tour leaves every hour, on the hour (10.00–18.00) and covers a route of 10 km.

Among the sights on the tour are a rare view of the *Malpais*—the immense, totally barren sea of black lava to the north—and the *Barranco del Fuego*, a 'river-bed' created by a flow of lava (the stalactite shapes formed here by the dripping lava are similar to those in the Cueva de los Verdes).

The climactic view is of the crater of *Timanfaya*, at the main centre of the eruption.

Jameos del Agua Grotto on north-east coast, 4km from junction with Arrecife–Bateria road 29km north of Arrecife.

This beautiful cavern was formed during a period of volcanic upheaval, when the pressure of steam arising from the combination of sea water and lava blew an opening in the rock. The sea water which filled the cavern remains as a dark, silent pool, habitat of a strange species of white, sightless crab.

The cavern has been cleverly transformed into a night-club by Cesar Manrique.

Janubio Saltponds (Las Salinas de Janubio) on west coast 33.5km west of Arrecife. These are the most extensive saltponds in Lanzarote.

La Geria Centre of Lanzarote's wine industry, in the volcanic region in the west of the island.

The resourcefulness of the local people in producing fruitful vines in an area of such desolation will greatly impress the visitor. At local *bodegas* he will have the opportunity to sample the speciality of the region, the sweet or dry *malvasia*.

Los Hervideros Natural phenomenon on west coast near El Golfo. The meaning of the name—'boiling spring'—aptly describes the effect of the sea churning furiously around the hollowed-out lava rocks which are a feature of this part of the coast.

Los Valles Group of villages in deep fertile valleys on route to Haria.

Montañas del Fuego (Mountains of Fire) The central feature of this volcanic island has become, in the past few years, a spectacular tourist attraction. The area was largely created in the eruptions of 1730–36, which obliterated what was once the most fertile part of the island. The legacy of this destruction—the gaping craters, the black and purple lava, the absence of any life, either plant or animal, and the total silence, is what casts such a spell on the visitor.

Camel rides, available on the road from Yaiza into the National Park, offer an opportunity for a closer view of this extraordinary terrain: also not to be missed is the coach excursion around the volcanic craters (see **Islote de Hilario**).

Mozaga Hamlet at crossroads 8km north-west of Arrecife, site of the *Monumento al Campesino*, a modern sculpture by Cesar Manrique dedicated to the country people. There is also a craft centre here and a restaurant with Canarian cuisine.

Playa Blanca This name applies to two different places. The first is a resort beach 5km south of Tias to the west of Arrecife (Puerto del Carmen), the second a small fishing village in the south-western corner of the island, 40km west of Arrecife. This is also developing as a resort, centred on its beach and the port which is the departure point for the Fuerteventura ferries. 4km to the east is the first of a series of wide sandy beaches surrounding the headland of the *Punta del Papagayo*.

Playa de Famara 5km stretch of sandy beach in the north-west of the island, reached by junction 3km west of Teguise. Its name has been adopted by the new resort development here, *Famara*.

Puerto del Carmen The island's major resort 16km south-west of Arrecife, centred on beach of *Playa Blanca*. The beach of *Playa de los Pocillos* to the east is the focus of another resort, the whole stretching along 6km of coastline (see also p.22).

Los Valles

Rubicòn The Costa de Rubicòn in the extreme west of the island was the site of the first settlement of Jean de Bethencourt, who built a castle here. This has since disappeared and it is difficult to imagine what attraction this desert area offered the early explorers.

2 km east of the village of Playa Blanca is a circular tower, the *Torre del Aguila* (1778).

Teguise Ancient capital of Lanzarote, 12 km north of Arrecife.

This sedate old town, marooned in the emptiness of Lanzarote's interior, is one of the most haunting places in the Canaries. Like Betancuria in Fuerteventura it was chosen as the original capital because of its security from coastal marauders. Replaced by Arrecife in the 18th c., it has attracted little development in modern times and retains much of the atmosphere of the days when it was the stately retreat of the island's Spanish masters.

The church of **San Miguel** in the main square (originally 17th c.) was rebuilt in the early 20th c. after a fire. Its interior has the oddly contrasting styles of Romanesque and Gothic. The figure of the *Virgin* on the high altar is 16th c.

Opposite the church is the 18th c. *Palacio de Spinola*, used for exhibitions. Elsewhere in the town are the old but sadly derelict convents of *Santo Domingo* and *San Francisco*. The main occupation of the town's 1500 inhabitants is agriculture. There is, however, one local craft which has survived the centuries: the making of the *timple*, a small instrument like a ukelele which is very popular throughout the islands.

Near Teguise (1 km to the east) is the 16th c. **Castillo de Guanapay**, built as a defence against the Moors. The castle, entered by a drawbridge, is perched on the edge of a crater. There is a fine view from the battlements of Teguise and the surrounding countryside.

Fuerteventura

Fifty miles from the north-west coast
of Africa (and the nearest of the
Canary Islands to the continent)
Fuerteventura is, in every aspect, like
a part of the Sahara that has drifted
into the Atlantic. With its low, rust-
coloured mountains and dusty
treeless plains it is the exact reverse
of the fertile La Palma, 200 miles to
the west. (Geological research has
shown that Lanzarote and
Fuerteventura were, in fact, once part
of the African land mass.)

The name of the island was inspired
by the words of the Norman explorer
Jean de Bethencourt, who on landing
on its shores in 1402 exclaimed
'Quelle forte ventura' ('what a great
adventure'). De Bethencourt had

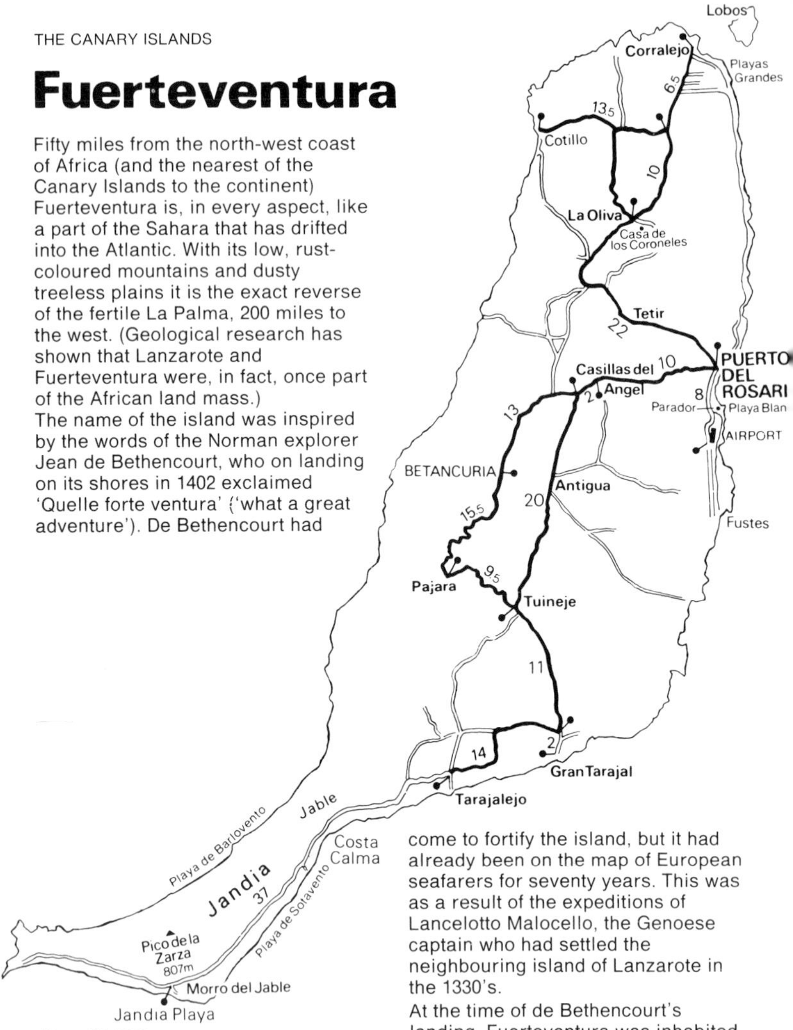

Pop: 19,500
Capital: Puerto del Rosario
Area: 2019 sq km
Highest point: Pico de la Zarza
(807m)
Nearest island: Lanzarote
Sailings: Direct to Las Palmas (10hrs),
Lanzarote (4hrs). For Jet-Foil service
to Las Palmas and Tenerife see p. 18
Flights: Direct to Tenerife, Las
Palmas, Lanzarote

come to fortify the island, but it had
already been on the map of European
seafarers for seventy years. This was
as a result of the expeditions of
Lancelotto Malocello, the Genoese
captain who had settled the
neighbouring island of Lanzarote in
the 1330's.

At the time of de Bethencourt's
landing, Fuerteventura was inhabited
by the Mahohs, descendants of
natives of the Roman province of
Mauretania who had been transported
here by the Romans as a punishment
for rebellion. Having established their
fortresses, de Bethencourt and his
followers (most notably his rival
Gadifer de la Salle) set about
pacifying the island, a task made
difficult by the Mahohs' ploy of
retreating to the barren, inhospitable

interior and waiting in ambush for their pursuers.

When the Spanish took over the island in 1414, however, most of the population had been successfully subdued. The final chapter was written when the *conquistador* Alonso de Lugo came to Fuerteventura in 1501 to formally take possession of the island as Spanish Governor of the Canaries.

The Spanish must have questioned, at times, the virtues of their possession. Although Fuerteventura is the second in size of the Canaries it is, after Hierro, the least productive. The sandy wastes and volcanic hills of the interior are features which, with the desert winds and almost total lack of rainfall, it shares with the Sahara.

With their limited resources, however, the people of Fuerteventura—known today as *maioreros*—make the most of this barren island. Unlike Lanzarote, Fuerteventura has some ground water, and by the use of artesian wells and wind-driven pumps the people are able to irrigate their smallholdings and make a modest living from growing potatoes, tomatoes and wheat. Many of the crops—notably tomatoes—are new to the island, but they have not supplanted the traditional rural industries, which in the western islands have been overwhelmed by the banana plantations.

As in Lanzarote, the cochineal insect (used for making dyes) is cultivated on the prickly pear cactus which abounds in the dry conditions of the eastern islands (the same conditions which have defeated the banana). Another cactus, the agave, also flourishes in the dry volcanic soil: from this comes the sisal fibre which is one of the island's main exports. Another successful industry is fishing, particularly on the north coast of Corralejo. A favourite haunt for underwater fishers is the strait between Fuerteventura and the little island off its north-east coast, the Isla de Lobos.

Apart from goats, which are found here in large numbers, the domestic animal most readily identified with Fuerteventura is the camel. These sedate creatures are used for farm work throughout the island, and bred for export to the other islands. Another animal associated with Fuerteventura is the *bardino*, a local breed of dog whose ancestors were the *canes* which gave the Canaries their name.

Geographically the island consists of two low mountain ranges running from north to south and divided by a central plain. The island is volcanic in origin and in the north and south there are a number of extinct craters surrounded by *malpais*, the deserts of lava which give a hostile appearance to the landscape.

At first sight, the interior of Fuerteventura is undoubtedly forbidding, but on further acquaintance its qualities can be recognized, particularly the extraordinary colours which different light conditions bring into play. Most dramatic are the reds of the volcanic ash and alluvium, which at sunset impart a fantastic glow to the mountains.

The most extraordinary feature of Fuerteventura is the Jandia, the narrow limb of land protruding from its south-west corner. This peninsula is really a mountainous island (its highest point, the Pico de la Zarza, is Fuerteventura's major peak), attached to the rest of Fuerteventura by a sandy isthmus (Jable). The Jandia is famed for its continuous white sandy beaches and is now a prospecting ground for private developers.

Fuerteventura's sparse population is mainly concentrated in the capital and main port, Puerto del Rosario. The airport is 8km from the town and the short flight from Las Palmas ($\frac{1}{2}$hr, three times daily) makes Fuerteventura possible for a day excursion from Grand Canary. However, this would hardly do justice to an island whose pleasures belong to the explorer who is prepared to hire a car and discover the unique qualities of the landscape.

Travelling in Fuerteventura The main roads are good, particularly those to Corralejo in the north and Tarajalejo in the south. The unsurfaced roads must be treated with caution. Many which appear driveable at the outset become impassable after a few kilometres. Others diverge without any indication of direction. Another unexpected hazard is the sand dunes which drift across the roads on the east coast (Playas de Corralejo) and south coast (Playa de Sotavento).

Although there are buses from Puerto del Rosario to the main villages, these are infrequent and car hire is recommended. (Cars are available at Corralejo and Puerto del Rosario.)

Hotels and restaurants

Fuerteventura has few hotels. The main ones are in the resort areas of Corralejo and Jandia Playa, where there are also apartments. There are hotels at Gran Tarajal and Tarajalejo, and Puerto del Rosario has a good Parador, 5km south of the town. (See also p. 23). The best restaurants are mainly in the hotels.

Beaches The best beaches in the Canaries are in Fuerteventura. These are in the Jandia peninsula in the south and at Corralejo in the north. Along the south coast of the Jandia is the seemingly endless *Playa de Sotavento* (25km of white sand) and on the north side the *Playa de Barlovento*. More white sand, piled in high curving dunes, lies along the north-east coast (*Playas de Corralejo*). There are many other superb beaches, but only a few are accessible. A popular one to the south of Puerto del Rosario is the *Playa Blanca*, the location of the Parador. There are also fine beaches at Cotillo in the north-west and Tarajalejo in the south.

Sports The sea provides most of Fuerteventura's sporting activities. Apart from the excellent swimming, skin-diving, etc. there is also some of the best fishing in the Canaries, particularly around the Isla de Lobos. For information apply to the Club Deportivo Unión Puerto in Calle General Linares, Puerto del Rosario.

Itineraries

North
Puerto del Rosario—La Oliva—Cotillo—Corralejo—return via La Oliva

South
Puerto del Rosario—Antigua—Tarajalejo—Tuineje—Betancuria—Casillas del Angel—Puerto del Rosario

Sisal plantation near La Oliva

Betancuria Village 30 km west of Puerto del Rosario, reached by surfaced road from Tuineje (25 km) or unmade road west of Casellas del Angel (13 km). (The latter road is shortly to be surfaced.)

Founded by Jean de Bethencourt, after whom it was named, Betancuria was the island's first capital. The choice of location was defensive, in the western interior of the island, and as a capital it was eventually superseded in more peaceful times by Puerto del Rosario. As a result of this isolation, Betancuria has remained a charming old town in which every detail is on an intimate scale.

Church of Santa Maria In recognition of Betancuria's status as the Canaries' first bishopric, this small church is often described as a cathedral. Built originally in the 15th c., it was destroyed by Moorish invaders in 1593 and subsequently rebuilt in a style closer to Africa than to Europe.

The church has three aisles, each with carved Mudejar ceilings. The gilded reredos is particularly fine. Of particular interest is the **sacristy** (entrance to left of high altar) with a carved and painted *artesonado* (panelled) ceiling. This is in the Berber style, as is the simpler ceiling in the adjoining vestry. Also in the sacristy are murals depicting the *Life of the Virgin*. The best preserved are those on the east wall, against the light.

A short distance to the north of the church on the east side of the *barranco* is the 15th c. convent of *San Buenaventura*. This Franciscan convent, now ruined, is associated with San Diego de Alcala, who was one of the leaders of the order and later Spain's patron saint. His *hermitage*, built in the 17th c. around the cave where he prayed, is on the opposite side of the *barranco*. This building has been recently restored.

5 km to the south of Betancuria a track leads in 4 km to the *Ermita de la Virgen de la Pena*, a cave in which the Virgin (patron saint of Fuerteventura) made a miraculous appearance to San Diego. The cave is on the north side of the *barranco* and only accessible by foot. In it is preserved an alabaster image of the Virgin (1500) to which the islanders pay homage every year on the third Sunday in September.

Corralejo Village on north coast 39 km north of Puerto del Rosario.

This fishing village, located near the superb beaches which take its name, is now rapidly changing its identity into that of a resort. To add to the attractions of the beaches it is also the departure point for boats to the Isla de Lobos, a favourite haunt of the underwater fishermen.

In 1402 Corralejo was the landing-place of de Bethencourt at the start of his conquest. Now it is a busy construction site for the villas and

hotels which are Fuerteventura's belated contribution to the Canaries' tourist boom. A link with the past is a local craft, the weaving of straw hats, which survives a pre-conquest tradition of rushwork. For accommodation see p. 23.

The east coast (*Playas Grandes*) is noted for its sand dunes, which are constantly shifting with the wind, occasionally making the coastal road impassable.

Cotillo Village on north-west coast 13.5 km west of junction 6.5 km south of Corralejo.

On the coast to the south of this fishing village stands a *watchtower* built as a defence against pirates in the mid-18th c. Like its sister tower, built at the same time on the east coast at Fustes, this building is perfectly preserved.

There are fine beaches of white sand to the north and south of the village.

Fustes Anchorage on east coast 15 km south of Puerto del Rosario.

An 18th c. *watchtower*, similar to that at Cotillo on the west coast, stands on the headland here. The flat sandy beach (*Playa del Castillo*) is sheltered and offers perfect bathing for those wishing to avoid Atlantic breakers.

A new road to Fustes has been constructed to the south of the airport. This links with the old coastal road, which starts immediately to the south of the Parador.

Church of Santa Maria, Betancuria

Gran Tarajal Port on south of island 45 km south of Puerto del Rosario.
Steamers from Las Palmas call here *en route* for Puerto del Rosario. Although a landing place for the south of the island, and possessing a reasonable beach, Gran Tarajal has no pretensions as a resort. Its activity is concentrated on the port and the local industry —tomatoes.

Jandia Peninsula in south-west of island, noted for its high *cordillera* and sandy coastline.
The curving mountain range of the Jandia (*Macizo de Jandia*) is thought to be part of the rim of an extinct crater, like El Golfo in Hierro, once standing proud of the rest of the island but now joined to it by a bridge of sand. Across this isthmus (known as the *Jable* or *Istmo de la Pared*) lie traces of an ancient stone wall which marks the boundary of an old Mahoh kingdom.
At the heart of the Jandia massif is the island's highest mountain, the *Pico de la Zarza*, which rises to 807 m. On either side of the peninsula stretch the longest beaches in the Canaries, the *Playa de Barlovento* (north) and the *Playa de Sotavento* (south). The latter beach, 25 km of white sand, has attracted considerable tourist development in recent years.
Much of this is centred at *Morro del Jable* under the heel of the peninsula. There can be few tourist complexes as remote as this. To the motorist who has driven the 37 km of bumpy, sand-blown road from Tarajalejo the façades of the apartment blocks and hotels rise like a white mirage. (See Accommodation, p. 23.)
Most of the Jandia (which used to belong to *one man*—a German) has now been sold to property companies—mainly English and German—who have predicted a glamorous future for the peninsula. The smaller speculators are here too, as shown by the isolated groups of chalets and notices declaring

'Prime Resort—Land for Sale'. The traditional life of the Jandia's 600 native people —mainly fishermen and shepherds—is now beyond recall. Most of the goats have been cleared from the land, and familiar occupations are being abandoned in favour of the tasks—building, catering, domestic service —associated with the new industry.

La Oliva

Village 22 km north of Puerto del Rosario at heart of volcanic, sisal-growing area.

Like so many churches in Fuerteventura, the *church* in this village has a striking and unique appearance, the square tower of dark lava contrasting with the white painted exterior.

To the south of the village, in splendid isolation, stands the 18th c. **Casa de los Coroneles** (House of the Colonels), the former residence of the military governors of the island. The house is in process of restoration.

Lobos, Isla de

Small island off northeast coast of Fuerteventura, reached by boat from Corralejo.

The name of the island relates to the *lobos* or seals which were once its only inhabitants. The island now has a small settlement of fishermen, who exploit the plentiful resources of the strait.

Pajara

Village 15.5 km south of Betancuria, most easily reached from Tuineje (9.5 km).

Pajara is the administrative capital of the south-western region of the island, including the Jandia peninsula. The centrepiece of this attractive village is the 17th c. *church* with its unusual carved stone façade, combining Aztec and Gothic features. The interior is unusual, with two equal naves. The wooden ceiling is of the Mudejar style.

Puerto del Rosario

(pop. 7500) Capital and main port.

Founded at the end of the 18th c., the Puerto Cabras (Goat Port) as it was then known, achieved status as the island's capital only when the need for an inland capital (Betancuria) receded along with the activities of the sea marauders.

This dusty, unattractive little port is now being furiously urbanized with most activity concentrated at *La Florida*, the new development on the hills to the west. The best place to stay is in the *Parador* to the south of the town (5 km) which overlooks the nearest good beach, the *Playa Blanca*. There is, alternatively, a limited choice of hotels and pensions in the town. (See Accommodation, p. 23.)

Bus services connect Puerto del Rosario with Cotillo and Corralejo (once daily) and with Gran Tarajal (twice daily). The buses usually leave the capital in the afternoon and return from their destination in the mornings.

Tarajalejo

Village and resort on south coast, 57 km south of Puerto del Rosario.

The isolated resort, situated next to a small fishing village, has a wide and beautiful beach, an excellent hotel—and little else. Ideal for the 'get away from it all' type. For accommodation see p. 23.

Jandia   Above: Pajara church

Madeira

Porto San►

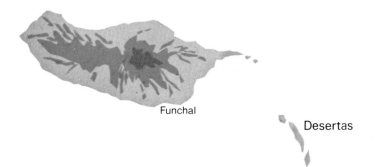

Funchal

Desertas

Introduction Two writers who best convey the charms of Madeira are the poets Diniz and Coleridge. To Diniz it was the 'Daughter of the Ocean, this country so full of flowers, gentle Madeira'. Coleridge, with special reference to the climate, wrote: 'I should think the situation of Madeira the most enviable on the whole earth. The seasons are the youth, maturity and old age of a never ending, still beginning Spring.'

Others have described Madeira as the 'Pearl of the Atlantic'—an appropriate name for an island which offers an encounter with something rare and beautiful. Few people who have visited Madeira do not voice a desire to return, and the mention of the island is sure to inspire the expression of that truly Portuguese emotion 'saudade'—the sweet longing for a place that is dear to the heart.

It is hoped that the modern traveller, arriving by jet aircraft or cruise ship, will experience the same feelings of pleasure that Madeira has given to so many visitors since the day that Zarco sailed round the tip of the island on his voyage of exploration.

The island is situated in the Atlantic Ocean, 338 miles north-west of the African coast, 674 miles south-west of Lisbon and 275 miles from Tenerife. It is the largest of a group of five islands. The others are Porto Santo (28 miles to the north-east) and the three Desertas (12 miles to the south-east). Three more islands, the Selvagens, lie 146 miles to the south. The main island is 57 km long and 22 km at the widest part. Its area is 741 sq km. The islands were formed by volcanic eruptions, which threw up Madeira's great peaks. The main island, rising sheer from the Atlantic, is in fact the summit of a great mountain range, four miles above the ocean floor.

From Madeira's peaks, torrents of rain carved the deep ravines which are the island's most striking feature, terraced and cultivated by the industrious islanders. Lava streams can be seen on the coast, breaking the line of the cliffs, and in the mountainous interior lies further striking evidence of the scale of the upheavals. No volcanic activity has been observed on the islands of the archipelago since the landing of the Portuguese in 1418, but earthquakes have occurred, the last tremor as recently as 1975.

There are two fairly flat inland areas: Santo da Serra in the east and the moorland of Paúl da Serra in the west. On the north and south coasts the sea cliffs rise to great heights above the rocky shores. The cliff at Cabo Girão, west of Funchal, reaches a dizzy 550 m, and is believed to be the second highest sea cliff in the world.

The highest inland point is the Pico Ruivo (1862 m). Not far away, to the south-east, lies the slightly lower peak of Pico do Areeiro (1810 m). No visit to Madeira is complete without a trip to one of these points, to view the island's extraordinary mountain panorama.

The deepest valley is the Curral das Freiras, or the Grand Curral as it is sometimes called. This is, in fact, the floor of an extinct crater, surrounded by a wall of peaks and reached by a steep winding road. It is an exciting drive, leading down through tunnels cut in the mountain spurs.

Considering its small area, the variety of Madeira's landscape is remarkable. The mountains and plateaux of the interior, the wild rocky coastline, the great pine and eucalyptus groves, and the fertile cultivated regions on the lower levels provide the visitor with innumerable scenes of great beauty.

One of Madeira's greatest riches is her flowers. Few houses lack the adornment of a vine or flowering shrub, and potted plants abound in every courtyard and terrace. In the towns two of the most popular shrubs are hibiscus and bougainvillea. Other popular varieties, seen in the gardens of the *quintas*, are jacaranda, strelitzia and wisteria. In the country areas mimosa is followed by agapanthus, hydrangeas and pink lilies.

On a visit to Madeira in 1768 Captain Cook wrote of the island as being the 'recipient of Nature's most liberal gifts', commenting on the richness of the soil and the variety of trees and plants. The same impression is conveyed to the modern visitor, and it is not difficult to imagine Madeira as a virgin island, as it was in the 14th century.

The tranquillity of another age is reflected in the people of Madeira themselves. To wander through the market of Funchal and see them at work is to return to the Middle Ages. The scene—the men in their strange caps, carrying the great baskets of produce, the women in their dark shawls—might be taken from a Bruegel painting. The gentle pace of life, the pleasantries, are things that are lost to the modern world: in Madeira we can recapture them.

The people The inhabitants of Madeira (pop. 310,000) and Porto Santo (3000) are Portuguese. They are descended from the original settlers who came to the islands with Zarco in 1419, and from the Italians, French and Flemish who were granted land rights during the 15th and 16th centuries by the Portuguese.

After the introduction of sugar cane slave lavour was imported from Africa and the Cape Verde Islands, and traces of Moorish and Negro blood are sometimes seen in the present population. Other residents who left their mark were the Spanish and English soldiers who were stationed in Madeira from time to time.

The Madeirans are a sturdy, virile race. Courteous in manner, and independent by nature, they are friendly and helpful to visitors. Being proud of their beautiful country they appreciate any expression of pleasure in its attractions.

Women gathering osiers near Santana   Right: Funchal Market

The economy Although tourism has taken over as Madeira's chief source of income, agriculture is still important in this highly fertile island. Chief crops are bananas, sugar cane, grapes, vegetables, fruit and cut flowers. Derived from Madeira's many natural products are her craft goods — wickerwork, embroidery and knitwear — which are in great demand as practical gifts. Madeira wine maintains its prestige as one of the island's chief exports, and cut flowers, always popular with the home market, have found ready outlets in Europe with the advent of air freight. Happily the growth in tourism, concentrated in Funchal, has done little to mar the charms of the island. In addition to earnings from these sources, the island receives a considerable amount of money from Madeirans working abroad. The majority of these emigrants go to Venezuela, Brazil or South Africa.

The problems of maintaining a balanced economy exist in Madeira as

in most countries. Despite the advance in such modern industries as tourism, the need for agricultural labour will always be great. Some improvement in conditions for farm workers will be necessary if an adequate labour force is to be maintained. In Madeira's difficult terrain, mechanization is impractical — but the resulting demand for manual labour must contend with a sharp decline in the number of people willing to work on the land. As standards of education improve (each child must attend school for a minimum of nine years) the tendency to work in less arduous industries will increase, as will the drift to other countries with a higher standard of living.

History

Discovery To the maritime explorers of the 14th century the horizon of the Atlantic was the edge of the world. It took a brave—or a storm-tossed— voyager to venture beyond the coasts of Iberia or Africa. The easternmost Canaries, visible from the sea off the African coast, were the first temptation—and it was the Italian explorers of these who first charted Madeira and Porto Santo to the north. The actual exploration of Madeira did not occur until 1419. This was during the golden age of Portuguese navigation, when her seafarers— inspired by Prince Henry the Navigator—were venturing further into the Atlantic. Madeira's 'discoverer' was João Gonçalves Zarco, who arrived at the island of Porto Santo in 1418 and went on to Madeira the following year.

Although Zarco found no trace of human habitation on Madeira it is by

no means certain that he was the first man to set foot on the island. It is possible that the Phoenicians knew of Madeira, but unlikely that they settled it. Pliny wrote of the 'Fortunate Islands' which were almost certainly the Canaries, and he also mentions the 'Purple Island' which could have been Madeira. The English traveller T. E. Bowdich suggests that 'If Homer's beautiful description of the Phoenician Isle, where fruit succeeded fruit, and flower followed flower in rich and endless variety, be applicable to any modern one, it is Madeira.'

The Machim legend One of the most persistent legends about the discovery of Madeira is that of the English adventurer Robert Machim (possibly a variant of MacKean). The story goes that in 1346 Machim sailed from Bristol with one Anne d'Arset, the lady of his heart, to escape the wrath of her father, who was strongly opposed to the match. They were aiming for Brittany, but a violent storm blew them off course and they arrived at Madeira. Here, at the site of the town of Machico, they landed, and were delighted to find themselves in a warm, beautiful country. Unfortunately the storm that had driven them ashore returned in full force and their ship, which had been anchored in the bay, was wrecked. Shortly afterwards the unhappy couple fell ill and died, and the members of their crew buried them near the shore. To avoid a similar fate, the crew then built a sailing craft by which they were able to effect their escape. Arriving on the shores of Africa they were captured and sold into slavery, and it was many years before they were able to find their way back to Europe. Here the story of their adventures, and the discovery of the mysterious island on which they had buried Machim and his bride finally reached Portugal and the ears of the Court. If the story is true, it undoubtedly stimulated the interest of the Portuguese navigators in the unknown Atlantic isle. (See **Machico**, p. 139.)

Statue of Zarco, Funchal

Zarco's voyages On his first voyage of exploration Zarco sailed along the coast of Madeira as far west as Cabo Girão. On the way he landed at the sites of Santa Cruz and Funchal, later to become important settlements. Funchal, the ultimate capital of the island, was named after the fennel plant (*funcho*) which grew there in great abundance.

The name of the island itself is the Portuguese for 'wood'. At the time of its discovery Madeira was covered by dense forest, only a small part of which remains today. After collecting samples of wood, soil and plants from the island, Zarco returned to Portugal to tell the King (João I) and his son Prince Henriques (Henry the Navigator) of the wonders of the island. A year later (1420) he was sent back to claim it for Portugal and to found a colony.

Settlement On his return Zarco divided the administration of the island between himself and his lieutenant Teixeira. Zarco's 'Captaincy' was the western half of the island, governed from Funchal, and Teixeira's the eastern half, governed from Machico. A third territory—Porto Santo—was allotted to Bartolomeu Perestrello, whose position of Captain or Governor of the island was held by successive members of his family up to the mid-18th c. Perestrello's further claim to fame was that his daughter married Christopher Columbus, who lived for a while in the island.

The basis of the island's administration was its division into plantations, in the European tradition. To create these plantations the forests had to be cleared, a task which Zarco's followers set about with disastrous enthusiasm. Fires were started to clear the timber, but these got out of control and large areas of forest were destroyed. The rich deposits of ash, however, greatly increased the fertility of the soil.

One of the first crops introduced was sugar cane. This was brought from Sicily in 1425, and proved to be easy to grow in the temperate climate. Sugar mills were built, using water power to crush the cane. Vines were later introduced from Cyprus, and they too were easily acclimatized. Thus the famous Madeira wine was first produced. A lucrative trade with England, Italy and Flanders soon became established.

The rich new land became increasingly attractive to Portuguese settlers, and during the first century after its discovery representatives of many of the noble families of Portugal settled in Madeira. They were joined by other Europeans, who being granted land, settled and later became Portuguese. The present Madeirans are a mixture of several nationalities, inheriting the character and skills of their different cultures.

Owing to the mountainous nature of the interior, road building presented great difficulties, and early communications were largely by sea. The most important towns on the island were also ports—Funchal, Machico, Santa Cruz and Ponta do Sol. In 1508 Funchal was made into a city, and in 1514 a bishopric (the *Sé*, or bishop's seat).

Foreign occupation For over a century and a half Madeira prospered under Portuguese rule. Ultimately, however, it fell prey to the attentions of pirates and rival powers.

In 1566 the island was invaded by a French freebooter named de Montluc. Driven by a storm to Madeira, the Frenchman decided to raid Funchal for supplies and booty. The people of the city barricaded themselves in their houses as best they could, but for fifteen days the French went on the rampage, plundering the houses and killing many of the inhabitants. The invaders did great damage to the cathedral, then newly built, but luckily a large number of its treasures had been carried away to safety in the interior of the island and were later restored after the departure of the raiders.

In 1580 Madeira, together with the rest of Portugal, fell under the rule of

Philip II of Spain. For 60 years the Spanish administered the island, and during their occupation built the fort which stands on Pico São Jorge, where they had a large garrison of troops to control Funchal. (The fort today is used as a radio station.)

On December 1 1640 an uprising in Portugal threw off the Spanish yoke. The Duke of Braganza (João IV) was proclaimed king, and after a series of wars and treaties Portugal's Atlantic possessions, including Madeira, were restored to her. (Today December 1, National Independence Day, is celebrated as a public holiday in the island.)

Alliance with England In 1660 the marriage of Charles II of England to Catherine of Braganza was arranged. By the terms of the marriage treaty England was granted many important territories, and it is said that the Portuguese were considering the addition of Madeira if the English did not accept the first offers.

The alliance brought many privileges to the English merchants in Madeira. It was the time of the development of the wine trade with England and the establishment of a prosperous English community in the island.

In 1768 Captain Cook visited the island in the *Endeavour*. He was on his voyage round the world, and put in at Funchal for supplies and water. The botanists accompanying this and a later voyage (1772) managed to collect a wide variety of specimens of Madeiran flora. Accounts of these voyages published shortly afterwards give an interesting picture of the island in the 18th c.

Napoleonic wars In 1801 the British Government (allied with Portugal against Napoleon) sent a force to garrison Madeira against possible occupation by the French. After the signing of the Peace of Amiens these troops were withdrawn, but in 1807, during the French invasion of the Peninsula, Admiral Hood was sent with a fleet carrying 4000 soldiers to take military control of the island.

When this force arrived a form of capitulation was signed by the citizens which was a token of allegiance to the British monarch, George III. This agreement was made in December, but in April the following year the island was formally returned to Portugal, with an arrangement that the British garrison should remain. The force was finally withdrawn in 1814 when there was no further threat from France. As an alliance existed between Britain and Portugal in 1807, and since the latter was militarily weak at the time, the protection of Madeira and its trade was necessary for both countries.

The British troops were well received in the island and many stayed there and married Madeiran girls. Traces of their sojourn can be seen in the names carved on the old drinking fountain at Santo da Serra. The Taylors, Hardys and Turners who scratched their names on the stones were probably members of the garrison there, and their continuing presence must account for the fair hair and blue eyes often seen in the people of the village. Similar characteristics may be found in the inhabitants of other villages such as Monte or Camacha where there was a British garrison.

On August 23 1815 the British ship *Northumberland* with Admiral Sir George Cockburn in command arrived in Funchal. She anchored offshore, but no one was allowed aboard except the British Consul, Henry Veitch.

He arrived to pay his compliments to the chief passenger, Napoleon Bonaparte. Apparently he pleased the ex-Emperor by addressing him as 'Your Majesty', and offering to obtain for him any articles which would make the remainder of his voyage more comfortable. It is recorded that Napoleon asked for some fruit and books. These Mr Veitch sent on board, together with some of the best Madeira wine. They were paid for by Napoleon in gold Louis, and the Consul kept the coins until 1822, when he laid them under the foundation stone of the new English church.

Relations with Portugal For all her geographical isolation from the mother country, Madeira could not escape involvement in Portuguese affairs. In 1828 the rivalry between the traditionalists and the advocates of a democratic constitution came to a head when Dom Miguel, at the time Regent in Lisbon, dissolved the courts and declared himself absolute King. Miguelist forces arrived in Madeira with a new governor appointed to the island by the regime. After meeting some resistance they took over the island. Four years later the supporters of the constitutional government in Lisbon sent a relief force to Porto Santo and Madeira, but this was repulsed. It was not until 1834 that Donna Maria II, the legitimate successor, was proclaimed Queen and the civil war ended.

Later disasters were of a natural order. In 1852 the vines and potatoes were destroyed by plague and had to be replanted. In 1873 the vines were again destroyed, this time by phylloxera, the disease which had already ravaged many of the vineyards of Europe.

1856 saw a serious outbreak of cholera in the island. The disease spread rapidly and in a few weeks caused more than 7000 deaths.

A closer link with Portugal was achieved with the laying of a telegraph cable in 1874, which greatly facilitated the administrative control of the island. In 1902, however, Madeira was granted self-government. Later on, after the fall of the monarchy, it became a part of the Portuguese Republic.

At the outbreak of the First World War Portugal remained neutral. Her sympathies, however, lay with the Allied cause, and the facilities she offered allied shipping caused Germany to declare war on her in 1916. In December of that year Funchal was bombarded by German submarines, and some damage done to the town. A second attack came in 1917, when once again Funchal was shelled and buildings damaged, among them the church of Santa Clara.

Foreign trade and tourism After the war Madeira returned to a period of quiet prosperity. Agriculture was still the main source of income, but additional revenue came from the growing number of visitors from Europe, attracted by the warm winter climate of the island.

In 1921 the former Emperor Charles of Austria arrived with his wife in the island after the collapse of the Austro-Hungarian Empire (his father, the great Franz-Josef, had been here in the 1860's). The royal couple resided first in Funchal and then in Monte, where Charles died in 1922.

In the 'thirties Madeira suffered from the effects of the world slump, and there was considerable emigration from the island. During the Second World War Portugal remained neutral, but her trade with Britain and America virtually stopped. In 1943, at the request of the British Government, 2000 evacuees from Gibraltar were given shelter in the island. These were mostly women and young girls, and they helped to fill the gap left by the absent tourists.

One of the island's most famous visitors was Winston Churchill, who holidayed in Madeira in 1949 and 1950. The statesman painted a number of pictures of Camara de Lobos, which has put the little fishing port on the map.

The age of air travel (heralded in 1921 by the arrival of a hydroplane from Lisbon) has transformed the life of Madeira. The seaplane route (Southampton-Lisbon-Funchal) inaugurated in 1949, was replaced by jet services when the landing strip was built on Porto Santo (1962). From here visitors had to travel to Madeira by boat, but this changed with the opening of the airport near Santa Cruz in 1964. Since then traffic has increased steadily, and charter flights as well as the regular schedule from Lisbon are available to visitors. It is also possible to fly to the Canary Islands and the Azores from Madeira. The resulting tourist trade has made an important contribution to the island's economy.

Climate The popularity of Madeira as a winter resort is largely due to its climate, which is pleasantly mild throughout the year. 400 miles out in the Atlantic, it is little affected by the climate of the African continent.

It also enjoys the benefit of the warm Gulf Stream and—in the summer—the cooling effect of the trade winds. The average monthly temperature varies little: from 61°F 16°C (January) to 70°F 21°C (August).

There are occasional sea mists and cloud tends to form at the higher altitudes. Rainfall is moderate, although higher than in the Canaries, and is usually confined to the winter months.

Cultivation The cultivation of the land in Madeira presents special problems. The rocky and precipitous terrain imposes great limitations on agriculture, which have tested the ingenuity of the Madeirans to the full. Over hundreds of years the people have built up innumerable terraces supported by rock walls, on which small plots have been created.

Lack of pastureland has forced the Madeirans to keep their livestock permanently in sheds. The manure, however, is spread over the terraces and this, together with the fertile volcanic soil and even temperatures, ensures the crops' rapid growth.

In such difficult terrain, farm machinery is impractical. Most of the work is done by hand, the farm workers using a tool called the *enchada*. This has a pick-like head, either flat or pointed, with which they turn over the ground.

The patterns of cultivation are varied to fit the conformation of each piece of land, so that when the irrigation channel is opened to allow the water to flow on to a property it runs along the furrows to every plant.

The most important fruit of Madeira's soil—as the lovers of her wines will appreciate—is the grape. Vines were introduced to the island from Crete and Cyprus in the 15th century. Second to the vine is sugar cane, the first crop to be introduced to the

island by the Portuguese. It is used for domestic consumption and in making brandy and rum. Recently sugar has become a less profitable crop, and large areas where it was grown are being turned over to vegetables and flowers for export. Bananas are also a large crop, but are subject to intense competition from other countries, particularly the Canaries.

Vegetables are widely grown. Many of these, especially onions, potatoes and tomatoes, are for export. The sweet potato is a staple item of the peoples' diet, and the green tops are used for cattle fodder.

The fruits grown include oranges, lemons, avocados, cherries, apples and pears. Custard apples, loquats and prickly pears grow wild in many places, though custard apples are also planted in gardens. Pumpkins and yams—grown for domestic use—are found all over the island.

The bananas, sugar and vines grow at fairly low altitudes, while fruit and vegetables do well on all levels. A common pattern of cultivation on the lower slopes is that of sugar or bananas on the terrace plots, with vines grown on pine pole supports around the perimeter—a practical method of conserving land.

Madeira wines are famous all over the world. The vineyards are mainly in the south (Estreito de Camara de Lobos, Estreito da Calheta) and in the west (Ponta do Pargo) but there are some in the north as well (Seixal, Faial, Porto da Cruz).

The unique flavour of Madeira wine can be attributed to its unusual process of production.

The harvest takes place between August and October and the grapes pressed either by mechanical means or—in the remoter areas—by the old foot presses. This activity is accompanied by much singing and guitar playing. The *mosto* (grape juice) is then conveyed to the wine lodges, and here again one might catch a glimpse of tradition in the *borrachieros*, the men who carry the

juice on their backs in goatskins capable of taking as much as 50 litres. In the lodges the juice is fermented and fortified with brandy spirit. It is then subjected to the special process known as *estufagem*. This involves putting the wine in a hot store (*estufa*) in which it is kept at a temperature of 50°C/122°F for a period of six months. (The idea for this came about as a result of the great improvement noticed in the wine during the days of sail, when the contents of casks that had travelled in the tropics were sampled on their return to Madeira.) This heating process, and the degree with which it is controlled, is responsible for the very special characteristics of Madeira wine. After the *estufagem* the wine is kept in the lodges for a minimum of 13 months before shipping.

Plants and flowers Almost any kind of tree or plant will grow in Madeira, and this applies as much to the wild as the domestic varieties. The changes in the natural vegetation are regulated by the altitude, and there are distinct zones in which certain types of tree and plant flourish.

The highest peaks are nearly bare of all forms of plant life, but below them there is a wide area densely clothed with heather, broom, blueberry and other low-growing shrubs. At the tree line the pines predominate, but lower down are eucalyptus, chestnut, mimosa and juniper.

Among the interesting native trees are many species of laurel, notably the Til (*Ocotea foetens*) which has been much used for building and

furniture. The juniper too has been widely felled for domestic use.

The story of the great fire which is supposed to have burned for seven years at the time of Madeira's first settlement may well account for the lack of native woods on the south side of the island. The fire was started in order to clear the lower slopes for cultivation, and got so out of control that large areas were totally denuded of trees. The best specimens of large native trees are to be found in the ravines in the north of the island.

The character of Madeira's native vegetation was for many years thought to have been due to an ancient land communication between southern Europe, North Africa and the Canary and Madeiran archipelagoes. This would account for the large proportion of southern European plants in Madeira's vegetation. But this theory of a connecting land mass has since been discarded in favour of the more conventional idea that natural agencies such as birds, winds and tides carried the seeds of Madeira's ancestral plants to the island.

It is difficult to establish which of Madeira's trees and plants are truly native. In such a temperate climate the process of naturalization is very rapid, and many species which might be thought indigenous were probably introduced by man. There are, however, a number of characteristic oceanic plants which unmistakably belong to this latitude. Among them is the *dracaena draco* (dragon tree), endemic to Madeira and the Canaries. Nearly fifty species of ferns are found in the island, two of which—*Polystichum falcinellum* and *Polystichum frondosum*—are endemic. There are nearly a hundred species of mosses and seven hundred species of flowering plants, many of them not found elsewhere.

Captain Cook's botanists were the first of a procession of writers who have extolled the beauty of Madeira's flowers. Subsequent writers have tended to concentrate on the cultivated species, which is perhaps inevitable in an island with such fine parks and gardens. Only visitors who explore the coastal regions or manage to get into the interior of the country will be able to appreciate the extraordinary range of Madeira's wild flowers.

One of the most striking of these is the Pride of Madeira. This is a species of *echium*, a native of Madeira and the Canary Islands. It grows in profusion on the cliffs of the south coast, and in the early spring its sturdy blue-grey bushes are covered with masses of purple flowers, which make a brilliant show against the dark rocks.

Along the levada paths there are always wild flowers growing in the cool shady spots which remain damp throughout the year. Forget-me-nots, foxgloves, wild cinerarias and tiny strawberries mingle with the luxuriant ferns. Also found on levada paths are wild orchids, arum lilies and hydrangeas. The latter flourish in a semi-wild state, and are particularly fine in Santana and Monte.

In April and May the yellow-flowered broom blazes across the higher slopes. In the autumn the belladonna lilies appear in pink drifts beneath the chestnuts and pines in the forests (notably in the Jardim da Serra and the Poiso region).

Many of the Madeiran roadsides are planted with flowers, most commonly hydrangeas and blue or white agapanthus. Travelling through the island it is difficult to see where the cultivated species end and the wild ones begin, since so many plants which would be regarded as garden specimens in Britain have taken to the countryside in Madeira. Where else would one find great cascades of nasturtiums of every hue falling over walls bordering farm plots, or goats plucking at arum lilies beside a country stream?

The country people have some charming names for the flowers which grow round their cottage homes. The decorative agapanthus are known as the 'Crowns of Henry' from their resemblance to the crown worn by the Portuguese Prince Henry the Navigator, whose sailors discovered Madeira. The bright red, yellow and orange nasturtiums which climb everywhere in the early months of the year are referred to as the 'Wounds of God', and the tall white spikes of the *Watsonia* are known as the 'Staff of St John'.

Gardens in Madeira show little conformity to the usual seasons. Roses bloom throughout the year, and in the winter one can see delphiniums flowering beside geraniums and marigolds. The plants which make the gardens such a delight have been introduced from all over the world. Where in one corner the garden may have the appearance of a prim English plot with its daisies and petunias, in another corner the exotic cacti and bird-like strelitzia give it a tropical character.

Some of the most brilliant floral displays are provided by the innumerable species of flowering trees, shrubs and plants which grow so freely in the island. Each season brings its special display of these beauties. At the end of the year the poinsettias are in their glory, and the bombax trees are covered with their coral pink star-like flowers. From December to March orange bignonia trails over walls and trellises, and is followed by the delicate wisteria.

During April and May the streets of Funchal are misted with the blue of jacaranda trees, and later on the bougainvillea splashes its rich colours over walls and balconies. At any time of the year the visitor will find an abundance of flowers to welcome him to the island.

The levadas One of the world's most remarkable systems of water supply is found in Madeira.

It was started by the early settlers who discovered that, although there was heavy precipitation of water on the northern slopes and on the high peaks of the interior, this moisture was not so plentiful on the south side of the island or on the lower levels where cultivation was easier.

Before describing the levada system

it is necessary to know something about the natural sources of Madeira's water.

Clouds carried to the island by the westerly winds meet the barrier of Madeira's land mass. The rainfall, seeping through the top layers of soil, finally reaches the impenetrable layers of laterite, where it is forced up in a series of springs. These appear at altitudes of about 500 m. The island is thus a huge reservoir, with an estimated 200 million cubic metres of water stored below the surface.

Before the levada system was started, all the water ran back into the sea through the ravines which it had cut in the sides of the hills. The introduction of the network of aqueducts (Portuguese *levadas*) diverted water to the areas where it was needed for irrigation. The construction of the artificial channels, started by the early colonists, has since been continued and improved over the years. Today the system comprises many hundreds of kilometres of levada channels which carry the precious water to the cultivated areas.

In 1939 the Portuguese Government sent a mission to Madeira to study a scheme for the complete irrigation of the island and the creation of an efficient hydro-electric system. As a result of this mission several major projects were completed, and practically the whole island now has a good supply of water and electricity.

The original levadas were channels cut out of the rocky hillsides. They started from the highest springs, and gradually descended in great bends and loops round the sides of the hills and ravines to the lower levels, where the water was then taken off in small aqueducts and channels to irrigate the arable areas. As time went on many concrete levadas were built, and where it was necessary the water was taken through tunnels cut in the hills. (One of these underground courses, passing through the central mountain range, is over 4300 m long.) For centuries the water system has been operated under a series of

complicated laws. The object of these laws is to ensure that the supplies so laboriously collected should be fairly distributed. The actual method of distribution is simple, a block being inserted in the main channel and a sluice opened in a side channel to divert the water to an individual plot. The amount of water diverted is strictly related to the size of the land area to be irrigated, and an appropriate water tax is paid.

While the whole elaborate system is purely practical from the point of view of the inhabitants, it provides continuing fascination for the visitor. Some of the loveliest walks on the island can be enjoyed along the courses of the levadas, most of which have paths running beside them. The routes of these channels take the keen walker into areas that he would otherwise never see, and offer intimate views of the island's superb scenery.

Madeira's skies From the first pale light of dawn breaking behind the Desertas to the last evening ray, Madeira's skies present ever-changing panoramas, matched only by those of the landscape itself.

The great masses of cloud which pass occasionally over the island play strange tricks with the light. The narrow shafts of sunlight piercing through them on to the surface of the ocean produce a theatrical effect, like 'spots' playing over a vast amphi-theatre of sky and sea.

The dawns are mystical, with the growing light spreading like a line of mercury over the sea behind the Desertas. Strengthening, it suffuses the sky with a soft gold light which is picked up by the tips of the mountains.

Sunsets are magnificent too, presenting a complete canvas ranging from the crimson of the western horizon to the soft reflected light in the east. The pattern of light changes every second, until at last the sun sinks below the horizon. At this moment one may with luck observe the strange 'green flash' which sometimes follows a Madeira sunset.

Practical information

TRAVEL

Air

Scheduled services

Air Portugal runs two direct flights weekly (Thurs & Sun) to Funchal from London (Heathrow). Flying time: 3hrs 20min. Flights can also be arranged to Madeira via Portugal, transferring to domestic flights at Lisbon for Funchal or Porto Santo.

Twice-weekly flights operate from Funchal to Las Palmas, Canary Islands in summer (once weekly in winter). Flying time: 1hr.

Charters

A list of companies offering charter flights (inclusive holidays) to Madeira is on p. 120.

Internal flights

Porto Santo Flights at least four times a day (not Tues) from Funchal. Flying time: 20min.

Airports Funchal's airport, Santa Catarina, lies 22km east of Funchal. Porto Santo airport is used for internal flights only, and by some charters.

For details of bus services between the airport and Funchal, enquire at the airport or at the Air Portugal office in Funchal.

Sea

A number of tour operators/steamship lines operate chartered cruises to Madeira from the UK. Cruises are normally from 10–14 days and can include the Canary Islands and Moroccan and Iberian ports.

Companies offering cruises:

Abreu Travel Agency Ltd 109 Westbourne Grove, London W2

CTC Lines 1 Regent St, London SW1

Fred Olsen Travel 111 Buckingham Palace Rd, London SW1

P&O Canberra Cruises 77 New Oxford St, London WC1 (P&O's *Canberra* includes Madeira on its African and South American routes)

A popular cruise offered by the major lines is the Christmas and New Year cruise which takes in Funchal's spectacular firework display on New Year's Eve.

Rail and sea

An alternative route to Madeira is by rail London-Lisbon and then on by sea. The railway journey is by way of the night train from London to Paris and then to Lisbon via Hendaye. Details of fares from British Rail or travel agents.

The onward journey from Lisbon can be made by the following steamship lines:

Companhia Portuguesa Transportes Maritimos Rua S. Juliao 53, Lisbon

This line offers island tours which include Madeira (length of voyage 36hrs). Sailings are, however, infrequent.

Empresa de Navegaçao Madeirense Rua Juliao 5, Lisbon

This line offers a combined cargo and passenger service to Madeira, calling at Porto Santo. The boats are small (12 passengers only) and the voyage takes 2½ days.

A number of other lines run services from Lisbon to the Canaries and South America which stop at Madeira. Details of these services may be obtained from travel agents or the Portuguese National Tourist Office in London.

Inter-island boat services and sea trips

Porto Santo A boat service to Madeira's neighbouring island of Porto Santo operates on six days a week, returning to Funchal on the same day (voyage 1hr 20min). The boat, a jetfoil, leaves from the main quay in Funchal (*Cais*) at 08.00, returning from Porto Santo at 18.00. Tickets may either be bought at the *Cais* or reserved through the hotel.

Desertas see Gazetteer entry

Boat trips round the coast of Madeira offer a unique view of the island's dramatic coastline. Excursions cover the south-east coast as far as Ponta de São Lourenço and the south-west coast as far as Ponta do Sol. Deep sea and shark fishing trips are also available.

A company offering a wide range of sea trips from Funchal is *Amigos do Mar*. Apply to the Information Office on the town jetty (*Cais*) which is also the departure point.

In the small villages around the coast boat owners can be found who will hire out boats for fishing, etc. It must be remembered, however, that the weather can change very rapidly round the coast as well as inland, so it is essential to take the advice of local people before making any sea trips.

Motoring

Visitors wishing to drive in Madeira should be in possession of a current British driving licence. Those wishing to hire a car should be over 21.

Car hire

There are several car hire firms in Funchal, with representatives at the airport.

The cost of renting a self-drive car varies according to the type of car and the duration of hire. Rates usually start at around £20 per day for the cheapest category of vehicle. Unlimited mileage usually applies and rates are reduced after 7 and 14 days. Rates exclude personal accident insurance and collision damage waiver, which are optional, local taxes and petrol.

Some car hire firms in Funchal:

Hertz Rua Ivens, Av. do Infante (& airport)
Avis Largo Antonio Nobre (& airport)
Atlas Rua da Alegria, Avenida do Infante
Europcar Rua Ivens, Avenida do Infante

Roads

Considering the rugged nature of the terrain, the roads in the island are very good. A main road runs all round the island, connecting the coastal villages, and three main roads cross from south to north (Funchal–Camacha–Porto da Cruz, Funchal–Poiso–Faial, Ribeira Brava–São Vicente). Roads are well sign-posted and with the aid of a simple map the motorist who keeps to the main (surfaced) roads will have no difficulty in finding his way.

Roads tend to be narrow and winding, but the only steep gradients occur in the occasional places where the main road drops down to the sea.

Madeira has three categories of road:

1 *Estrada*
2 Secondary or *caminho*
3 Local or *caminho vicinal*

Madeira's *estrada* (main highway) runs from the airport to Funchal and from Funchal to Ribeira Brava. Although some of the secondary roads are cobbled (such as the one which zig-zags from Paúl da Serra down to the south-west coast) they are all suitable for motor traffic. Roads in the third category, running between the smaller villages, are usually very narrow, with cobbled or rough stone surface. They were built for bullock carts and sledges long before the age of the motor car.

Roads in Madeira occasionally become dangerous through bad weather conditions. These can be heavy rains causing rock falls, or ice on the higher passes. In such eventualities the road will be closed, and police will advise about alternative routes.

Maps

The 2-sheet, large scale map (1:50,000) of Madeira published by the *Instituto Geográfico e Cadastral* is available from their office in Funchal or in London from Edward Stanford, 12 Long Acre, WC2.

On a smaller scale the *Fairey Leisure Map* includes a town plan of Funchal.

Bus services

Madeira's bus services are concentrated on the more populated areas in the south and east of the island. The services are run by a number of independent companies, but fares and schedules are under Government control. They are punctual and cheap, and most lines operate from early morning until late at night. Frequency of buses depends on the route.

A booklet 'Madeira by Bus' with details of routes to places of interest and timetables is available from the Tourist Office in Funchal. Visitors should be warned that on market days (Fri & Sat) the buses get very crowded.

All buses leave from the Avenida do Mar, the orange ones for routes within the Funchal area, the others to country destinations. The numbers for the latter, with their destinations, are:

No.	Destination
2	Assomada
4	Babosas
6, 103	Bonaventura
154	Cabo Girão
29, 77	Camacha
1,4,6,7,27,107	Camara de Lobos
113	Canical
2,136	Caniço
96	Corticeras
81	Curral das Freiras
6	Encumeada
53	Faial, Igreja
30	Jardim Botanico
23,53,113	Machico
4	Madalena do Mar
20, 21	Monte
155	Ponta da Oliveira
4	Ponta do Sol
107	Ponta do Pargo
1	Ponte dos Frades
53	Porto da Cruz
150	Porto Moniz
103	Ribeiro Frio
67	Santa
23, 53, 113	Santa Cruz
103	Santana
77	Santo da Serra
103	São Jorge
5, 150	São Vincente
150	Seixal

Taxis

Taxi services in Madeira are very good. Taxi stands may be found not only in Funchal but in the smaller towns and villages. Taxis are painted in the island colours — orange and blue — which makes them easy to identify.

In Funchal the taxis work on meters. Fares for country trips should be agreed with the driver before taking the journey, and will vary according to the number of passengers, amount of luggage, waiting time, etc.

For visitors with limited time taxis are the most convenient way of seeing the beauty spots in the vicinity of Funchal. Popular taxi excursions are to Monte, Eira do Serrado, Cabo Girão, Camacha and Pĺco do Areeiro. An all-day trip round the island can also be made.

Hire charges for taxis are regulated by the regional tourist board, with an official hourly rate. Details of approved charges for excursions by taxi from Funchal may be obtained from the Tourist Information Office.

Sightseeing tours

Coach tours to places of interest in Madeira are offered by various companies. These tours can vary from short local trips to full-day excursions, and coaches will collect passengers at their hotels. Reservations may be made through the larger hotels who will have details of the excursions. Most hotels provide a packed lunch for guests taking the tours, but restaurant stops are included in the full-day excursions.

Some companies in Funchal (Agências de Viagens) offering excursions:

Atlantica Rua dos Ferreiros 177
Blandy Avenida do Mar 1
Companhia de Automoveis de Turismo (CAT) Avenida Arriaga 62
Savoy Travel Agency Savoy Hotel
Panorama (Gray Line) Rua Dr J. Camara 3

INCLUSIVE HOLIDAYS

A package tour including flight, accommodation and food is the quickest and cheapest way of holidaying in Madeira. Tour operators specialising in the island are:

Arrow Holidays and **Suntours** Romeland House, Romeland Hill, St Albans, Herts
These two subsidiaries of the Arrow Leisure Group offer comprehensive brochures on Madeira and Porto Santo, with accommodation from 5-star hotels to self-catering at competitive rates.

Cadogan Travel 9/10 Portland St, Southampton, Hants
Countrywide Holidays Birch Heys, Cromwell Range, Manchester
Destination Portugal Madeira House, 37 Corn St, Witney, Oxford
Enterprise Holidays Ground Star House, London Rd, Crawley, Sussex
Hayes & Jarvis 152 King St, London W6
Horizon Holidays and **Wings** Edgbaston Five Ways, Birmingham
Just Portugal 170 New Bond St, London W1
Martin Rooks Holidays 204 Ebury St, London SW1
Merchant Travel Service/Villa Connections 55 Rathbone Place, London W1

Portugala Holidays 14 Collingwood Ave, London N10
Portugal a la Carte J3 Beauchamp Place, London SW3
Ramblers Holidays Box 43, Welwyn Garden City, Herts
Saga Holidays The Saga Building, Middelburg Sq, Folkestone, Kent
Thomas Cook Holidays PO Box 36, Thorpe Wood, Peterborough, Cambs
Thomson Travel Greater London House, Hampstead Rd, London NW1
For cruise specialists, see p.118

ACCOMMODATION

For many years accommodation in Madeira was confined to a small number of hotels in Funchal and Monte, serving the wealthy few — many of them invalids — who sought the benefit of the warm winter climate. Subsequently, in response to the increasing popularity of the island to both winter and summer visitors, a number of new hotels have been built, mainly in the Funchal area. The range of accommodation is wide, from the 5-star luxury establishments to the small 1 or 2-star *pensãos* (pensions).

A complete list of all hotels, pensãos, apartment hotels and villas can be obtained from the Portuguese National Tourist Office, 1 New Bond St, London W1. This gives details of rating and facilities.

Apart from the hotels on the south coast at Machico, Matur and Ribeira Brava, privately-run accommodation outside Funchal can only be found in the small pensãos (see list below). Accommodation is simple, but the advantage of these places is that food can usually be obtained in them, as they are often also the local restaurant.

The Government runs a *pousada* (Pousada dos Vinhaticos) at Encumeada on the main north-south road across the island. This hotel is dramatically situated on the high central ridge of mountains, and is an excellent place from which to take some of the finest walks. Reservations should be made through the Tourist Office in Funchal.

Hotels

Hotels in Madeira, like those in mainland Portugal, are graded on a star system. This is similar to that operating in Spain, though with slight variations (see Hotels in Canaries section, p. 21.)

Some popular hotels in **Funchal**:
Reid's (5-star)
Internationally famous British-owned hotel, one of the oldest in the island. Situated on a cliff to the west of the town overlooking the sea and harbour, the hotel has beautiful sub-tropical gardens with two swimming pools (one heated) and tennis courts. Access to beach and water-skiing facilities.

Savoy (5-star)
Luxurious hotel with old-style decor to west of town on Avenida do Infante. Most famous for its superb complex of sea-level swimming pools. Views of Bay of Funchal and access to beach and water-skiing facilities.

Madeira Palacio (5-star)
On the Estrada Monumental to the west of Funchal, this hotel faces west towards the pretty fishing village of Camara de Lobos. Its three restaurants offer local and international dishes. A heated swimming pool and tennis courts are further attractions, and the hotel offers a free bus service to Funchal.

Madeira Sheraton (5-star)
This newly-built luxury hotel stands on the west side of the Bay of Funchal, within ten minutes' walk of the town centre. Three swimming pools, artificial sandy beach and various sports facilities.

Casino Park (5-star)
Madeira's newest luxury hotel was designed by Oscar Niemeyer, architect of Brasilia. Near the casino, only 10 min walk from town. Superb facilities, panoramic view of harbour.

Vila Ramos (5-star)
Some height above the sea to the west of town (15 min walk or free transport). Attractions include the 'tipico' restaurant *O Tonel*.

Girassol (4-star)
Near the sea to the west of town (10 min by bus). Heated swimming pool and sun terrace.

Santa Isabel (4-star)
Also near the Savoy. All rooms have balconies, and there is a heated roof-top pool.

Santa Maria (3-star)
Visitors wishing to stay in Funchal itself will choose this hotel, situated on the shady Rua de João de Deus at the eastern entrance to the town. It has a roof-top swimming pool with good views of the town.

Penha de Franca (4-star Albergaria)
This charming small hotel, in an old *quinta* with attached bungalows (near the Savoy) has a sea-water pool. Bed and breakfast only.

Outside Funchal

Machico

Atlantis (5-star)
The tall white tower of this hotel dominates the tourist complex of Matur near the airport. Indoor and outdoor pools, wide range of entertainments. Good location for walks.

Dom Pedro (4-star)
Overlooking Bay of Machico to the east of the airport. Interesting if obtrusive design with panoramic restaurant, solarium, heated swimming pool and private beach. Water sports.

Ribeira Brava
Ribeira Brava (3-star)

Porto Moniz
Pensão Fernandes (2-star)

Porto Santo
Porto Santo (4-star)
Opened in 1979, this is the island's first hotel, situated on the beautiful 10 km beach. The hotel has 90 rooms and is within easy walking distance of the town.

Pensão Central (3-star)
Pensão Palmeira (1-star)

Apart-hotels
These offer self-catering as well as normal hotel facilities. Most *hotel apartamentos* are located in the new hotel development west of Funchal. Self-catering needs are supplied by local mini-markets.

Apartments and villas
Along the south coast east of Funchal a large number of apartments and villas are available for sale and to rent. Most apartments and villas can be rented for a week or more, and offer maid service.

Swimming is either in private pools or lido, and restaurants, shops and other services form an integral part of the complex.

Three of the larger developments to the east of Funchal are:

Atlas International Garajau
Matur Agua da Pena, Machico
Reis Magos Ponta d'Oliviera (Contracta)

FOOD AND DRINK
Madeira's prolific natural resources (fruit, vegetables, abundant fish) provide visitors with a cuisine which virtually excludes canned or processed food. To the visitor who is accustomed to the latter, the taste of the *espada* fish, served with sweet potato fritters, or chicken cooked Portuguese style with vegetables, wine and brandy is a revelation. For all its variety of ingredients, Madeiran cooking has a simplicity which appeals to the average visitor. Meat is not plentiful but served in many different forms.
Some typical local dishes:

Açorda Soup with egg, bread and spices
Caldo verde Potato soup with finely
  shredded cabbage
Sopa de tomate cebola Onion and tomato
  soup
Bifes de atum Tunny fish steaks
Bacalhau pudim Dried cod soufflé
Espetada Various meats cooked on laurel
  spit over charcoal
Carne de vinho e alho Pork in wine with
  garlic
Frango na pucara Chicken and ham
  casserole
Arroz de frango Chicken in white wine with
  garlic
Milho frito Fried maize sticks
Pudim Madeira Caramel flan with Madeira
  sauce
Pudim de laranja frio Orange pudding
Bolo de Mel Madeira cake made with
  honey, cinnamon, spices and nuts

Madeira wines are drunk chiefly as aperitifs or after dinner. The four main types are:

Sercial (pronounced sir-sheal) Driest of the wines, of light or golden colour. This is Madeira's most popular aperitif. Origin of grape: Rhineland.

Verdelho (Ver-day-lio) Slightly sweeter than *Sercial*, with a colour varying from gold to purple. Drunk as an aperitif or with soup course. Origin of grape: Iberia.

Boal (or bual) A medium sweet wine, both sweeter and darker than *verdelho*. Popular as dessert wine. Origin of grape: Iberia.

Malvasia (malmsey) The most famous of the Madeira wines. A sweet wine, popular as after-dinner drink. The grape was introduced from Crete in the 15th c., and the wine became particularly popular with the British.

Madeira wines may be sampled at various wine lodges in Funchal. The best-known is the Madeira Wine Association near the tourist office.

The main table wines drunk in Madeira come from Portugal, and are of good quality and reasonable price. Beer (*cerveja*) is made and bottled locally, but imported lagers and stout are available at most restaurants. An unusual local drink is *maracuja* (passion fruit juice).

English pubs In addition to the local bars there is now a new craze for the imitation British pub—particularly popular with the natives of that country. There is one in the Sheraton Hotel and another—the *Prince Albert*—near the Savoy.

Casino da Madeira Situated in the gardens of the Quinta Vigia at the west end of Funchal, Madeira's casino offers a wide range of evening entertainment.

Restaurants

All the big hotels have dining rooms with international menus. Most of the 5-star category offer a choice of main restaurant, grill room and coffee shop.

Popular restaurants in the island:

Funchal

International

Apolo	Av. de Almeida
Caravela	Av. do Mar 15
Casa Velha	Near Casino Park Hotel
Estrela do Mar	Largo do Corpo Santo
Funchal à Noite	Rua das Pretas
Gavinas	Near Lido (fish)
Romana	Largo do Corpo Santo

'Tipico' (regional)

A Seta	Livramento (north of town)
Boa Vista	São Gonçalo (east of town)
Espadarte	Estrada de Boa Nova 5
Doca dos Cavacos	2km west of Funchal at Ponta da Cruz (fish)

Arco de São Jorge	**Machico**
A Cabana (west of village)	*O Facho, Mercado Velho, O Pescador*
Camacha	**Matur** (Agua de Pena)
Relógio	*Matur, O Cacto*
Camara de Lobos	**Portu da Cruz**
Riba Mar	*Penha d'Agua*
Caniço	**Porto Moniz**
Galo, Girassol, Jardim do Sol, O Boierio	*Cachalote, Pensão Fernandes*
Faial	**Polso** and
Casa de Chá	**Encumeada** (pousada) have government-run restaurants

Hotel School The old British Country Club in Funchal, now the *Quinta Magnolia*, offers excellent 4-course lunches cooked and served by students at a reasonable price (not Sun). The elegant dining room looks out over beautiful gardens.

FOLK ART

The main crafts of Madeira are embroidery, tapestry and wickerwork. These crafts are still carried out by the people in their homes, as well as in the factories which have been created to meet the demands of the tourist and export markets (notably USA and Canada).

Wickerwork Basket-making came about from the need of the country people for some indoor occupation during the wet weather. The craft began in Camacha and other villages where the willows grew locally. Today Camacha is still the centre of the industry, producing about 80% of the total output. Visitors can watch baskets, furniture and other articles being made in the workshops in this attractive village.

Embroidery Introduced in the early 19th c. as an occupation for the peasant women, embroidery has now become one of the island's major industries with an export potential of £2m. yearly.

An English lady, Mrs Phelps (whose name is commemorated in one of the streets of the capital) was largely responsible for the promotion of embroidery in the island in the 1850s. Although much of the needlework is done by the village women in their homes, a number of embroidery factories have been opened. Here visitors may see the embroiderers at work and can if they desire place individual orders. Among the factories and showrooms in Funchal open to visitors are *Brazao & Freitas* Rua do Conselheiro 39 (west of Jardim de São Francisco) and *Teixeira* Rua do Aljube 13/15 (opposite cathedral).

Tapestry Another speciality of Madeira is hand-worked needlepoint, *petit point* and Gobelin wall-hangings, cushions, etc., which may also be seen in showrooms in Funchal.

UNUSUAL TRANSPORT

Although travelling on foot has always been the most successful way of coping with Madeira's difficult terrain, some special — and peculiar — methods of transport have evolved to cope with the steep, uneven gradients. Until recently a special example which could be hired by tourists on the Avenida do Mar in Funchal were the *carros de bois*, or bullock carts, specially designed to shift heavy loads over hilly ground. Small open carriages on runners, like sledges, were drawn at a walking pace by a pair of oxen led by a boy in front with the driver alongside prodding the animals. To assist progress the driver would occasionally grease the runners by slipping a roll of sacking filled with tallow beneath them.

In the age of the four-wheel drive these vehicles are now, sadly, redundant: so too the equally bizarre, but highly practical *rede*, or hammock. This method of transport, greatly favoured by well-to-do ladies for their city rounds or for trips into the country, involved a long pole with a suspended hammock carried by two bearers.

Carros de Vimes (or *carros do cesto*) Still in commission for the tourists are the famous toboggans used for the descent from Monte to Funchal. Originally used for carrying produce down to the coast from the heights above Funchal, they are now a great novelty for visitors. The basket or running car has a wide seat for two or three people and is mounted on runners, with ropes attached to the corners. Two men control the carriages by means of ropes, pushing off with their feet to start them on the descent. The downhill run is a great thrill, the men running alongside and shouting 'Afasta!' ('Out of the way!') as the toboggan hurtles down the steep Caminho do Monte.

LANGUAGE

The language spoken in Madeira is Portuguese. In most of the shops and hotels in Funchal the staff speak English and some French. Most taxi drivers speak a little English. In the country districts a few words of Portuguese are necessary when ordering meals, arranging accommodation etc. A knowledge of Portuguese numbers, times, days of the week and a few simple phrases will enable the visitor to make himself understood. The people are quick to understand signs and gestures, and enjoy communicating with visitors. They are very pleased to hear the stranger use a few words of Portuguese, such as 'Bom dia' (good morning) or 'Boa tarde' (good afternoon). The word for 'thank you' is a necessary courtesy: a man should say 'obrigado' and a woman 'obrigada'.

Other useful words for those travelling in the island are:

Achada small plain	*Paragem* bus stop
Boca gap	*Paúl* marsh
Cabo cape	*Pico* peak
Caminho, calçada road	*Ponta* point
Capela, Ermida chapel	*Praça, largo* square
Encumeada summit, pass	*Praia* beach
Igreja church	*Quinta* villa, farm
Jardim garden	*Ribeira, ribeiro* ravine, river
Levada aqueduct	*Rua* street
	Serra mountain range

POPULAR FESTIVALS

No visit to Madeira is complete without the spectacle of one of the island's colourful festivals.

One of the largest and most important is the two-day *festa* held at Monte on August 14–15 (Feast of the Assumption). Thousands of people from all over the island attend this event. Many of them camp out all night in the vicinity of the church, and at daybreak attend the first Mass. For two days there is a continual procession of people going through the church, and the whole village is *en fête* for the occasion. Electric lights are threaded between the trees; flags and garlands of greenery adorn the streets, and stalls selling a multitude of goods are set up. In the main square and side streets one can buy freshly-baked country bread, meat on sticks for cooking over charcoal braziers, fruit and cakes. At one side of the square local produce and livestock is auctioned for the benefit of charity, and there is usually a commotion when a pig or goat is sold and the purchaser tries to lead it away through the dense crowd of onlookers.

Other festivals are held at different times throughout the year in every town and village to honour the local patron saint. At all of them the village and church are beautifully decorated with greenery and flags, and a bandstand and street market are set up. The local people come out in their best clothes: the older folk in sober black and the young ones in the bright colours the Portuguese love. Everyone walks up and down greeting friends and neighbours. Fire crackers and rockets are let off, and the small bars are crowded.

Monte's famous toboggan ride

A feature of some of the festivals is the intricately-patterned floral path which is laid along the street leading to the church steps. This forms a route for the procession to the church in honour of the saint.

Main festivals and events:

Feb/Mar	**Carnival**	
	Throughout island	
Apr	**Funchal**	
	Flower show	
Jun 12	**Funchal**	
	Santo Antonio	
Jun 28	**Funchal**	
	Sao João	
Aug 14–15	**Monte**	
	Nossa Senhora do Monte	
	(Feast of the Assumption)	
Sep	**Porto Moniz**	
	Cattle Show	
Sep	**Funchal**	
	Wine festival	
Sep 7	**Calheta**	
	Nosso Senhora do Loreto	
Sep 9	**Machico**	
	Nosso Senhor das Milhagres	
New Year's	**Funchal**	
Eve	Firework display	

The main tourist attraction is the famous fireworks display which takes place on New Year's Eve in Funchal. On the stroke of midnight the whole town bursts into a great blaze of exploding lights, as thousands of fireworks are exploded about the bay. All ships in the harbour are dressed with lights to add to the shore illuminations, and they too let off fireworks and sound their sirens to welcome in another year.

FOLK DANCING

The inspiration for many of Madeira's folk dances lies in the daily work of these hardy people. One, the 'Heavy Dance' imitates the crushing of grapes with the feet—a practice still seen in some parts of the island. Another, the 'Carrier's Dance' imitates the jogging movement of the farmworkers carrying their heavy loads. Other dances are of Moorish origin, introduced by the slaves brought to Madeira from Africa by the early colonists.

The centre of the island's folk dancing is Camacha. Dancing groups from this village can usually be seen at one of the main hotels on most nights of the week.

SPORT AND RECREATION

Beaches and swimming pools

Madeira's only sandy beach is on the south side of the Ponta de São Lourenço. Porto Santo, however, has a fine beach, about 10 km long, on the south coast.

The other beaches in Madeira are shingle, but there are, alternatively, some excellent natural swimming pools in the rocks at some points on the coastline. Changing facilities are usually available at these and in villages with accessible beaches. In the hotels the pools are usually for hotel guests only, but some will admit visitors on payment of a small fee.

In *Funchal* there is one public swimming place (Socorro) on the east side of the town and an excellent Lido on the coast west of the capital. There are also swimming pools open to visitors in the Clube Turismo da Madeira, the Quinta Magnolia and the Clube Naval, all on the west side of the town. Outside Funchal three bathing places should be mentioned:

Santa Cruz The beach here has good facilities (summer only). These include changing rooms, children's enclosed pool and restaurant.

Machico has good bathing facilities at the west end of the beach which include changing cabins and ladders out into deep water. There is a refreshment kiosk and picnic area. Although the beach is pebbly at Machico there is a sand bar a few metres from the shore.

Porto Moniz Here a magnificent series of pools have been created out of the volcanic rocks which lie along the shore, and sea bathing can be enjoyed in perfect safety. Facilities at the pools include changing rooms, sunbathing area, restaurant and bar.

Sailing is one of Madeira's most popular recreations, centred on the harbour of Funchal. Arrangements for sailing may be made through the major hotels (Savoy, Sheraton, Reid's), also through *Amigos do Mar* (Marina, Avenida do Mar).

Fishing Madeira is famous for its ocean fishing, with tunny and swordfish as the most popular game. Boats equipped for fishing can be hired in Funchal (apply to Tourist Office for details) while in the coastal villages local fishermen can usually be found to take visitors out for fishing trips.

Amigos do Mar (see above) organise fishing excursions, including big game and shark fishing.

Water skiing and **wind surfing** are also available at Reid's Hotel, the Savoy and Sheraton and at the Hotel Dom Pedro, Machico.

Golf There is an attractive 9-hole golf course at Santo da Serra (see Gazetteer). Visitors are always welcome to play there on payment of a moderate green fee. Caddy service is available, and the club house has a restaurant and bar.

Tennis There are good hard courts at the Quinta Magnolia, Savoy, Sheraton and Reid's hotels in Funchal, and at Ponta d'Oliveira near Caniço.

WALKS

Walking is one of Madeira's greatest pleasures. For years visitors have enjoyed exploring the country on foot, and since Victorian times many authors have recorded their walks in diaries and journals.

The island is one of the few remaining holiday places where traffic does not spoil the pedestrian's outings. The paths and small local roads are too narrow and steep in most places to permit vehicles, and walkers can roam at leisure, stopping to admire the wonderful views or watch the country people at work. Most of the best walks are along tracks or beside levadas which reveal the beauties of the countryside at every turn.

Walkers are advised to carry a stick, and should always wear stout rubber or rope-soled shoes, as the paths are often very rough and can be slippery when wet. The more arduous walks in the interior should only be undertaken after the visitor has become accustomed to the extreme inclines, rough paths and often precipitous surroundings of the trails. These walks should never be made unaccompanied, and a competent guide is necessary for the routes to the highest peaks. The weather can change very rapidly at the higher altitudes, and when rain clouds close in one can become totally lost.

Recommended walks are from Camacha, Machico and Ribeiro Frio (see Gazetteer entries). More strenuous routes not recommended to elderly or novice walkers are to the Pico Ruivo and Paúl da Serra (see Gazetteer entries). See also *Guides*, below.

WEATHER

The conditions affecting Madeira's climate (see p. 114) make it one of the most pleasurable places to live in or to visit at any time of the year.

Average temperatures (near sea level) in Fahrenheit are:

Jan	Feb	Mar	Apr	May	Jun
61	61	61	62	65	67
Jul	Aug	Sep	Oct	Nov	Dec
71	71	71	70	67	62

Prevailing winds are from the north-east, and sea temperatures range from 17°C/64°F (Mar) to 22°C/72°F (Sep). Hours of sunshine are at their peak in July with an average of 7.5 hrs per day. There is however little variation in this at other times of year, and there are few days without sunny periods. Heaviest rainfall is in December, January and February, and in the summer months practically nil. Over the last 20 years the average rainfall for the period Apr–Sep has been only .2 inch.

An interesting feature of the weather in Madeira is that it varies greatly within very short distances, so that if it is a poor day in Funchal, it is usually fine and sunny a little way along the coast or inland. As it is never very hot, excursions are comfortable all the year round, and walking very pleasant even at the height of summer.

CURRENCY, BANKS AND SHOPS

The unit of currency in Madeira is the *escudo*, for which the dollar sign ($) is used. The escudo is divided into 100 *centavos*, and the dollar sign is placed between the escudos and centavos, thus: 1$50. There are banknotes for 20, 50, 100, 500 and 1000 escudos, and coins for values between 10 centavos and 25 escudos.

Foreign currency and travellers cheques can be changed at any bank or *cambio*. Banks are open 08.30–11.45 & 13.00–14.30 Mon-Fri; *cambios* 08.30–19.00 Mon-Fri, Sat 08.30–13.00.

There is an excellent range of shops in Funchal. In addition to modern department stores such as *Camachos* (near the cathedral) there are the smaller speciality shops where one can purchase embroidery, basketwork and other crafts. Two shops which have a selection of all these crafts under one roof are the *Casa do Turista* in the Rua do Conselheiro (west end of the Avenida do Mar) and *Jabara* in the Rua Fernão de Ornelas near the market. Both shops will arrange to send gifts by post.

GUIDE AND REFERENCE BOOKS

There is very little about Madeira in print, in the English language. One or two guides to Portugal contain a section on Madeira, but for background reading one has to resort to books now out of print, available in the larger libraries.

The following are recommended reading:

Madeira, Its Climate and Scenery by Yate Johnson (Dulau, 1885)

Madeira, Its Scenery and How to See It by E. Taylor (Stanford, 1889)

A Glimpse of Madeira by C. Miles (Garnett, 1949)

Madeira and the Canaries by Elizabeth Nicholas (Travel Book Club, 1953)

An excellent guide to walks and picnics in the island, *Landscapes of Madeira* by John and Pat Underwood, is available from all good bookshops and from A&C Black, PO Box 19, Huntingdon, Cambs PE19 3SF.

REGISTRATION

All visitors are required to register with the police within 48 hours of arrival in Madeira.

TOURIST INFORMATION

Information on all aspects of either visiting or residing in Madeira can be obtained from the Portuguese National Tourist Office, 1 New Bond St, London W1.

In Madeira the Tourist Information Office is at Avenida Arriaga 16/18, Funchal.

Exploring Madeira

A map of Madeira presents few obstacles. Its small size, however, is deceptive and the visitor arriving for the first time on this island massif will be astonished by the variety and complexity of its terrain.

The routes to its discovery are equally diverse. The most obvious are the roads, which follow the coast for a circular tour or cut corners through the mountain passes in the centre of the island. The method of transport depends on personal preferences and time available. Coaches, local buses or taxis provide good services to the more accessible parts, and hired cars are available for more independent spirits.

One does not have to search for the beauty of Madeira. Using a car one has only to follow the main roads to enjoy constant views of its dramatic coastline and interior. The winding and precipitous nature of the roads, however, makes it difficult to stop safely except at one of the *miradouros* or look-out points.

On road to Pico do Areeiro

The secondary roads, though often poorly surfaced, offer the most peaceful driving. On these one can wander quietly from village to village, to obtain a glimpse of the local life. All along the south coast west of Ribeira Brava, coastal villages can be reached by good secondary roads seldom used by visitors.

There can be few more dramatic routes than the one from the south coast up the central valley and the mountain pass at Encumeada to São Viçente, and west along the tall dark cliffs of the north coast to Porto Moniz. Another road, from Santa Cruz in the south to Faial in the north via Santo da Serra and Portela has gentler attractions and offers beautiful picnic places. On many stretches of coast in the south the old road runs nearer to the sea than the new highway or *estrada*. It is always worth exploring these old roads. They are usually built of stone blocks, and are quite safe for driving.

The organized coach trips from Funchal provide a good opportunity for visitors with limited time to see the main places of interest. A more thorough exploration requires a self-drive car, or the services of a congenial taxi driver. Taxi drivers naturally tend to take visitors to the well-known spots along the best roads, but if one can be found who speaks English it should be possible to agree a more adventurous itinerary to remoter areas. It is also much more restful than doing the driving oneself, in a strange country where the roads are narrow and winding.

A cheaper, if more time-consuming way of seeing the island is by local bus. The whole country is covered by an excellent bus system run by different companies which have the franchise to cover certain routes. Fares are low, and the service is punctual. Tickets can be booked in advance at the appropriate office for any long-distance trip. (See Bus Services, p. 119.)

Other—less obvious—ways of seeing Madeira are by boat or on foot. A boat trip offers a different aspect of the island. The extraordinary geological formation of the cliffs is best viewed from the sea, as are the impressive heights of the central mountains. (For details about arranging boat trips see Boat Services, p. 118.)

Undoubtedly the best way to explore Madeira is on foot. It is not necessary to be a sturdy hiker to do this, as there are plenty of walks on level ground, such as those which follow the levadas. All along the coast there are cliff paths and roads which lead the walker safely from one village to another, and walking down to Funchal from any point above the town, such as Monte or Camacha, is always perfectly safe. The more spectacular walks do, of course, require extra agility. One of the finest is the path from Pico do Areeiro to Pico Ruivo, the two highest points on the island.

A combination of driving and walking will provide the traveller with the best opportunities for exploration. Some suggested itineraries are given below. For Walks, see p. 125.

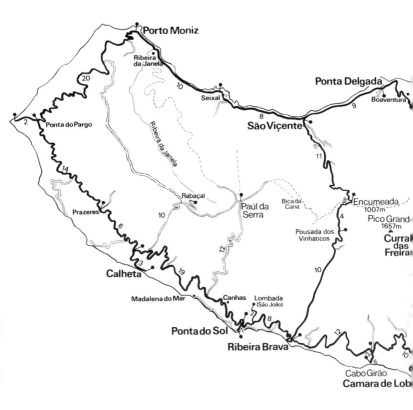

Porto Moniz

Ribeira
da Janela

20

10

Seixal

Ponta Delgada

Boaventura

8

São Viçente

9

2

Ponta do Pargo

11

14

Ribeira da Janela

Encumeada
1007m

Rabaçal

Bica da
Cana

Pico Grand
1657m

10

**Paúl da
Serra**

4

Prazeres

6

Pousada dos
Vinhaticos

**Curral
das
Freira**

3

12

10

19

Calheta

Madalena do Mar

Canhas

Lombada
(São João)

Ponta do Sol

8

12

10

Ribeira Brava

Cabo Girào

Camara de Lob

— Itinerary route
· · · · Levada walk
- - - Trails

Madeira

Pop.: 310,000
Capital: Funchal
Area: 741 sq km
Highest Point: Pico Ruivo (1862 m)
Other islands in Madeiran
archipelago:
Porto Santo, Desertas

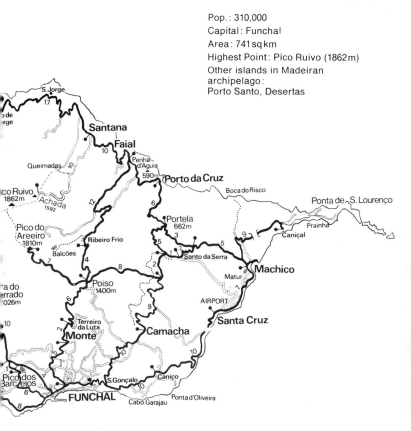

Itineraries (from Funchal)
1 *Funchal — Camara de Lobos —
Cabo Girão — Ribeira Brava — Ponta
do Sol — Calheta — Ponta do Pargo
— Porto Moniz — São Viçente —
Ribeira Brava — Funchal*
A full day should be allowed for this
route around the west coast of the
island returning to Funchal via
Encumeada. The drive is consistently
rewarding, offering a cross-section of
the island's extremely varied
landscape.
The terraced hills of the south, where
every piece of land is cultivated, give
way to the wilder, more forested

region of the west. After Porto Moniz on the north coast the nature of the route changes dramatically as the road winds around the base of the stark cliffs, softened here and there with white waterfalls. At São Vicente the road turns inland and enters the beautiful valley leading up to the Encumeada Pass, a vantage point from which one can see both the north and south coast of the island. From here the road descends to Ribeira Brava to rejoin the coastal road to Funchal.

This route, which includes the attractive fishing villages of Camara de Lobos and Porto Moniz and the spectacular cliff of the Cabo Girão, demands a leisured approach, as the road from Punta do Sol to São Viçente (84km) is very slow, following the indentations of the numerous valleys on the south and west. Ideally a night should be spent at Porto Moniz so that one can enjoy even more fully this superb drive.

2 *Funchal — Ribeira Brava — Encumeada — São Viçente — (Porto Moniz — return to São Viçente) — Ponta Delgada — Santana — Faial — Poiso (Pico do Areeiro) — Monte — Funchal* (full day)
This route covers the central 'square' of the island with an optional diversion to Porto Moniz for those who are not approaching it by Route 1. In the coastline route to Faial with its great basalt cliffs and promontories of black lava, one can appreciate the truly volcanic nature of the island. The return drive to Funchal via Poiso offers splendid views of the mountainous hinterland, particularly above the tree-line on the diversionary route to Pico do Areeiro.

3 *Funchal—Monte—Poiso—Pico do Areeiro—Camacha—São Gonçalo—Funchal* (half day)
This short excursion, concentrated on the mountainous centre of the island, reaches its climax at the Pico do Areeiro with magnificent views of the island's major peaks. The return journey is via the village of Camacha, with its flourishing wickerwork industry.

4 *Funchal—São Gonçalo—Camacha —Santo da Serra—Portela—Porto da Cruz—Faial—Poiso (Pico do Areeiro) —Monte—Funchal* (half day)
This is an extension of Route 3 to the east and north, bringing in the attractive countryside around Santo da Serra and Portela and touching the coastline at Porto da Cruz.

5 *Funchal—São Gonçalo—Camacha —Santo da Serra—Caniçal—Machico —Santa Cruz—Funchal* (half day)

The eastern part of the island is covered by this route. The approach is inland via Camacha and Santo da Serra, continuing via the route to the north of Machico to the Ponta de São Lourenço. The return route follows the attractive coastal road from Machico via Santa Cruz. Stops should be made to explore both villages.

For itineraries in the environs of Funchal, see **Funchal** (Gazetteer).

View from Pico do Areeiro with plateau of Paúl da Serra in distance

Arco de São Jorge Village on north coast 17 km west of Santana.

The houses of this village are scattered over a wide area. It was in this region that a great landslip occurred in 1689, when—according to an eyewitness—the slide was so gradual that houses were carried along on it without being destroyed.

Areeiro, Pico do (1810 m) Second highest peak on Madeira. This is the most accessible of the peaks, with a motor road to the summit. The views from here are magnificent, and provide the best understanding of the island's volcanic formation.

On a clear day one can distinguish to the east the *Curral das Freiras* crater and the distant plateau of the *Paúl da Serra*. Immediately to the north are the *Torrinhas* peaks and the *Pico do Torres*. The latter peak masks the island's highest mountain, the *Pico Ruivo*. If conditions are good one can also pick out such features of the coastline as the *Penha d'Aguia* and the *Ponta de São Lourenço*.

One of the most dramatic walks in the island commences at this viewpoint. This is to the summit of the *Pico Ruivo*. It is well signposted and takes 6 hrs for the return trip.

To reach Areeiro from Funchal, take the route to Monte (Rua 31 de Janeiro, Rua do Til) and then to Poiso. From here, turn left for Areeiro. (Total distance 20 km.) There are no buses to Areeiro, but those with time and energy can take the Ribeiro Frio bus from Funchal as far as Poiso and then walk from there to the peak, a distance of 7 km.

In view of the unpredictable weather conditions at the higher altitudes there can be no guarantee of perfect visibility at the peak. However, the traveller should not be deterred by mist during the climb as this is usually confined to lower levels.

Barcelos, Pico dos (355 m) Viewpoint 6 km west of Funchal which offers superb views of the south coast and the mountains to the north.

Leaving Funchal by the Avenida do Infante, turn right after crossing the bridge. After 5 km the *Miradouro do Pico dos Barcelos* is reached. From here one can enjoy a panorama of the distant Funchal, set in its bay, and the surrounding villages, scattered over the green slopes.

The road continues a further 11 km to the spectacle of the *Curral das Freiras*

In the middle of the village is a large level area, which used to be referred to as 'the common' by English visitors. Now a park, it is the site of the field where football was first played in Portugal. The event is commemorated by a stone plaque.

The main folk dance group in Madeira comes from Camacha, and has toured all over the world.

The climate of Camacha (alt. 700 m) is drier than Monte or Santo da Serra, and several families from Funchal have country houses here, where they spend their summer vacations. It is a good centre for walking, the surrounding country offering fine scenery and many beautiful paths. There is a frequent bus service from Funchal.

There is a fine **levada walk** along the Levada da Serra from Camacha to Santo da Serra. (Buses return from the village to Funchal: times should be checked before departure.) Start behind the church in Camacha, where the main road forks right to the north. Climb the cobbled road to the right of the Quinta das Almas, to reach the levada in 15 min. At the outset the walk affords splendid views of the south coast and the Desertas Islands, as well as the beautiful valley of the Porto Novo River. The walk takes approx. $4\frac{1}{2}$ hrs: during the last hour the panorama changes to views over Ponta de São Lourenço and the north coast. The walk is well signed and at an easy level.

Cabo Girão (550 m) High cliff 20 km west of Funchal.

The world's second highest sea cliff, and the point where Zarco is said to have turned back on his first voyage of discovery (the name means 'Cape Turn Again').

The cliff is reached by turning off the main road at Quinta Grande. The views from the look-out are magnificent. To the east is the Bay of Funchal, to the west the Ponta do Sol. Inland the deep gorges with their closely-stepped terraces penetrate the flanks of the central range.

Calheta Village and port on south coast 60 km west of Funchal.

Calheta was one of the original *concelhos* (districts) into which the island was divided by the early settlers, and dates from 1511. The village, which lies at the centre of one of Madeira's principal grape growing areas, is best visited in September when the grapes are being harvested. The *church* (rebuilt in 1639) has a fine *ceiling* in the Mudejar style, like that in the cathedral of Funchal. It also possesses some fine sacred treasures, including a *tabernacle* of ebony and silver, given by King Manuel I.

Camacha Village 10 km north-east of Funchal, reached by good road from São Gonçalo.

This is the centre of the island's wickerwork industry. The osiers which provide the raw material for this craft are gathered locally, and there are several factories in the neighbourhood producing a well-designed range of wicker goods. Visitors are welcome to see the work in progress and to place orders.

Camara de Lobos Fishing village 8 km west of Funchal.

The name of this much-celebrated village means 'Seals' Chamber' and describes the little cove in which Zarco and his companions disturbed a number of seals during their first journey of exploration.

The picturesque bay, fisherman's quarter and brightly-painted boats have made Camara de Lobos one of the best-known places in Madeira. To add to its fame it was painted by Winston Churchill during his visits to the island in 1949 and 1950.

Caniçal Most easterly village in the island, 36 km from Funchal. (Buses from Funchal nine times daily.)

The village, situated at the neck of Madeira's barren eastern peninsula, is very poor. Fishing is the main industry, and there is a factory where whale oil and meat are processed. Both sperm and finback whales are caught locally.

Caniçal's main interest to the visitor is as a starting point for an exploration of the peninsula (see **Ponta de São Lourenço**).

Caniço Village 10 km east of Funchal.

The main part of the village lies to the south of the road, and is dominated by the *church* built here (1780) at the behest of Dona Amelia

Above: Cabo Girão Right: Camara de Lobos

I. The principal crop grown in the area is onions, many thousands of tons being exported annually.

Curral das Freiras

Village 19km northwest of Funchal, in extraordinary site on floor of extinct crater. Reached by winding mountain road which terminates at village. (Leave Funchal by Rua das Maravilhas and Caminho de Santo Antonio.) Buses four times daily from Funchal.

The name of this village means 'Nuns' Shelter' referring to an incident in 1566 when the sisters of the convent of Santa Clara took refuge here during the raid of the French pirates.

The crater in which the village lies is surrounded by peaks reaching up to 1500 m. The best viewpoint is from the *Eira do Serrado* (1026 m) just before the road descends to the village.

For many years the only way down to the village was by a steep track with over 30 hairpin bends, but now there is a good road. From the terrace of the church one can view many of the highest peaks of Madeira, including the Pico Ruivo and Pico do Areeiro to the east and the Pico Grande to the west.

Desertas

Group of three uninhabited islands (*Deserta Grande*, *Bugio* and *Chão*) 12 miles south-east of Madeira.

Soundings have shown that the Desertas are part of a mountain ridge, extending from the São Lourenço peninsula, connecting them to Madeira. The largest island, *Deserta Grande* (14.5 × 2.5km) reaches a height of 488 m.

Until 1972 the islands were privately owned, but they now belong to the Portuguese Government. Permission to land on them must be obtained from the authorities in Funchal. At one time they were inhabited by herdsmen who looked after the sheep and cattle kept there, and visited by hunters in pursuit of rabbits, wild goats and seals. Today their only inhabitants are sea birds and wild animals.

A boat trip to the islands can be made in the summer, but landing is only possible in calm weather. The climb from the rocky shore to the high ground is extremely steep and should only be attempted by the agile. It is probably better to settle for a boat trip around the islands, which makes a pleasant excursion. (Apply for details at Tourist Office.)

On the east side of the islands there are caves in which seals can sometimes be seen. Recently, however, their numbers have been much reduced by fishermen, who see them as a threat to the fishing stock in these waters.

Encumeada

(Encumeada de São Vicente) Pass at alt. 1007 m on main road from Ribeira Brava (14km) to São Vicente (11km).

The pass commands some of the most beautiful scenery in the island, and there is a fine *Miradouro* (look-out) from which visitors can enjoy the views. 4km to the south of the pass is the *Pousada dos Vinhaticos*, a Government hotel built in 1941 and recently renovated. It is a convenient place to stay for a few days, providing an excellent centre for some of the most exciting walks on the island. There is a good restaurant, open to non-residents.

For trails to *Pico Ruivo* and *Paúl da Serra*, see Gazetteer entries.

Funchal (pop. 180,000) capital of Madeira and seat of government.

Situated on the south coast, at the foot of steeply-rising hills, Funchal is the only large town in the island. The site of the first settlement, founded in 1420, was at the mouth of three rivers, whose dry beds cut through the modern town. The town has since spread along the coast to the west, with the addition of the many new hotels that have opened in the past ten years. To the east is the prominence guarded by the Forte São Tiago, to the north the steep hills rise to the mist-shrouded heights of Monte.

Beneath its tranquil atmosphere, Funchal is a busy place. Its population is more than half that of the whole island. As a commercial centre Funchal can look back to the original source of its wealth as the sugar industry that was started here in the 15th c. (commemorated by the four sugar loaves in the town's coat-of-arms). Now its trade is based on the export of wine and the many other varied products of the rich soil, as well as manufactured articles such as wickerwork and embroidery for which there is a world demand. It is also the focal point for the many thousands of tourists who come to Madeira every year, arriving either by the cruise ships or via the airport at Santa Cruz.

It is an extremely attractive town, with buildings on a human scale. The most imposing buildings, which would be lost in any modern European city, are here the dominant features: the Cathedral in the old town, the Governor's Palace on the seafront. The houses, too, can be enjoyed as individuals, particularly the orange-roofed, white-painted dwellings scattered on the green slopes above the town.

With the exception of the wide Avenida Arriaga and its tributaries in the lower part of the town, the streets of Funchal are mostly narrow and cobbled, and to climb them is both an exercise and a pleasure. The old balconied houses which line them belong to a more elegant and mannered age, of which one may have a more intimate glimpse through an open door or gateway. A cool interior, a flower-filled courtyard, give Madeira's capital an extra dimension that makes its exploration one of the real delights of a visit to the island.

It is a town in which the old blends happily with the new. The modern shops and offices, cheek by jowl with buildings of earlier centuries, are not incongruous, and the traditional products compete happily with the factory-made novelties. While the milkman carries his cans on a yoke across his shoulders the supermarkets make the same offering in plastic cartons.

Shops which specialize in Madeiran products are numerous. The best showrooms are at the Casa do Turista at the west end of the town near the seafront. Here one can find all the local products, as well as many items from the mainland of Portugal. Each room is devoted to a special craft, ranging from embroidery to wickerwork. Visitors interested in wine can sample the different varieties in special Madeiran glasses. (They can similarly indulge themselves in the town's numerous wine lodges.)

Another place worth visiting is the market, housed in a large building on the east side of the town. This is particularly lively on a Saturday morning and a visit here provides a good opportunity to study a congregation of the Madeiran 'types' — the women in their shawls and calf-skin boots, the men in their woollen caps and homespun trousers, energetically selling their wares.

The town's museums are varied and interesting, and range from the Sacred Art Museum with its fine Flemish collection to the Photographic Museum with its fascinating record of the Madeira of yesteryear.

The parks and gardens of Funchal are a great attraction for botanists and gardeners. The finest are the public gardens on the Avenida Arriaga (Jardim de São Francisco), the Park of Santa Caterina, the grounds of the Quinta das Cruzes, with its botanical garden and orchid house, the gardens of the Quinta Magnolia (formerly British Country Club), and the Jardim Botanico north-east of the town (bus from the Avenida do Mar).

Walking tour (see map)
Harbour — Governor's Palace — Sé (Cathedral) — Praça do Municipio — Museum of Sacred Art — Municipal Museum — Convent of Santa Clara — Quinta das Cruzes Museum — Parque Santa Caterina — Casa Turista — Avenida do Mar

Harbour The tour commences at the end of the *Cais*, the jetty opposite the end of the *Avenida Zarco*. To the south may be seen the great arm of the *Potinha*, the mole where the cruise ships dock. On a little island connected to the harbour by the mole stands a 19th c. fort. The point at the end of the mole offers a splendid panorama of Funchal. Running along the seafront is the wide *Avenida do Mar*. On the north side, to the west of the Avenida Zarco, is the impressive **Governor's Palace**. This was originally the fortress of São Lourenço (16th c.), the first fortification to be built by the Portuguese in Madeira. Reconstructed several times, the building now bears little resemblance to the original, although there is a memento in the arms of King Manuel on the south-east side. The building is now the residence of the Regional Governor.

The Avenida Zarco leads to the main shopping street, the *Avenida Arriaga*. At the crossroads is a statue of the first explorer of Madeira, *João Gonçalves Zarco*, by the modern sculptor Francisco Franco. To the west at No. 16/18 is the *Tourist Information Office* (09.00–19.00, Sun 09.00–11.00) and further on the *Madeira Wine Company*, where visitors are welcome to view the cellars and sample the different types of Madeira wine. To the east the street ends in the cathedral square. (On the north side stand the offices of the *Governo Regional*.)

Sé (Cathedral) Built between 1485–1514, during the reign of King Manuel I of Portugal, the cathedral reflects the 'Manueline' style current in the Portuguese architecture of the period. Its plainness is a little daunting, but the details are interesting. (Note particularly the use of local stone—the dark basalt and red tufa—in the exterior.)

The bell tower is square and has a short spire covered with glazed tiles. It contains four bells. As one may gather from the account of a Portuguese writer in 1590, it has lost some of its earlier magnificence:

'It has a lofty and beautiful spire, covered with Dutch tiles, which when the sun shines upon them appear as of silver and gold; in which is a large bell of magnificent tone, which may be heard two leagues away, and lower down the tower are two windows, in which are fifteen bells.'

The fifteen bells, destroyed in the French raid of 1566, were replaced by the present bells in 1814.

Interior The cathedral is in the plan of a Latin cross with a nave and two aisles. It has a fine *ceiling* of cedar wood inlaid with ivory, in the Moorish style. This belongs to the original building: of later date are the *choir* (17th c.) and the richly-decorated *Sacramento Chapel* (18th c.) to the right of the choir. Above the altar are 16th c. Flemish paintings.

(To the south of the cathedral square the Rua A.J. Almeida leads back to the harbour and the old *Customs House* (Alfandega), an 18th c. reconstruction of a 15th c. building. The original Manueline doorway, Mudejar roof and gargoyles survive. The building now houses Madeira's Parliament.)

Bay of Funchal viewed from the west
Above: Cathedral

135

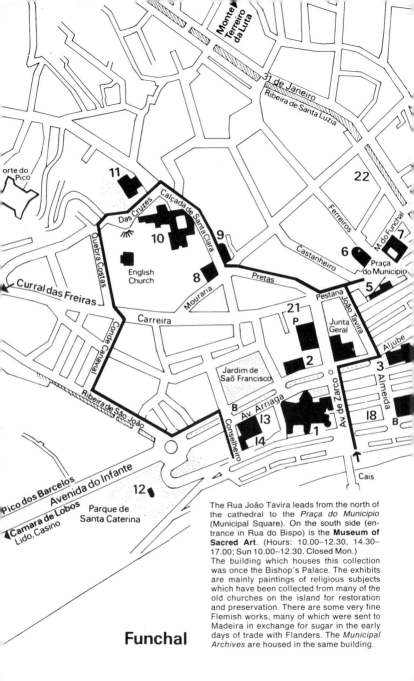

Monte
Terreiro
da Luta

31 de Janeiro
Ribeira de Santa Luzia

orte do
Pico

11

22

Calçada de Santa Clara

Das Cruzes

10

9

Ferreiros

M do Funchal

7

6

Praça
do Municipio

Castanheiro

5

Quebra Costas

English
Church

8

Mouraria

Pretas

Pestana

João Tavira

Aljube

Curral das Freiras

Conde Carvaral

Carreira

21

P

Junta
Geral

3

Almeida

B

Jardim de
Saõ Francisco

2

B

Ribeira de São João

Av. Arriaga

13

1

18

Conselheiro

14

Av. de Zarco

Cais

Pico dos Barcelos

Avenida do Infante

Camara de Lobos
Lido, Casino

Parque de
Santa Caterina

12

The Rua João Tavira leads from the north of
the cathedral to the *Praça do Municipio*
(Municipal Square). On the south side (entrance in Rua do Bispo) is the **Museum of
Sacred Art**. (Hours: 10.00–12.30, 14.30–
17.00; Sun 10.00–12.30. Closed Mon.)
The building which houses this collection
was once the Bishop's Palace. The exhibits
are mainly paintings of religious subjects
which have been collected from many of the
old churches on the island for restoration
and preservation. There are some very fine
Flemish works, many of which were sent to
Madeira in exchange for sugar in the early
days of trade with Flanders. The *Municipal
Archives* are housed in the same building.

Funchal

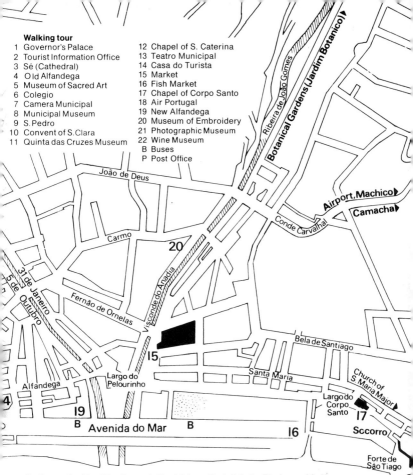

Walking tour
1 Governor's Palace
2 Tourist Information Office
3 Sé (Cathedral)
4 Old Alfandega
5 Museum of Sacred Art
6 Colegio
7 Camera Municipal
8 Municipal Museum
9 S.Pedro
10 Convent of S.Clara
11 Quinta das Cruzes Museum
12 Chapel of S. Caterina
13 Teatro Municipal
14 Casa do Turista
15 Market
16 Fish Market
17 Chapel of Corpo Santo
18 Air Portugal
19 New Alfandega
20 Museum of Embroidery
21 Photographic Museum
22 Wine Museum
B Buses
P Post Office

On the north side of the Praça do Municipio is the 17th c. *Colegio* (Collegiate Church). This has a fine Baroque interior, in which the *azulejos* (Portuguese decorative tiles) are a striking feature. On the east side is the 18th c. *Camara Municipal* (Town Hall), with an attractive courtyard and small museum.

To the right of the Colegio, halfway up the Rua dos Ferreiros, is the *Wine Lodge of João Pereira d'Oliviera*, where one may sample a glass of Madeira. (Those interested in the history of Madeira's wine industry can continue eastwards to the Rua 5 de Outubro, to the **Museum of Wine**, open 09.30–12.00, 14.30–17.00 weekdays only.)

The Rua C. Pestana leads west from the Praça do Municipio. Beyond the junction with the Avenida de Zarco (Rua Carreira) on the left, is the **Photographic Museum**, open 14.00–18.00 weekdays only. North of the junction, the Rua das Pretas leads up to the Rua da Mouraria. At No. 35 is the **Municipal Museum**. (Hours: 10.00–12.00, Sat & Sun 12.00–18.00. Closed Mon.) The collection (2nd floor) is devoted to natural history. On the 1st floor is the *Municipal Library*, and in a small but delightful *aquarium* on the ground floor one can see something of Madeira's marine life. A good time to visit the aquarium is 3pm (feeding time).

Opposite the museum, on the other side of the Calçada de Santa Clara, is the church of *São Pedro*, with an attractive tiled spire.

Ascending the steep Calçada do Santo Clara one reaches the convent of **Santa Clara**. This was founded in the late 15th c. by the two granddaughters of João Zarco.

137

It stands on the site of a church founded by the navigator as a burial place for himself and his family. The present *church*, built in the 17th c., contains Zarco's tomb, to the right of the entrance. The convent belongs to the Franciscan order and the nuns run a children's home here.

Quinta das Cruzes Museum Just above the convent of Santa Clara in the Calçada do Pico, this museum is housed in a 19th c. mansion which stands on the site of a house where Zarco once lived. (Hours: 10.00–12.30, 14.00–18.00. Closed Mon.)

The ground floor—originally kitchens and store-rooms—contains 16th c. Portuguese furniture, as well *objets d'art* from other parts of the world. On the first floor is a collection of English, French and Spanish furniture.

The house is surrounded by beautiful *gardens*. Scattered about them are a number of carved stone ornaments, doorways, windows and crests, which have been collected from old buildings demolished in Funchal and Santa Cruz. Many of these date back to the 15th c. There is a fine orchid house, and many interesting plants and trees from all over the world.

On the street to the south of the museum (Rua das Cruzes) is a *belvedere* offering a fine panorama of Funchal and the bay. An interesting detail immediately below is the dome of the *English Church* (1822). This recalls an edict of the Portuguese authorities that no non-Catholic church should be permitted a spire or bell-tower.

Turning left down the cobbled Rua de Quebra Costas one passes (at the bottom on the left) the gate to the English Church. Crossing the Rua da Carreira, one continues (first right) down the Rua de Conde Canavial. This joins the Rua da Ribeira de São João, from whence one continues south to the roundabout (Praça do Infante).

Parque de Santa Caterina Situated between the Avenida do Infante and the sea, this park contains the tiny chapel of *Santa Caterina* built in 1425 by Zarco (closed to public).

Continuing eastwards, one reaches the Rua do Conselheiro. To the north is the *Jardim de São Francisco*, the municipal garden: to the south the *Teatro Municipal*. This charming little opera house and theatre was founded at the end of the last century.

At the foot of the Rua do Conselheiro, below the Avenida do Mar, is the *Casa do Turista* (Hours: 09.30–19.00, Sat 09.30–13.00; closed Sun) where one can choose from a wide range of local crafts.

Other places of interest in Funchal

Instituto do Bordado, Tapeçarias e Artesanato da Madeira
Corner of Rua do Carmo and Rua do Visconte do Anadia. This museum of embroidery, tapestry and crafts is well worth a visit.

Market (Mercado dos Lavradores) The 'farmers' market is situated on the east side of the town by the Ribeira de João Gomes.

The market is housed in a building of two stories with a central courtyard. Around this courtyard are fruit and vegetable stalls, and in the centre the flower sellers, dressed in traditional costumes, display their blooms. Butchers and poultry dealers also have stalls.

On the second storey are more fruit and vegetable sellers, and a section where small livestock such as chickens, rabbits and pigeons are sold. In a separate hall, beside the main building, is the great fish market, where the local catch is laid out on huge slabs. Here is arrayed the harvest of Madeira's seas: the tunny fish, the wicked-looking swordfish, the brilliant red mullet. There is a continual hubbub as the fish sellers shout their wares, trying to catch the attention of a prospective customer, or yell for a boy to take the fish away to be filleted. The best time to visit the market is in the mornings—preferably a Saturday morning when there is most activity.

Fishermen's Quarter and Socorro

Between the market and the seafront lies the *Fishermen's Quarter.* Here is a view of the old Funchal—a 'village' of workshops, narrow cobbled streets, old stone arches framing glimpses of shady courtyards. At the east end of the Avenida do Mar is the wholesale *Fish Market.* This is situated by the beach where the catch is landed, and with a bit of luck one will see the fishing boats come ashore with their harvest.

Beyond the fish market a narrow street leads up to the Largo do Corpo Santo in the *Socorro* quarter. In the square is the chapel of *Corpo Santo*, the fishermen's and sailors' chapel. Further on is the *Forte de São Tiago*, the eastern fortification of the old town. This building has been largely reconstructed, but the turrets are those of the original 17th c. stronghold.

The Rua de Santa Maria leads eastwards to the Largo Socorro. The church of *Santa Maria Major*, with its onion-shaped dome, stands on the north side. This church contains a shrine to St James the Less, who is credited with the dispersal of two plagues from Madeira during the 16th c., and who is honoured at special celebrations in the church on May 1 each year.

Opposite the church, steps lead down to the public beach (*Praia de Barreirinha*) which has enclosed pools for children.

Botanical Gardens (Jardim Botanico) In the north-east of the town, reached by bus from the Avenida do Mar (Hours 09.00–18.00. Closed Sun.)

Quinta da Boa Vista In the same part of the town, this orchid farm has perhaps the finest collection of varieties in the island. (Hours: 10.00–12.30, 14.30–17.00 weekdays.)

Short excursions from Funchal

North

Quinta do Palheiro Ferreiro 10km from Funchal, off Camacha road (best reached by taxi). 30-acre flower garden of the Blandy estate. (Hours: 09.30–12.30 weekdays.)

Monte (see Gazetteer entry) 5km.

Terreiro da Luta (Gazetteer entry) 7km.

West

Camara de Lobos (Gazetteer entry) 8km.

Pico dos Barcelos (Gazetteer entry) 6km.

Hotels and restaurants

Most of the major hotels and apartments are on the west side of the town, the smaller hotels and pensions (*pensões*) in the centre. (See Accommodation, p. 120.)

There is a good variety of restaurants in Funchal, both in the town and its environs. The choice ranges from the small 'typical' restaurants which have geared themselves to the tourist trade without losing their identity, to the restaurants in the large hotels offering international cuisine. (See Restaurants, p. 122.)

Beaches and swimming pools

The only beaches in Funchal are the private ones belonging to the hotels to the west of the town and the *Praia do Barreirinha* to the east. The larger hotels such as the *Savoy* have their own swimming pools. By the sea 2km to the west of the town is the public *Lido.*

Bus services and local excursions

Most of the island's major towns and villages are covered by bus routes from Funchal. The terminals are located on the *Avenida do Mar* (see map and p.119). Local excursions by coach are available from agents in Funchal. Most will arrange to collect passengers from their hotel (see p. 120).

Garajau (Cabo Garajau) High cliff east of Funchal, reached by turning off main road (7km) and taking side road (2km).

The cape was so named by Zarco on account of the number of terns which he saw there on his first trip along the coast from Machico. It has also been called 'Brazen Head', and before there was a Protestant burial ground on the island it was the point from which bodies of non-Catholics were thrown into the sea for burial. There is now a large figure of Christ on the headland.

The name *Garajau* now identifies a new residential and tourist development behind the headland.

Janela see Ribeira da Janela

Machico Village on south-east coast 27 km east of Funchal.

This village has important historical associations. It was here that Zarco first landed when he reached Madeira in 1419, and if the legend is fact, is the site of the graves of the ill-fated Robert Machim and his bride. Machim (whose name might suggest an origin for the name of the village) was supposed to have been shipwrecked here in the mid-14th c., before the arrival of the Portuguese.

Machico was the Captaincy of Tristão Vaz Teixeira, who was appointed to rule the eastern part of the island while Zarco took over the west. For many years it was a flourishing place, but its prosperity declined as that of Funchal grew. Today it is a modest but attractive village situated in a wide fertile valley. The river (*Ribeira de Machico*) divides the old and new parts of the town.

In the old town, in the Praça Municipio, stands the **parish church**, built in the Manueline style (1499). The King of Portugal (Manuel I) was its benefactor and inside the church one can see his special gift, the statue of the *Virgin* over the high altar. (The side *doorway*, with its white marble columns, was also his gift.) On the altar of the chapel on the left is a painting of *Christ and the Apostles* (School of Van Dyck). An interesting detail, found in many of the old Madeiran churches, is the gallery reserved for the gentry on the south side of the church.

On the eastern side of the bridge stands the little *Chapel of the Miracles* (Capela dos Milhagres). This was one of Madeira's oldest buildings (constructed by Teixeira in 1420) though all that remains of the original is the Gothic portal. Reputedly, Teixeira sited the building on the last resting place of Robert Machim and his bride.

To the east lies Machico's fishermen's quarter, the *Banda d'Alem*. Beyond it, on the headland, stands a small *fort*. Near here was the historic landing place of Zarco.

To the west, on the other side of the bay, lies the chapel of São Roque, also founded by Teixeira and rebuilt in 1739. The ceramic tiles (*azulejos*) on either side of the presbytery are particularly fine.

The best view of Machico and the bay is from the *Miradouro* to the west, reached by a side road 1km from the village (near the *Atlantis*). An alternative view from the east is from the *Pico do Facho* (5km, turn right before Caniçal tunnel).

Walk A strongly recommended walk from Machico is up the Ribeira Seca to the northern coast (*Boca do Risco*). There is no road along this coast so the walker has the unique advantage of seeing a part of the island missed by the motorists.

To reach the start of the walk, take the road out of Machico to the north. From the junction of the road to Caniçal measure 2.4km, at which point a cobbled road leads off to the left. If going by bus, ask for 'Ribeira Seca'. At the end of the cobbled road, the walk commences.

The route follows the valley of the *Ribeira Seca*, which despite its name is a fertile valley lined with farm-houses. Further on there is a forest—pine and mimosa—and a gentle uphill climb to the sea-cliffs at *Boca do Risco*. From here the view extends to the *Ponta de São Lourenço* in the east and *Porto da Cruz* in the west. (One can continue the walk along the cliff-face to Porto da Cruz if desired, or cross-country to Caniçal.)

Matur Large tourist development at Agua da Pena, to the north of the airport.

Here, by the main road on a hillside overlooking the sea, is a holiday complex consisting of a hotel (the 5-star *Atlantis*), villas and apartments, and an Olympic-size swimming pool. Future development has been inhibited by proposals for the enlargement of the airport.

Monte Village 5km north of Funchal. Leave Funchal by Rua 31 de Janeiro, turn right at Rua do Til. Buses from Avenida do Mar.

Set on the heights above Funchal, Monte is the most popular short excursion for visitors to the capital—particularly for those who stop off for a few hours on the cruise ships. Once the fashionable resort for European visitors, it has now relapsed into its pre-19th c. calm, hardly stirred by the comings and goings of the tourists.

Arriving in the shady square at the summit of the climb from Funchal, the visitor will immediately fall under the spell of this remote, cloud-covered retreat. Following a pathway through the adjacent park he will reach the broad flight of steps leading up to the church of **Nossa Senhora do Monte**.

For generations this church has been a landmark for sailors arriving at Madeira. Founded in 1470, it was rebuilt in the 18th c. On the high altar is a jewelled image of *Our Lady of the Mountain*, the patron saint of Madeira. This is credited with miraculous powers and is the object of the veneration of thousands of pilgrims on August 15 (Feast of the Assumption). The church also contains the tomb (in chapel on left of nave) of the last Emperor of Austria, Charles IV, who died here in 1922. (The exiled Emperor had brought his family to Madeira the previous year, to live at the Quinta do Monte).

In the village itself the *gardens* are very fine. Below the main square is a park full of flowers and great ferns, which flourish in the damp atmosphere. There is a restaurant in the square, and walks in all directions offer wonderful views.

Monte's most famous attraction is the **toboggan ride** down to Funchal. This starts at the bottom of the church steps, where relays of doughty Madeirans—two to each toboggan —guide their charges down the steep cobbled streets to the capital. Before motor vehicles arrived on the island this novel form of transport was used for centuries by the Madeirans as the most practical means of bringing heavy loads down from the higher levels.

The run extends above Monte to the village of Terreiro da Luta, although toboggan rides are confined to the Monte-Funchal descent. The visitor who prefers a more leisurely return trip to the capital can follow the route of the toboggan downhill.

Paúl da Serra (Marsh of the Mountain) Plateau in western half of the island, approx. 5km long and 3km wide.

Madeira's moorland has the remote aura of the Scottish Highlands. It is accessible by car from the north and south coasts, and there are paths from Rabaçal and Encumeada (see below) which in fine weather provide good walking. (Remember the mists come down very quickly here.)

Approaches to the Paúl da Serra

By road There are routes to the Paúl from Ponta do Sol and by the old cobbled road west of Canhas. The 12km journey by the latter, though steep, is one of the most beautiful drives in the island, with splendid views of the furrowed southern coastline. At the top the road crosses the plateau of the Campo Grande to the Paúl da Serra crossroads. From here a scenic route continues west above the valley of the Ribeira da Janela to Santa.

On foot The nearest point of access to the plateau is by a trail from *Encumeada* on the road from São Vicente to Ribeira Brava. This trail, which offers spectacular views, leads up to the *Bica da Cana* at the east end of the plateau. From this point it is possible to walk across the plateau in a westerly direction and go down to *Rabaçal*, or on to *Janela* on the north coast.

Pico do Areeiro see **Areeiro, Pico do**

Pico dos Barcelos see **Barcelos, Pico dos**

Pico Ruivo see **Ruivo, Pico**

Poiso (1400m), at junction of roads to Pico do Areeiro and Faial, 13km north of Funchal. Excellent restaurant and bar.

Ponta Delgada Village 9km east of São Vicente on north coast.

Situated on a promontory of black lava, this village has a number of houses from the early colonial period, when it was an important settlement. The *church*, dedicated to São Jesus, was built in 1745. On the first Sunday in September it is the scene of a great popular gathering, the Festa do Senhor Jesus.

Ponta d'Oliviera Point on south coast east of Funchal, reached via Caniço (2km). This point derives its name from the olive tree which was planted here by the first settlers to mark the dividing line between the two 'Captaincies' into which the island was divided for administrative purposes. It is now the site of a large tourist development comprising houses, apartments, villas, a restaurant, swimming pools and tennis courts. The name of this development is 'Contracta' (see p. 121).

Further east along the cliffs there are some beautiful walks. On the shore, at the end of the new development area are the remains of an old *fort*, built in the 16th c.

Ponta do Pargo Most westerly village in the island, situated on coastal road from Funchal to Porto do Moniz.

This village, which has a 16th c. church, is in the middle of a rich agricultural area. 2km from the village, at the extreme western tip of the island, stands a lighthouse. At this point one can enjoy spectacular views of the rocky coastline to north and south.

Ponta de São Lourenço Pointed promontory at eastern tip of island.

The peninsula is a great attraction for walkers. It also has the only sandy beach on the island, at Prainha Bay to the east of the village of Caniçal. This can be reached by going to the end of the road beyond the village, and then walking a short distance through sand dunes to the sea.

The paths which traverse the peninsula command fine views of the rocky coast on both sides. The whole area is of great interest to the geologist, who will enjoy studying the varied strata.

The peninsula is extended by two islands to the east. The easternmost of these, Fora, has a lighthouse.

Ponta do Sol Village 39km west of Funchal. The coast road which leads here from Ribeira Brava is rather rough but offers delightful sea views.

Situated on the south coast at the mouth of one of the streams running down from the Paúl da Serra (Ribeira da Ponta do Sol), this village began life as a sugar plantation in the 15th c. Its founder was Jean d'Esmenaut, a Fleming who was granted a large area of

Church at Monte

land here by the Portuguese. (He and his family later took the name of Esmeraldo.) The village, dramatically sited on either side of a ravine, has a church of the 15th c.

Church of São João This little chapel, built by one of his descendants on the site of a church founded by Esmeraldo, is situated at *Lombada*, to the east of Ponta do Sol. It is reached by a cobbled lane $\frac{1}{2}$ km from the Ponta do Sol/Porto do Moniz junction. This lane should be followed for 2 km, turning left when the church comes in view. The church was built in 1720 and has fine gilding, *azulejos* and other decoration. From the courtyard are superb views of the ravine up to the east end of the Paúl da Serra. Nearby are the ruins of the family house, bearing the Esmeraldo coat-of-arms, and a little water-mill—one of the few remaining in the island.

Portela (662 m) 'The Little Gateway' is a pass on the road which runs across the eastern corner of the island from Machico to Porto da Cruz. At the junction of the road from Santo da Serra, there are beautiful views towards the coast and inland.

Porto da Cruz Village on north-east coast, 16 km east of Santana.

One of the few villages on the north coast at sea level, Porto da Cruz boasts a small port and accessible beach of black sand. To the west the great rock of *Penha d'Aguia* makes a striking landmark: to the east are views of the Ponta de São Lourenço. The village has a restaurant.

Porto Moniz Northernmost village of the island. 75km from Funchal via Ribeira Brava and São Vicente.

The life of this village, attractively situated on a shelf of land beneath the mountains, re-volves around its vineyards and fishing. For the visitor, its attractions lie in the natural features of its coastline. Just off shore is a huge basaltic rock with a lighthouse, the haunt of innumerable sea birds. Along the coast is a volcanic reef: a barrier for some natural rock pools which provide some of the best swimming in the island.

The village itself has a pretty square and a 17th c. church. The old houses lean over the narrow cobbled streets, offering endless subjects for the artist and photographer. Two good *pensãos* provide accommodation for visitors who wish to stay to enjoy the swimming and scenery.

Buses to Porto Moniz are infrequent. The best way to reach it from Funchal is via the central route to São Vincente, passing through the island's most varied scenery. A pleasant alternative is to take one of the coach tours which go several times a week from Funchal, and from which a stop-over can be arranged if desired.

Porto Santo (pop. 3000, area 75 sq km) Island 28 miles north-east of Madeira.

In 1418 this was the first landfall of the Portu-guese explorers Zarco and Teixeira in their voyage of discovery. Blown here by a storm, they named the island Porto Santo or 'Holy Port'. A year later, they sailed on to Madeira. The new settlers offered the administration of Porto Santo to Bartolomeu Perestrello, an Italian sea captain in their service. His title, Captain of Porto Santo, was inherited by his descendants until the mid-18th c. Peres-trello's daughter, Doña Felipa Perestrello y Moniz, married Christopher Columbus, who came to live for a period in the island.

Porto Santo is approx. 15km long and 5km wide. It is much flatter than Madeira, although there are mountain formations to the north and south (the highest point, the *Pico do Facho* in the north is 507 m). On the south side of the island is a fine sandy beach.

The little town of *Vila* (otherwise known as *Vila Baleina* or *Porto Santo*) boasts the *house* in which Columbus is thought to have lived during his stay in the island. Behind the town the land rises to the *Pico do Castello* (438 m), crowned by the ruined stronghold built as a defence against raiders in the 16th c.

Porto Santo is a much poorer island than its fertile neighbour. The land is too flat and the soil too sandy for effective irrigation on the lines of the levada system and the island is as a result largely uncultivated. The flatter terrain, however, makes grain production more feasible and the island has windmills —unknown in Madeira—for grinding the maize.

The water of Porto Santo has excellent mineral properties and is a popular drink in Madeira. Limestone is quarried on the little islet known as *Ilheu de Baixo*.

For the visitor who can spare the time a few days spent on the smaller island offers a very different experience from Madeira. Though unfortunate for the island, the lack of com-mercial development in Porto Santo en-

hances its appeal to those in search of a quiet and simple holiday.

There is one hotel (*Porto Santo*) and two *pensãos* in or near the town. The swimming is excellent, and one can walk all over the island without any difficulty.

There are four flights a day to Porto Santo from Funchal. One can also go by boat (see Boat Services, p. 118). If the sea is rough the passage can be very uncomfortable, but it is usually a quiet trip of about $2\frac{1}{2}$ hrs.

As the island is very popular with Madeirans for summer holidays it is usually necessary to book well in advance for a visit in July or August, but at other times of the year there is no difficulty.

Rabaçal (1070 m) Refuge west of the Paúl da Serra in west of island, reached by track from Calheta (10 km). (For other approaches, see **Paúl da Serra**.)

From Rabaçal there is a levada walk to the '25 Waterfalls', the largest of which has a drop of over 100 m. The scenery, at the head of the mighty gorge of the Ribeira da Janela, is superb.

Ribeira Brava Fishing port 30 km west of Funchal, situated at foot of river valley of same name. It is from here that one can travel north to São Vicente (25 km).

The beach here is wide and clean, and at the eastern end a tunnel runs through the cliff to a large quay where local boats discharge their cargo.

Ribeira da Janela Madeira's major river in west of island.

The source of the river is in the Paúl da Serra and from here to the coast runs through a deep gorge. At the point where the river runs into the sea, below the village of *Janela*, a passage cut through the cliffs gives access to the shore. Here one can view the group of basaltic rocks which stand offshore—a superb subject for artist or photographer.

Ribeiro Frio ('Cold River') River valley north of Poiso.

Here, on the road to Faial, is the *Government Trout Hatchery*. From here the fish are distributed to streams throughout the island. There is also an experimental garden area, 'Flora of Madeira', with a collection of indigenous plants.

Walk In the vicinity is one of the loveliest levada walks in the island. A little to the north of the tiny chapel beside the main road is a path which follows the *Levada do Furado*. After 2 km the *Balcões* look-out is reached, a vantage point for one of the most breathtaking views in Madeira. At a great depth below is the *Metade valley*, winding away to the north, while opposite is one of the new power stations, dwarfed by its mountain backdrop.

Ruivo, Pico (1862 m) Situated in the centre of the island, the 'Red Mountain' is Madeira's highest peak.

Approaches to Pico Ruivo

Three trails lead up to Pico Ruivo, from *Pico do Areeiro*, *Queimadas* and *Encumeada*. The shortest route is from Santana, picking up the Queimadas trail: the more direct approach from Funchal is via Areeiro.

From *Areeiro* look-out the path is well marked, and unless there have been recent heavy rains to cause rock falls or to make it slippery the walk is within the scope of any reasonably active person. There are, however, several very steep inclines and flights of steps on the trail, and it is not recommended for anyone who suffers from vertigo. The scenery along the trail is superb, with glimpses of the coast all round the island, and views of the deep gorges which lead down to the villages on the lower slopes. (A minimum of 3 hrs should be allowed for this walk.)

At the base of the peak a *Government Rest House* offers complete accommodation facilities for those who wish to stay overnight or longer. There is no food here, but cooking facilities are available for those who bring their own rations. To reserve a bed in the Rest House, at least two days notice should be given to the office of the Department of Tourism in Funchal.

From *Santana* a road joins the trail to Queimadas at Pico das Pedras (4 km) and then continues 6 km to Achada do Teixeira (1592 m) from whence one can walk in 1 hr to the Pico Ruivo Rest House.

From *Encumeada*, the longest and most strenuous route (6 hrs) a guide is recommended. Either of the last two routes may be used as return routes by those approaching Pico Ruivo from Areeiro. There are buses back to Funchal from Encumeada and Santana, but it is advisable to ascertain the times in advance.

At Queimadas there is another *Rest House*, operated by the Camara do Funchal, which offers accommodation to the visitor who wishes to stay overnight prior to exploring the beautiful levada walks in the locality.

Santana Village on north-east coast, 39 km north of Funchal.

Reached by the road from the south via Ribeiro Frio, Santana represents the typical Madeiran village, with a small church at the roadside and houses scattered over a wide area. Many of these houses are thatched—a traditional feature now little seen in the island—and the roadsides are planted with flowers and shrubs.

Santana is a good centre for some of the best walking country in the island. The road to *Queimadas*—starting point for the climb to Pico Ruivo, runs south-west from here. A faster approach to the peak is by the road to Achada do Teixeira, south of Santana.

Santa Cruz Village 20 km east of Funchal, on coast near airport.

This was the second landing-place of Zarco and his companions during their voyage of discovery. They raised a cross in commemoration, and it is from this that the village gets its name.

Founded in 1515, Santa Cruz was one of the original districts established after the first settlers arrived. The well-preserved church of **São Salvador** dates from 1533, and contains the tombs of its founders. There are also some paintings of the Renaissance period. The *sacristy* (reached by door to left of chancel) has some beautiful tiles which were originally in the local monastery but were removed when these institutions were abolished (1834).

The central square, lined with a favourite Madeiran laurel—the til—is very attractive. Of special interest is the *Paços do Concelho*, a 16th c. public building with Gothic features. From the square one may reach a small esplanade overlooking the beach. During the summer months this beach has excellent facilities; including changing rooms and an open air restaurant, located at the east end of the village.

Santo da Serra Village in centre of small plateau in west of island 7 km west of Machico.

The name of this village (a shortened form of Santo Antonio da Serra) is identified with Madeira's only *golf course* (18 holes) situated nearby. Bus services are infrequent, so players are dependent on taxis or their own transport. The surrounding country is very pretty (views of the *Machico valley* to the north) and the tree-lined roads pleasant for easy walks. In the ravines and glades in this neighbourhood are some of the rarest ferns in Madeira.

The village, which is a good excursion centre, has a small hotel.

São Vicente Village in north of island, 56 km north of Funchal. The road across the island via the Encumeada Pass emerges on the north coast at this point.

Situated in the fulcrum of the north coast, within reach of some of the island's most dramatic countryside, São Vicente stretches for 3 km along the valley. The *parish church* in the main part of the village has one interesting feature: a picture of the village painted on the ceiling.

The curious little chapel of *São Vicente* stands at the junction of the main roads by the sea. The chapel, hewn out of the rock, was constructed in 1692.

Seixal Village in north of island 8 km west of São Vicente. This village, built on a bed of lava, is well known for its vineyards, which produce some of Madeira's finest wine. It is worth pausing here for views of the coastline: on the drive along the coast, to east and west, one passes beneath, and even *through* dramatic waterfalls.

Selvagens The 'Wild Isles' are a group of three uninhabited islands approx. 150 miles south of Madeira, 100 miles north of Tenerife. They are Portuguese, but administered separately.

Terreiro da Luta 2 km north of Monte, at an altitude of 876 km, this is the site of a huge *statue* raised to commemorate World War I. There are wonderful views of Funchal from the road here. Beside the memorial is a tea-room.

Thatched house at Santana,
with 'Staff of St. John'